The Tightrope of Trust

A memoir about the life that shapes a man and the career that tests him

Dan Evans

Ginger Jar Publishing
Portland, Oregon

This is a work of non-fiction. The events and conversations in this book have been set down to the best of the author's ability and memory. In some cases, names and identifying characteristics have been changed to protect the privacy of individuals.

Cover illustration generated by Gemini

Ginger Jar Publishing
Portland, Oregon

Library of Congress Control Number: 2026913031

ISBN 979-8-9961363-0-8 (paperback)
ISBN 979-8-9961363-1-5 (hardcover)
ISBN 979-8-9961363-2-2 (electronic)

First Edition: June 2026

TABLE OF CONTENTS

PART 1

THE FORGE

DEDICATION TO PART 1

Throughout her life, my mother tucked away memories related to her children. Each child had their own unique box. Inside it were tangible fragments that included letters, pictures, school projects, and every time a child's name appeared in a church program or newspaper article. Most special of all was a Baby Book, whose loose pages captured those unique moments in her own words.

As my mother aged, she repeated the same thing to me during almost every visit and every phone call. She said, *"You should write a book."* I always thought telling someone to write a book was like telling a bored child to go clean their room. I never took her seriously.

My mother passed away several years ago, and only recently have I thought about acting upon what she said. This memoir is inspired by her words. It doesn't aim to capture every memory. Instead, it reaches for key moments that shaped who I became. Maybe, somewhere in those moments, a reader might uncover a memory of their own.

Dedicated to my mother, who collected pieces of my childhood, and passed them along.

PROLOGUE

I sat silently at the kitchen table. The morning was halfway over, and except for a few carefully composed lines in an email, I hadn't accomplished much. It wasn't the first time I'd written these words. Work had lost its excitement long ago. I closed my eyes and tried to focus, but the only thing I could hear was a small voice whispering,

Press the button.

My eyes opened slowly as I turned to stare out the window. Leaving home with only a few days' notice to travel across the globe wasn't unusual. Managing hundreds of people in high stress environments came with the territory. With my wife by my side, I thought I could handle just about anything. Yet, this wasn't anything. It was a decision that would separate me from a career built over three decades.

Across the valley on a distant hillside, a stand of Douglas fir trees rhythmically swayed in the breeze. It wasn't long before I could almost hear them saying,

It will be okay.

The calculations had been gone over many times. I knew my expenses and had established a generous emergency fund. A risk assessment had been conducted, identifying every scenario that could possibly go wrong. It didn't change the math. The numbers added up.

I used to love my job, didn't I?

Fifty-five years old is too young to retire, isn't it?

A decision had to be made. I already knew the answer.

My finger hit send.

CHAPTER 1

BEGINNINGS

My childhood memories are fragments, scattered and incomplete, like puzzle pieces spread out across an expansive floor. Although the earliest memories remain shrouded in fog, one stands out.

At the top of the kitchen stairs, a 3-year-old boy stands unsteadily, one hand on the banister, both eyes staring down. My father, a distant figure, pauses at the bottom of the dimly lit steps. He looks up, staring, his face lacking any expression. For a brief second, it feels like the world has stopped. All I know is that he is leaving. Then, he's gone.

At the time, our family consisted of two sets of boys. John was the oldest at age 9, followed by Mike at age 8. Rick was toddling around at age 4, with me not far behind at age 3. Four months later, Kathy arrived. She was the girl my father always said he'd hoped for.

I was too young to remember what it meant to have a father, so I didn't feel any sense of loss. As the sudden departure rippled through our household, my mother remained steady.

Something in our family had permanently changed, and the weight of his absence would shape us in ways I wouldn't grasp until much later in life. That moment may always live in fog, but as time moved forward, other memories found clarity. Before we get to those stories, I need to show you where I began.

Setting the Stage

Pittsburgh was a city built on hard work and pride. That same energy ran through the sports teams. Pirates and Steelers games filled the air. These were the days of world championship teams. Roberto Clemente stepped up to the plate. Terry Bradshaw hurled passes at Three Rivers Stadium. Sporting events were more than just entertainment. Whether I was at a game or watching from home, they became part of me.

While the city's spirit echoed in stadiums, my family's spirit echoed in something simpler, our house on Lovingston Drive. It wasn't much to look at from the outside. Inside, it held everything that shaped our daily lives. There were arguments, jokes, and constant teasing, which wasn't always a good thing.

The building itself was a three-story structure. Some called it a cracker box because of its plain square shape. The upstairs floor held two larger bedrooms connected by a Jack and Jill bathroom along the front of the house. Toward the back were three smaller bedrooms and a hallway bathroom. The main level contained the formal living room and dining rooms. Except on special holidays, children were not allowed to play in these spaces.

The two noisiest rooms were also on the main level, the family room and the kitchen. Thankfully for the neighbors, they were located at the back of the house. The family room held a fish tank, a television, and a bookcase filled with Junior Encyclopedias for children. It was our main playroom. The lower level had a partially finished basement and a two-car garage that housed a single car.

The front yard had a large oak tree and a driveway that ran down the side of the house into the back. That space would one day hold laundry lines, endless ball games, and a talking tree.

Our neighborhood was full of kids my age. There was never any problem finding somebody to play with. My best friend Stephen lived directly across the street. We were inseparable at that age, and if I wasn't inside my house, I was likely in his.

The house on Lovingston Drive was a wonderful place to grow up. Even as an adult, the home remained a safe harbor. When I moved away, it stayed a steady place in my mind. I knew I could come back if life got too hard or the wheels fell off my wagon.

Meet the Parents

My father was a veterinarian who left the family while my mother was pregnant. There was no real explanation. I was told that he wanted to travel more, but no one ever understood that. The family had taken vacations to Virginia and Florida. It made no sense. Not to his mother. Not to my mother. Not to my older brothers. Decades later, just before her death, my mother still wrestled with the same unanswered question: "What went wrong?"

After he left, his world moved on. He swapped out his old family for a sports car with gull-wing doors, a single-engine plane, and a house with a new wife and her children. It might have looked like freedom. He never came back.

My mother called him "your father," never "Dad." I didn't think much of it then. It was just how things were. To me, my mother was Mom, and he was Dad. Only later did I learn his other family's children called him "Doc." It was oddly comforting to hear him being called by a different name. It marked a line. Dad was a name reserved only for the children he left behind.

He did not come to Little League games, choir recitals, or band concerts. He did not attend church with us. He was more like a visitor than a parent, always distant, never fully in the frame.

Those early years weren't shaped by only a single male role model. They weren't family, but coaches and counselors guided me in ways they probably didn't even realize. From them I learned how to slide into a base, how to paddle a canoe, and how to fix a bike. These men weren't replacements for a father. They were part of my village.

My mother was the center of our family. Raising five young children in the shadow of a father who walked away still seems like a small miracle. She was loving, steady, and always kept us moving forward.

One of my earliest memories with her is toddling through the living room. I was helping at a neighborhood ladies' group tea by bringing a tray of cookies from the kitchen. She seemed so alive in that moment. I can't recall her ever hosting another tea after my father left. It was as if the door closed behind that version of her. She abandoned the teacups and never looked back.

The silver trays from that day still sit on my dining room table. The teapot, the sugar bowl, and the tiny milk pitcher were part of her wedding set, and outlasted the gatherings themselves. They haven't poured tea in decades, but they've never stopped reminding me of those days.

There is another early memory, just as strong. One day, after hearing noisy children playing and arguing upstairs, she decided I was the cause. I didn't think I'd done anything so wrong, and it was more likely an older brother was to blame. My mother, stern but unwavering, called me over and delivered a spanking. With a deep sense of injustice swelling inside my tiny four-year-old self, I cried out, "I hate you, I hate you, I hate you."

I don't know what else was going on in my mother's life, but those words were more than she could bear. She started to cry. Through a gentle stream of tears she wrapped her arms around my body and whispered, "Please don't hate me."

My anger faded. It was replaced by love. I hugged her back and said I was sorry. Her embrace tightened slightly. She taught me how powerful a simple hug could be.

Just as my mother's love spoke volumes, so did her writing, and she was a prolific writer. Every week she would send letters out to family and friends, and for each child she created a Baby Book. The Baby Book contained things like height, weight, doctor appointments, and vaccinations, but added something special. Her loose pages of notes recorded birthday dinner menus, gifts, summer camp adventures, and her own personal observations. Looking back, writing might have been her way of coping with the loss of a husband, and the strain of raising five children alone. At the same time, she kept our household running smoothly, making sure life moved forward despite whatever challenges arose.

Years later, I asked her what she remembered about the turmoil outside of our household, like the civil rights protests, the Kennedy assassination, or the hippies. Her answer was always the same, "I was too busy raising a family to notice any of those things."

Despite whatever storm she was weathering, love filled our home. I remember sitting at the kitchen table as she gently brushed her hand across my arm or the back of my leg. Her touch always calmed me. I'd freeze in place, not wanting it to end. Even now, I can still recall the warmth of those touches, and the comfort they still carry.

A Smattering of Siblings

John, the eldest boy, carried the weight of our father's absence more than anyone. He was born the same day they buried our grandfather, and from early on, he was expected to step into both of their shoes. My grandmother used to say, *"When God closes a door, He opens a window."* For John, it felt as though the weight of two generations had settled on his shoulders. The legacy of our grandfather wasn't offered. It was assumed. With our father gone, the pressure only grew. He never seemed to want that role, and maybe that was why he always had an air of grumpiness about him. One of the first ways he showed stress was by tugging at his hair. I remember it always looking slightly disheveled. It was a visible sign of how tangled life would eventually become for him.

John found refuge in electronics. His room was filled with parts from old radios and televisions. I never understood what he did with all those things, and he never cared to explain.

Even with his tendency to withdraw, John had moments of unexpected magic. One summer, he hid a speaker in a backyard tree and ran a cord from his upstairs window. Rick, Kathy, and I would stand outside, laughing as the tree spoke, knowing full well it was John, but never caring. Even though we usually steered clear of him, the grumpy brother could still delight us.

Mike lived in his own world, and when he engaged, it was unpredictable. Sometimes he showed a caring brotherly love, but more often he teased, and not in a way that felt playful. Of all my brothers, he was the worst, and often found ways to get under my skin. Some of his jabs went beyond teasing. They were words meant to wound, and they did. It became a game for him. He seemed to enjoy how much it hurt me, and encouraged others to join in. I learned early on that not all pain came from accidents or scraped knees. Some of it arrived on purpose, in words that lingered long after the room went quiet. He might have been kind to others in the family, but that rarely applied to me.

My mother said I could tease back with equal intensity, but she never quite understood how much his words stung. If there was any lesson learned from Mike, it was that life was not always going to be fair.

Rick offered a camaraderie that buffered the sharp edges of the older two. Rick liked to tell everyone he was the middle child. He'd say that meant he got the least attention, but it wasn't really true. He was just working the referee, our mother. I followed him everywhere. Sometimes he liked it and sometimes he didn't. Sometimes, he used it and I became the fall guy, the tagalong conveniently nearby when something broke or went missing.

Despite his games, we were close. Our survival practically depended on it. Since John and Mike had their own brotherly alliance, Rick and I formed an unspoken one of our own. To avoid the grumpiness of John or the teasing of Mike, we escaped outside, or hid in our room.

Our room was a great place to be because it contained something special, bunk beds. The day the bed arrived, it felt like we owned a castle. Rick ruled the tower, and I ruled the dungeon. Every night, his arm would swing down like bait, silently daring me to tug. I always did. He would tumble off the bed in exaggerated agony, shrieking with laughter. Then we'd do it again, until our mother's voice put a stop to the fun. That game wasn't about winning or losing. It was about two brothers packing as much fun as possible into every day.

When Kathy arrived, it wasn't in a disruptive way. Rick and I kept carving out our domain, but now it had another player. The noise got louder and new alliances would be formed. Rick remained somewhere between strategic and chaotic. Always in the middle.

Kathy arrived as a baby, not a force of personality, at least not yet. My mother documented our first interaction. She wrote:

"New baby sister home Sept 13 – Danny loves her dearly, can't get too close because of cough and cold. Doesn't want her to go back to hospital."

I don't know how my brothers felt, but from that first moment, I cared about her.

Even though Kathy mostly just lay there, everything revolved around her. She didn't compete or command attention. She simply existed, and somehow, that was enough to change the feel of the house, especially for me. Overnight, I lost my spot as the youngest child and suddenly found myself at the mercy of three older brothers. I never resented Kathy, but I did miss the protection that came with being the youngest.

She faced turmoil too, especially when John and Mike decided she needed toughening up. One night at dinner when she refused to eat, Kathy stormed up to her room in protest, stomping her feet in frustration. John and Mike climbed onto chairs, smacking the ceiling with their hands, knowing it would drive her crazy. Kathy screamed louder. The house erupted into laughter and chaos as our mother tried in vain to restore order. As far as I know, that kitchen ceiling still contains indented handprints from my brothers.

It wasn't always tough for Kathy. She had her moments. When our grandmother visited, she gave Kathy a full one-pound bag of M&M's. She alone decided if, when, and how much to share with her brothers. Being the only girl in a sea of boys clearly had its privileges. As my mother watched over the ritual to ensure fairness, Kathy held the upper hand. Nobody minded her newfound power. Instead, we all enjoyed the game she commanded.

CHAPTER 2

THE EARLY YEARS

There's a line scribbled by my mother. It was a quote from a toddler too young to understand words, but somehow old enough to know what love should feel like:

"Don't pank me, hug me, luff me." - Baby Book 1967

That simple and instinctive plea became the undercurrent of everything that followed. Before bunk bed laughter, baseball games, and cartoons, there was this: a child asking the world to be gentle.

Visits and Sanctuaries

Time with my father was measured in hours, not days. Sometimes we went to his house, other times to a show. There always seemed to be something new.

One visit came in 1973, when he took me to Heinz Hall to see Marcel Marceau, the famous French mime. As an eight-year-old, I loved the performance, but something was missing. I don't remember laughing or sharing reactions. We just arrived, sat in silence, and left. It felt like something we were supposed to do, not something we shared.

Another time, he took us to a cabin on a lake stocked with fish. The only fishing I'd known up to that point was a plastic board game we played at home. It had a toy pole and colorful magnetic fish. At the lake, our pole was a stick, a piece of fishing line, and a cheeseball-baited hook. My father stayed in the cabin, so it was my brothers who showed me how to fish. I caught one sunfish. The thrill didn't last long. When the hook was pulled loose, I watched the fish gasp for air and felt a sharp pang of guilt for the pain I'd caused.

As interesting as a visit could be, sometimes it was the ride home that was memorable. One Saturday, I asked him a small question, maybe about the drive or the week ahead. Nothing that should have provoked anything. He gripped the steering wheel tighter and exhaled sharply. His eyes stayed fixed on the road. Then, without any softness, he surprised me by saying:

"I am never coming home."

I was five or six years old, and the words didn't make sense. I hadn't asked about him coming home. What lingered after that drive weren't his words, but the awkward silence that followed.

After he dropped us off, I was glad to get back to the sanctuary of the house, and the predictability that came with it.

Part of that predictability occurred every Sunday. My mother raised me to have a deep respect for the church. To her, the denomination mattered less than a person's spiritual grounding. Whether it was Presbyterian, Methodist, or Lutheran, she believed religion served as an anchor in life. She passed that belief on with deliberate intention. To encourage us to learn the Bible, she made a deal: if any of us could recite the books of the Old Testament or the Ten Commandments, we'd get first pick of the cereal box toys. The toys were collected and set aside. I don't remember fighting over them, or ever being disappointed about not getting one I wanted. They were always a thrill to receive.

We belonged to a small congregation that met in a traditional red brick church tucked into a quiet neighborhood. It had a tall white steeple and recorded bells that chimed through the streets every Sunday morning. The building wasn't grand, but it had a dignity.

Sunday mornings, our whole family sat together in the same pew off to the side. I always thought it was about keeping five fidgety children from disrupting the service. Even after we had all grown up, that pew remained ours. On some Sundays, one of us would sing in the children's choir. Ten or twelve kids in purple robes stood in front of the congregation, uncomfortably shifting from foot to foot. Our voices barely made it to the back of the church.

Midweek also had its place in church life. On Wednesdays after school, I went to Youth Club, followed by choir practice. Youth Club felt like a livelier version of Sunday school, with snacks and games added in.

Just as we all knew our place in the church, we also knew a chicken dinner would be waiting for us once we arrived home. My brothers devoured the legs, thighs, and breasts, while I was given the backbone. My mother wanted me to have a piece that was "special," and even though I later learned it wasn't exactly a prized cut, I appreciated that it was uniquely mine.

Sunday dinners were predictable. My brothers were not. At times, they would knock me down, pin my arms, and mercilessly tickle me until I couldn't breathe from laughing so hard. Somehow, I always managed to escape, into the safety of my mother's arms. Once she calmed everyone and sent me on my way, it wasn't long before the game started all over again. Was it roughhousing or my brothers trying to stop me from bothering them? I didn't care. All that mattered was how much fun it was.

Once Kathy learned to walk with confidence, she was pulled into the game too, only now, I chased her. Chasing and tickling her brought the same joy my brothers must've felt running after me. It was a similar kind of bond, one wrapped in giggles and shrieks. Those times with Kathy made the house feel full.

Not all the fun came from family, some of it was beamed straight into our living room. Our mother only had so much time in the day and when she was keeping home life running smoothly, we had to find our own way to fill the gaps. The television became an unofficial babysitter. It was my guide to every kind of comedy, from people tripping over their own feet, to jokes so bad you couldn't help but laugh.

Some mornings began with Captain Kangaroo and the ping-pong balls that rained down on his head. Other times I watched Abbott and Costello or The Three Stooges. They mixed fast talk and goofy slaps until the nonsense felt normal. Saturday mornings were more special. They belonged to cartoons. I watched Bugs outsmart everyone in his way while Scooby-Doo unmasked "monsters" to a catchy tune every week.

While laughter filled our home, an unexplored world waited outside. One early adventure was walking with my brothers to the local barbershop, about half a mile away. Keeping up meant no dawdling. It took all my energy to match their long strides, and by the time we arrived, I was exhausted.

Being exhausted wasn't a bad thing. Nobody wanted a small child running around the barber shop. While waiting our turn, old men paged through newspapers and magazines as a transistor radio filled the air with songs from another era. My brothers tried to scare me by saying the men with the clippers were butchers who would cut off my ears. I wasn't scared. The barber who worked on me was a kind Italian man named Tony.

I watched in fascination as Tony worked. He sometimes used an open razor, gliding it across faces in smooth strokes. When my turn came, I could still smell the aftershave he had slapped on their cheeks. I sat in the chair as he wrapped me in a cape, then out came the clippers. By the time Tony finished, my soft curls were gone. They were replaced by the crisp, bristly feel of a crew cut. I grinned, thinking of the song about *Fuzzy Wuzzy*. Unlike him, at least I still had my hair.

With our heads freshly shaved, we set off on the fast-paced journey home. As an adult, people told me I walked quickly and with purpose. It all traces back to those days when keeping up with my brothers was a matter of necessity.

Years later, after returning from college, I stopped by the old barbershop. I hadn't been there since elementary school. Tony was still behind the chair, his hair more gray, his voice still commanding the space in rolling Italian. A line of old men waited patiently. The transistor radio played the same kind of songs. I'd always wondered where my love of artists like Sinatra, Crosby, and Nat Cole had come from. Standing in that shop again, the answer was clear. It had been there all along.

Holidays

Each holiday brought its own special routine. Out would come the Super 8 camera. Only my mother and John were allowed to operate it, but they recorded all the controlled chaos and excitement that every celebration brought. A few times per year, we'd gather around the projector as reels of film were loaded. With popcorn and a root beer float in hand, the lights would go out, and we would all watch home movies.

Since there were no holidays or birthdays early in the year, the first time the camera would come out was Easter. The house was decorated with bunny shaped candles. Hard-boiled eggs were dyed, and baskets were hidden throughout the house. When morning came, there was a great rush down the stairs to find our baskets and discover what the Easter Bunny had brought. Nobody ever questioned what a rabbit had to do with plastic eggs full of jellybeans, and nobody cared. After church, we gathered around the formal dining room table for a lamb dinner. As a finishing touch, my mother brought out her special homemade Easter Bunny cake with jellybean eyes and spaghetti whiskers.

The Fourth of July was less about inside decorations, and more about what was going on outside. We would walk to the main street of our suburban town to watch horses, fire engines, and marching bands. Shriners wearing their funny tasseled hats waved at the crowds as they drove their miniature toy cars down the center of the road.

As each of us entered high school, we all participated in the parade as a part of the marching band, but in those early days the parade was full of wonder. The evening always ended with a trip to watch the local fireworks display and listen to our mother "ooo and ahhh" with every explosion of light.

During the month of October, the house came to life once again. My mother pulled out all sorts of decorations to liven up the rooms. Ghosts made with Kleenex were taped in every window. Vintage Gurley candles shaped like pumpkins, and witches decorated shelves. School projects of construction paper black cats and pumpkins with dangling feet covered the walls. Picking a pumpkin and carving it was a required ritual.

In the early years, we had Halloween parties. The basement was converted into a haunted house. Blindfolded neighborhood children reached their hands into bowls of cooked spaghetti masquerading as slimy worms and zombie brains made of cold Jell-O. After hands were cleaned, everyone went upstairs to bob for apples and play games.

My oldest brothers stepped up on Halloween. With my father gone, they had the responsibility of escorting Rick and me through the neighborhood. They always navigated us with care.

Every year, upon returning from our trick-or-treating, Rick feared his older brothers were going to take his candy. He would eat as much as he could as quickly as he could. The result was a one-day tummy ache. Rick never learned. After his candy was gone, he would always try to sneak some from the other family members. I didn't mind and was always willing to share, as long as it was only one piece at a time.

As October gave way to November, Halloween decorations were packed away, and Thanksgiving took over. Pilgrims, Native Americans, and turkeys would find their way into every corner of the home's main level, and at the center of it all was a fold-out paper diorama of the first Thanksgiving. I still have the diorama, and it still comes out every fall.

Whether it was my grandmother from Florida or my Great Aunt from across town, a big holiday meal always featured one or more guests. Thanksgiving dinner was held in the formal dining room and had all the traditional fixings. For the main course, a turkey adorned the table, and that meant a big responsibility for John. We had an electric knife for carving meat, and it was the responsibility of the oldest boy to cut the bird with care.

Most of the year, dinner meant instant mashed potatoes, but on holidays they were real and full of lumps. To top it all off, there was typically at least one small mishap like the rolls getting slightly burned, affording the family some gentle teasing amidst the holiday cheer.

My mother had been raised in a household where alcohol was strictly off-limits. Our glasses never clinked with wine, but instead sparkled with ginger ale. Holidays were the only time of year this bubbly treat made an appearance, turning simple moments into small celebrations that felt special.

During the meal there was always a phone call from a relative wishing us all a happy holiday. One by one, each child was expected to leave the table and spend a few polite minutes reporting how we were doing in school. Then, after the plates were cleared, came the dreaded adult conversation. We sat squirming, dying to escape the boredom and get back to playing. Finally, we'd look to our mother and one by one ask: "Mom, may I please be excused?" As long as enough time had passed, the answer was always yes.

When December settled over Lovingston Drive, the house began its slow transformation. Glass Christmas balls shimmered in every window. The front door was wrapped in shiny green foil and had a Styrofoam snowman attached in a way that permitted him to mischievously grin toward the street. In the yard, a multi-colored wheel cast red and green waves of light across the front of the house.

Inside, the air turned sweet with the smell of fresh-baked cookies. My mother, armed with her legendary sweet tooth, put herself into production mode. Tin after tin was filled with peanut butter blossoms, thumbprints, snowballs, and lemon bars. I positioned myself near the kitchen, keeping just far enough to stay out of the way, but close enough that if a gingerbread man needed decorating or a spoon of batter needed licking, my support was at hand. All the cookie tins were labeled. Some were for immediate enjoyment but most were stacked in the downstairs freezer for Christmas and New Year's Eve. Despite five children in the house, no one dared sneak a cookie. Everyone had too much respect for our mother.

We waited to buy our Christmas tree until the last minute, after the prices dropped. When it arrived, a whirlwind of activity ensued. Popcorn on thread, construction paper ornaments from school, handmade crafts from church, and the ever-tangled lights with one or two broken bulbs were hung on the boughs. Once the last decoration had been placed, we carefully draped it with long strands of tinsel. An old model train was placed around the bottom of the tree, the type whose cars had small moving parts and pieces.

On Christmas Eve, paper bags would be filled with sand and a single candle to make luminaria. They were then placed along the front curb to light the way for Mary and Joseph on their journey to Bethlehem. Once the candles were lit, we dressed in our best and headed to church. At the end of the service, each person lit a candle, an act meant to honor the journey of Jesus. There was something special about being in a crowded sanctuary and seeing a light passing from person to person, each face glowing in candlelight. As more and more candles were lit, the congregation sang Christmas hymns.

Back home, dinner was served in the formal dining room. A white linen tablecloth anchored the room, while good china and fine silverware were drawn from the side cabinets and drawers. John, as "man of the house," sat at the head of the table and read aloud the story of Mary and Joseph's journey to Bethlehem. Once the record player clicked on with Bing Crosby or a symphony of carols, the meal began.

Christmas morning meant waiting in the hallway at the top of the stairs for permission to rush down and descend upon our presents sitting patiently under the tree. Within a short time, the living room floor was covered with torn-up wrapping paper and endless toys. John and Mike acted indifferent, although they never ruined the magic, not even when I started to suspect that Santa might be the work of my very tired mother. Our stockings were each individually made by our Great Aunt Mary. Each one hung from the stair railing, weighed down with candy and a Florida orange stuffed into the toe. Mine, inexplicably, featured a little girl. I was a little boy!

How could my aunt give a stocking with a little girl on it to a little boy?

Recognizing the displeasure I had with the stocking, my mother removed the little girl after my aunt passed away.

My mother always told me I appeared more excited about my birthday than Christmas, and she was right. With my birthday being the day after Christmas, people always tried to combine the two. My brothers and sister all had their special day of the year, so it was only fair that I got one also. I never really asked for much, but I asked for that special day. A day that was mine and not shared.

My mother recognized this, and was careful to make sure that gifts were not combined. My gifts weren't placed in the formal living room with the Christmas tree. They were given to me in the family room at the back of the house. Balloons decorated the walls, and gifts were not wrapped in old Christmas paper. Even the birthday dinner was of my own choosing, and it wasn't ever leftovers from the day before. My mother really worked to make the day special.

For years, one birthday stuck in my memory like a thorn. My father said he was giving me an organ as a present. This was incredibly exciting because an organ is quite a fancy gift. As my birthday came and went, no organ arrived. My father said there had been a problem. To make it up to me, he promised a bigger and better organ that had pre-programmed rhythms and more buttons and knobs than I could imagine. My excitement built again, but there was a catch. When the organ arrived, I was told it was not only for me, but was also for the family. Since it was supposed to have been a gift for my birthday, I would get the "biggest piece."

Biggest piece?

It wasn't as if the organ wouldn't have been shared. My father had violated a sacred rule: Never combine my birthday gift with Christmas, and especially do not combine it with my siblings. I never considered the organ mine, and came to understand that my father didn't really know me.

As my birthday passed, one final holiday awaited: New Year's Eve. Dinner consisted of pork and sauerkraut. We were told those foods were Danish traditions, and eating them would bring good luck in the coming year. Nobody but my mother liked the sauerkraut, but for the sake of good luck, and to be polite, we all managed at least one small bite. To top the meal off we were provided with a rice pudding she called Ris-Ras. Within the pudding was a hidden almond, waiting to crown someone with good luck. Once dinner finished, the best part was yet to come. We were allowed to stay up way past bedtime.

To prepare for New Year's, my mother set up a snack table. Chips, crackers, and all kinds of home-baked Christmas cookies were placed on card tables in the formal living room. Our big color TV console sat at one end of the room, flanked by an integrated record player and radio. Lawrence Welk or Guy Lombardo conducted their countdowns as the ball in Times Square started to drop. At midnight, we ran to the front door banging pots and pans to welcome in the New Year. As the echo faded into cold night air and the front door clicked shut, we had all grown a little older, a little tougher, and were ready to welcome the challenges brought on by a new beginning.

Years later, I reached for what remained from those holidays. After our mother passed, and with my wife's encouragement, I gathered up the old holiday decorations. Those decorations were the physical reminders of who we'd been and how we'd celebrate the holidays together. The wax candles and paper diorama still reemerge from their boxes every year to join the other decorations in my home.

Kindergarten to 4th Grade

Once I was old enough for kindergarten, the adventures of growing up expanded beyond home. The elementary school was located in a residential neighborhood. To the delight of every child, including me, a candy store stood right next door. By this time, my allowance had grown to one shiny dime per week, to be saved or spent. That dime was a small fortune, and when asked what I wanted to be when I grew up, the answer was not a noble profession like a doctor or an astronaut. I wanted to be a millionaire. The allowance provided quite a dilemma. Should I save my weekly allowance to achieve the goal of becoming a millionaire, or spend the money after school at the candy store. I bought candy once in a while, but more often than not, the dime went straight into the piggy bank.

When school was not in session, more choices arose. My mother would keep cans of pop in the basement, and on warm summer Saturdays, I was given the opportunity to buy a can from the pantry for ten cents. Another option was to chase after the randomly appearing musical ice cream truck that slowly drove down the street. Even in summer, with more choices, I chose to mostly place my allowance aside for a rainy day. That small weekly decision, save or spend, was training I didn't recognize until much later.

While some lessons came one dime at a time, others were stitched right across my chest. There's a saying about how clothes make the man. I don't know if that's true, but I do remember a shirt from the early '70s that filled me with pride. It was a Smucker's promotion that played off their slogan: *"With a name like Smuckers, it has to be good."* If a customer sent in jelly jar labels, they would mail a T-shirt. Mine was white with blue lettering, except for my name, which was red. It proudly declared: *"With a name like Danny, I have to be good."* I wore it constantly, not because it was stylish, but because it said something I believed. That little line, meant to be clever, became part of me. No matter what kind of mischief I got into, I told myself I had to live up to the shirt. Wearing the promise of goodness on my chest I stepped into the world.

Parents always talk about how special their child's first day of school was. I really don't remember much about mine. My elementary school was located one mile away, and the district expected everyone to walk. Kindergarten start times were different from the older grades, so the journey to school wasn't with my older brothers. It was with a friend who lived across the street. Unlike the quick paced, direct barbershop walks, these trips were full of possibility. Without anybody driving me forward, the wonders of the outside world were mine to explore. My mother never had anything to worry about. To paraphrase Winnie the Pooh, *I always got to where I was going by walking away from where I was.*

With a bit of help from Bob the Crossing Guard, my friend and I always made it to class on time. Bob was located a few blocks from the school. Always patient, he would kneel down, help tie my shoes, zip my coat, comb my hair, and send me off with a reassuring nod. I know I left the house put together quite well. It's just that a lot can happen on the way to school. I'll never know what he thought of me, but I remember his kindness.

As challenging as the walk to school was, the trip back home with my friend was even more so. My mother recorded our journey.

"It has taken them 1-1/2 hours to walk home. After 6 weeks they whittled it down to a half hour. It took talks from teachers, a policeman and parents, plus a little bribery, but they finally made it."

Baby Book 1969

At four years and eight months, I had been right on the cusp of kindergarten age. By year's end, my teacher and mother agreed I wasn't quite ready for first grade. They asked what I'd like to do. Looking back, I'm sure they steered me gently, but it felt like my choice. I chose to return to kindergarten for a second year.

Shortly after that, my best friend Stephen moved away. Losing my classmates and my best friend hit hard, but I made new friends when school started in the fall. Having already completed the assignments, my new teacher called me the smartest kid in the class. That year gave me a confidence that never left.

Sometime during first grade I learned how to read. I was sitting on my mother's bed, staring at a book. The letters didn't slowly come together, they struck like lightning. Shapes I had only known by sound suddenly formed clear, familiar words, and I understood them. A rush of excitement surged through me. My mother was delighted. I couldn't get enough. Books began piling up beside my bed, and library visits became a regular part of life.

As second grade rolled around, even as I raced ahead with reading, basic fashion sense still eluded me. My mother recorded a brief note that made me laugh.

"Danny is a very little boy, very naïve, sweet, and smart. His schoolwork is tops. The only thing his teacher was concerned about at the April conference was that he can't seem to get his shoes on the right feet. This is typical Danny to some extent, as he puts his shoes on at the last minute he goes outdoors and really couldn't care which foot they're on."

Baby Book 1972

Maybe I couldn't get my shoes on right, but at least one of my brothers could. Watching how Rick transformed a baseball diamond into something artistic was special. While batting, he would bounce up and down to distract the pitcher. As the ball approached the plate, he stopped, and like a tight spring suddenly uncoiling, his body would unwind. When he made contact, the ball would sail into the outfield as I watched with pride. I might have been too small to do much for the team, but cheering my brother on was something I could handle.

It was nice to think a small part of his success started in our backyard. Hours were spent playing a baseball-themed game with a softball-sized orange Nerf ball. Rick was older, so he batted most of the time. I didn't mind. I loved pitching. Fastballs, curveballs, sliders, and sinkers were all wildly exaggerated by the soft, spongy Nerf ball. It gave Rick a great eye by the time Little League rolled around. That same year, we landed on the team that won our championship. The trophy settled into its permanent spot on a shelf in our childhood bedroom.

Years later, Rick forgot all about our old trophy. I never did. After moving into a new home as an adult, the shelf might have changed, but the trophy is still there.

During third grade, I wrote a report about our family background. My grandfather immigrated from Denmark as an electrical engineer. He passed away before I was born. Our Danish heritage was a source of family pride. When he came to America, he immersed himself in his new country and only spoke English. His native tongue wasn't taught to his children, but traditions were. Though I never knew my grandfather, my mother shared one of his beliefs that stayed with me:

"Success in life is built on both patience and time."

It may sound like a fortune cookie, but I carried that idea with me, especially in my approach to saving, investing, and dealing with people.

Sometime during fourth grade, another best friend moved away. Jason wasn't a neighbor, but we saw each other in my class at school, and in church at Youth Club. Then, one day, without warning, he was gone. It wasn't the first time a friend had disappeared. Stephen had moved away in kindergarten. Losing Jason confirmed it. Best friends didn't always stay. After that, I learned to keep a little distance. I had plenty of acquaintances, but not a lot of close friends.

Even though there was a hesitation to make close friends, I never stopped looking for places to belong. Music became one of those places. The school offered instruments to students who wanted to learn. My brother John started on the alto horn, and following in his footsteps would have been okay, but the real instrument I wanted to play was the saxophone. Unfortunately, to play the saxophone, you needed to own one.

Looking back, the choice of the alto horn wasn't about wanting it. I chose it because it was free. Increasingly, my mother could be found staring at bills with a worried look on her face. There was no way I could lift that weight, but at least I wouldn't add to it. Picking the instrument that came without expense was its own kind of love. By the end of fourth grade, the world inside our house still felt intact, but signs of a subtle, slow-building strain were starting to show.

Seeing Cars and Cracks (5th Grade)

The summer of 1975 was the last time I remember the entire family taking a vacation together. On one summer trip, we crowded into the car and headed north on a two-hour drive to the Pymatuning Reservoir. In the trunk were paper bags filled with crusts of bread we'd saved all year in the basement freezer. As we passed cornfields, my mother would sing the opening lines of a song from the musical *Oklahoma*, about the corn being as high as an elephant's eye.

At the reservoir, each handful of bread we tossed onto the glassy water unleashed a frenzy of thrashing fish. As the food quickly disappeared, the surface returned to its calm state. There wasn't any fighting over the scraps, there was only the joy of watching the fish churn at the surface. It felt like every other family trip, with our mother singing her songs and laughing with my siblings, except that visit to Pymatuning marked the end of a special kind of togetherness.

Long before and long after that last family vacation, the car stayed constant. It was a yellow Rambler. The Rambler carried us to drive-in movies, petting zoos, church picnics, and school concerts. It was in the background of nearly every memory. Our car was part of the family. No matter how packed the back seat or how much it groaned on cold mornings, it never left us stranded. With its boxy frame and dull yellow paint, it waited in the garage.

After we saw *Herbie the Love Bug*, we were convinced the Rambler had a soul. It never spoke or blinked its headlights, but it had a certain way of coughing to life. When we pushed it too hard, it rattled as if it understood us.

Around that same time, cracks beneath the paint began to show, not just in the Rambler, but in everything. Visits with my father became more sporadic. He was divorcing his second wife, and his lack of child support payments caused stress in the house. The word "mechanic" started appearing more often in everyday conversation.

In the house on Lovingston Drive, new cars weren't discussed. They weren't even dreamed of. The family focused on keeping the Rambler alive, mile by mile. Our local mechanic became something of a physician, doing all he could to keep our aging companion alive on a budget that shrank by the month.

Years later, my father told me the only thing he fought to keep in that divorce was his animal hospital. He was willing to give up the house, the sports cars, the plane, everything but the business. "I could always buy another car," he once said. He was right. He could. We couldn't.

As fifth grade approached, the elementary school seemed like a new place. The older students were all on the main building's third floor, far from the lower grades. By then, Rick had moved on to junior high. With a new set of friends, he no longer wanted his younger brother around bothering him. Our alliance seemed to fade overnight, and I went from being a trusted companion, to being an adversary.

John and Mike also pushed me away. They had started a Dixieland Band with their friends. John played trombone and Mike played the piano. One corner of the basement was converted into a music studio, where their songs were perfected. Going anywhere near the basement when they played was strictly forbidden, so all I could do was listen from a distance.

That year, it wasn't just the Dixieland Band that made life at home feel more divided. Our father bought John a car, and it didn't get much care. While playing in my upstairs bedroom, I sometimes heard John and my mother yelling in the basement. I didn't know what the fights were about. All I knew was that yelling did not belong in our house, and especially not at my mother. Those moments left my whole world feeling off-balance. All I could think of was that John was breaking one of the Ten Commandments, *"Honor thy Father and Mother."* His behavior didn't improve.

In the fall, John got into a fight at the local McDonald's and shattered his jaw. Drinking his meals through a straw and mostly staying in his room further isolated him from his brothers and sister. I could hear even more arguments through the house as concern grew about whether his grades were good enough to graduate. He did graduate that year, but all the turmoil surrounding our home raised my awareness of the struggles our family was going through. I lowered my head and kept a low profile, all to make sure I would not be the cause of any added stress on the family.

When the house got louder, I retreated to the backyard and focused on baseball. The days of being able to barely swing the bat were gone. My coordination and athleticism were developing quickly, and I went from being the little kid who gets placed in deep right field away from the action, to being the kid at the center of the field on the pitcher's mound. Rick moved to a more advanced league. With older brothers becoming less and less available to play with, I turned to my next best friend, the house.

The home's red brick walls made perfect targets for a tennis ball. With a Pittsburgh Pirates game playing on the radio, tossing a ball against the wall just right sent fly balls arcing back. It was practice I never tired of. For pitching practice and ground balls, the area under the kitchen window was perfect. Hours were spent outside practicing. I'd like to think the sound of the ball against the house was comforting to my mother, because as long as there was the sound of a ball hitting the wall, she knew exactly where her youngest boy was and what he was doing.

As I threw tennis balls against brick, my mother worked numbers in her checkbook. My grandmother's saying, *"When God closes a door, He opens a window,"* became relevant once again.

The last of my mother's Danish aunts passed during this time, and my mother inherited silver keepsakes along with a modest sum of money. Although the silver would gain a mythical status, it was money that had the most influence. The cash had been placed in a trust, then distributed to my mother at the beginning of each year. The amount was just enough to clear old bills and cover the basics, like groceries. The arrival helped balance the inconsistent child support from my father, and kept the family moving forward to fight another day.

Fists and Footlights (6th Grade)

Sixth grade was about holding my ground and expanding my boundaries. Whether it was in the classroom or on the playground, boys tried to show who was the toughest, and sometimes, it led to a fight. During those years, I only got in one. A boy who had been bullying other classmates decided to try bullying me. I had three older brothers who had toughened me up, so his efforts didn't work.

One day while walking home, he started pushing me. Classmates surrounded us, chanting, "Fight, fight, fight!" As we stared each other down, he pulled back to throw a punch. I lunged forward first. Before he knew what was happening, I had him on the ground, his arms pinned by my knees. His surrender came quickly. When I let him up, he skulked away. I knew fighting was wrong, but he attacked me, and running wasn't an option.

Not all confrontations ended that way. Some never made it that far. Seeing my success at defeating the bully, classmates tried to arrange another battle. This time it was with a boy whose path barely crossed with mine. Sal was a proud Italian boy. He was strong, athletic, and a fierce competitor on the playground. On the day of the fight, Sal and I saw each other in the hall before school ended. I told Sal I didn't know why we were going to fight, because I wasn't mad at him about anything. He looked back at me with the same uncertainty. We gave each other a nod of respect, and moved on.

While Sal and I chose respect over rivalry, the playing field offered another kind of challenge. On the backdrop of changing dynamics at home, I was slowly developing into quite an athlete. By sixth grade, despite being smaller, there was not a single classmate of mine who could best me during gym or on the playground, and my Little League reputation was well known. The sixth-grade coach asked me to join the football team. Rick had played in elementary school, and I inherited his old plastic pads. The problem was that Rick was much taller than me, and the football pads didn't fit.

After one step onto the field in oversized gear, I knew I didn't belong. As loose pads awkwardly clattered around my shoulders, I could see the coach looking at me with concern. After those first practices, he pulled me aside and offered to help get pads that fit. I knew my family didn't have money to spare for new football equipment. The embarrassment of accepting charity was too great. I politely declined the help, and stumbled through the rest of the season.

Around the same time, my mother took on extra work. None of it was glamorous. She sold Avon, assembled Welcome Wagon baskets, and delivered thick stacks of phone books to doorsteps. She rarely worked alone. I was often with her, running catalogs to porches or keeping her company in the car.

She had earned a master's degree in the 1950s, when most women didn't even finish college. Taking on odd jobs must have been humbling, but degrees didn't pay the bills. She did what was needed to keep the family afloat. Without knowing it, she was teaching me the importance of a strong work ethic, and that any job could be done with dignity.

School on the other hand, offered a chance to show a different type of strength. At Christmas, the sixth-grade students put on a play for the rest of the school. Tryouts for the part of Santa Claus were highly competitive, and I was in the running for the starring role. This was my shot at fame. Unfortunately, there was another boy with a stronger voice. I ended up with the role of the family dog, Ponto.

It helped that the dog had a singing part, but everyone knew the role of Santa was the real prize. I wasn't going to let disappointment affect my effort. When performance day came, I clearly spoke my lines, sang my song, and even improvised by playing with some presents under the tree.

Afterward, the younger students wrote letters to the performers. To my surprise, they liked Ponto better than Santa. During tryouts, I thought I had lost the part that mattered. As it turned out, the one I got was the one that stood out most. I'd barked loud enough to be remembered, and with junior high ahead, standing out would soon matter even more.

The summer before seventh grade brought one last simple thrill. I joined my Boy Scout troop ushering Pitt football games. Tony Dorsett was in the backfield that year, running through defenses without slowing down. We watched the games and sometimes received tips. Being helpful came with rewards. That stadium held special meaning since both my mother and father had gone to Pitt. My parents may not have been together, but being at their old university made me feel like I was sharing something with them. Those Saturdays felt easy, like I belonged there.

By the end of summer, everything felt less certain. John had disappeared into college life at West Virginia University. Occasionally we'd hear updates, but mostly he lived in a world apart.

Mike was absorbed in the high school glory of being drum major and receiving scholastic honors, his success feeding a streak of arrogance that required caution at home.

I remember my mother telling us about my grandfather. He loved collecting stamps. His collection was given to Mike. One day I entered Mike's room without permission to look at my grandfather's collection. When he found out I had violated his kingdom, he unleashed a violent attack. Mike punched and beat me as I curled up at the bottom of the entryway stairs. His twelfth grade fists and feet pummeled my sixth grade body. Boys my age didn't run to their mothers for protection, so there was nothing I could do but survive the onslaught. It was something I wouldn't forget.

Rick wanted less to do with his younger brother as he started high school and drifted into a life of his own. Meanwhile, Kathy stayed close to our mother, still under her protective wing.

We weren't the only ones adjusting. When the school year approached, my mother decided to return to teaching, the career she had before starting a family. Not wanting to be too far from home, she applied for a job as an elementary school substitute. It was strange to imagine her standing in front of a classroom, but part of me was glad she was stepping back into the world again.

Family still shaped my world, yet I had begun looking for more. I didn't know if school would give me that, but seventh grade was my chance to find out.

CHAPTER 3

ON TO JUNIOR HIGH

Junior high was not an extension of elementary school. Family faded into the background, and friends became more important. Not like Stephen in kindergarten or Jason in fourth grade. Those bonds were pure and uncomplicated. By seventh grade, everyone was jockeying for position, popularity, attention, and identity. Belonging took on new meaning. Some days I found that at wrestling practice or in the band room. Other days, one wrong outfit or a joke that fell flat made me feel like an outcast.

For the first time, I walked to class without a brother or sister in the building. The comfort of one teacher all day was gone, replaced by the shuffle of changing classrooms and new rules. The halls buzzed with unfamiliar voices and locker slams. It was a time of trial and error. There was no way to study for the social tests that happened in the hallways. I didn't really try to fit in. I was just being me.

French Horns and Cinnamon Sticks (7th Grade)

My brothers had always been the ones to caulk doors and repair whatever broke. The only thing I was allowed to do was watch. Junior high changed all of that. I still carried the image my family had painted me with. I was the kid who spilled milk, and who wasn't allowed near the kitchen except to lick a spoon or wash the dishes. My new classes offered space and opportunity to do things I'd never imagined, like baking muffins, making wood boxes, and pouring molten metal into a coin mold. Those opportunities were exciting.

Other opportunities were less appealing. Gym class was supposed to be about athletes showing off their skills in fierce competition. Ours included square dancing. It wasn't fierce, and there was no score or strategy. We stood in a circle, boys and girls staring blankly at one another. Then it got worse. We were each assigned a partner, not someone we knew or liked, just a random girl. I remember learning the steps and wondering why we were being taught to square dance. We lived in the suburbs, not on a farm. The only useful lesson seemed to be how to ask a girl to dance without embarrassment. That part didn't work either.

Fortunately, band wasn't about asking someone to dance. It was familiar and comforting. After graduating from the alto horn, I joined the French horn section alongside two girls who played the same instrument. Having them beside me was less awkward than square dancing, and talking with them came naturally. They were the only two girls I dated during those years. There was no drama when things ended. The experience became the beginning of friendships that lasted through high school.

There was more to band than just meeting girls. I remember one practice when our director was out sick. Teaching band was one of the toughest assignments a substitute could get. We were an unruly group, and it was common to switch instruments. A student didn't have to know how to play the instrument, they simply had to be good at pretending. In fourth grade I had wanted to play the saxophone, and now an opportunity appeared. Like many classmates, I switched instruments with a friend and took my seat in the appropriate section. This was a chance to find my hidden talent. Unfortunately, the talent stayed hidden.

The teacher started conducting, and the awful sound of out-of-tune instruments filled every corner of the room. I tried my best, but the only notes bleating from my friend's saxophone were sad little squeaks. To my surprise, the substitute teacher complimented my playing, and gently scolded me for missing a note. After class, my friend and I laughed at the trick we played. That was the end of a not-so-promising saxophone career, brief and squeaky as it was. My French horn didn't object that I'd let somebody else play it. It was quickly becoming a friend that felt right.

Band had been my first choice for an elective. The second was a new language. I'd always enjoyed puzzles, and a language felt like solving one. My mother had taken Spanish when she went to school, and my brothers had all taken German. I chose French for its connection to my band instrument and its reputation as the language of love. I figured that couldn't hurt.

In class, our teacher planned to inspire us by putting on a mock French wedding, complete with food. Nobody wanted to act as the pretend bride or groom. We were just settling in with the idea of boys and girls going on dates. Marriage, pretend or not, was a bridge too far. Thankfully, I wasn't chosen for one of the starring roles, and I don't remember the food. It must not have been too bad, though, because I kept studying French. Learning a language turned out to be more useful than I ever expected. It didn't lead to romance, but it did give me a sense of how foreign languages worked, and stirred a desire to travel.

Sports, on the other hand, made my world feel more unforgiving. All the practice of throwing a ball against the wall at home started paying off, and I was the only seventh grader on the school's softball All Star team. The coach placed me at second base, a position I'd never played before.

The first batter up hit a line drive so hard it looked like a rocket coming off the bat. I ducked my head and held up a glove as the ball shot into right field. Despite my embarrassment, nobody laughed. The game went on, but my confidence had been damaged. It was the kind of moment when having a father around might have helped. I needed someone to pull me aside, tell me to shake it off, and get back out there.

When the spring baseball season arrived, money was tight at home. Sign-ups came and went without a sound. Upon realizing the opportunity to play in the league had passed, I wasn't upset. Sometimes in our house, unspoken sacrifices had to be made. Playing in organized leagues ended there for me.

The next big opportunity at school had nothing to do with sports. It came wrapped in foil and smelled like cinnamon. Word had spread that soaking a toothpick in cinnamon oil gave it a kick, and the flavor lasted a lot longer than a piece of bubble gum. Even though there was competition, I saw an opportunity. I bought a bottle of cinnamon oil, soaked a handful of toothpicks, wrapped them in foil, and started selling dozen-sized packs for a quarter each.

The demand was there. The money flowed. For a few brief days, I had a booming business. Then rumors started swirling about students getting rashes on their legs from cinnamon oil leaking through their pockets. The school cracked down. The principal summoned the offending entrepreneurs, but I wasn't one of them. My product was clean, neatly packaged, and complaint-free. It didn't matter. The safe choice was to shut down, and that's what I did.

Wrestling, A Kiss, and A Connection (8th Grade)

By eighth grade, the family drifted further apart. Mike left for college and my mother, tired of hearing Rick and me constantly bickering, moved me into Mike's old room. My view of school and family was changing. Seventh grade had given me a taste of independence, and I was no longer willing to do things just because an adult said so. I needed meaning. It didn't have to be deep or important. Sometimes just having fun was enough, but there had to be a purpose, or I lost interest. I wanted to know why something mattered, how it would be useful, or why it was worth doing at all. If I lost interest, mischief appeared. When that happened, the line between funny and hurtful blurred.

It is difficult for anyone to make English interesting, and my eighth-grade class wasn't any different. The teacher was young, pretty, and energetic. Despite teaching a boring subject, she related so well with her students that it was almost like she was one of us. She wasn't.

One day after class, while displaying a pen with disappearing ink, I sprayed some on her blouse. Except, the ink didn't fully disappear. My friends all thought it was funny. I did not. I could see a look of disappointment on her face and immediately apologized. I even offered to pay for dry cleaning or replace the blouse. I just wanted to fix what I had done. She politely declined. She also didn't report me for any bad behavior.

The next day, the teacher came back to class as if nothing had happened, except something had happened. That was the hardest part. There was no discipline, no lecture. The only punishment came from me. I felt a heavy, unshakable guilt. My teasing and joking had gone too far, and the guilt ran deep. After that, I was on my best behavior for the rest of the year. I'd learned what crossing the line felt like, and I didn't want to feel it again.

I needed somewhere to put my energy, to prove I could do things right. That place became the wrestling mat. Growing up with three older brothers who were often trying to hold me in one place prepared me for wrestling. Fortunately for me wrestling didn't come with tickling. The practices were after school. They were physically exhausting tests of strength and endurance that often went on well past 7:00. I won every match except one, which happened to be the last match of the year.

The match was a battle between seventh graders and eighth graders. My opponent might have been in my weight class, but he was both bigger and stronger than me. He was one of the most athletic and popular kids in seventh grade. Heck, even the eighth graders liked him. As the match started, I carefully sized him up. Wrestling was all about speed and technique, and I had the edge on both accounts. The score was going my way until the final minute, when I applied a move that should have guaranteed victory. Even though my instinct told me to do it my own way, I used the move exactly as the coach showed us. A victorious result did not follow. My opponent broke the hold, and I quickly went from two points up to one point down.

I sat on the mat after the whistle, watching the referee raise his arm while catching my breath. Everything had been done as taught, but maybe that was the problem. Sometimes doing everything as instructed isn't good enough. Instincts aren't guesses. I had ignored the voice telling me to do it my way. Although it would take making many more mistakes for that concept to fully sink in, that was the moment I started to learn the cost of ignoring instinct.

The lessons didn't stop with the school year. I'd learned to trust my instinct on the mat. Off the mat, especially with girls, I was still figuring them out. A first kiss can be both exciting and exhilarating. That's not exactly how it went for me.

By the end of the year, I was dating the girl who sat next to me in band. We found common ground in playing the French horn, having older siblings, and not being one of the rich kids in school. Kids bragging about how rich their parents were was common. Some days, I walked Holly home from school, and like any gallant young man, I carried her books. Carrying books for a girl was a true sign of affection, but there was another sign I wasn't quite ready for.

One day, while walking to her house, she started to talk about kissing, French kissing. That was new. I was already playing the French horn and taking a French language class, but nothing was ever mentioned about a kiss. I knew about the kiss on my forehead my mother gave me before going to bed, or a relative giving a peck on the cheek. I thought I knew what to do. Besides, kissing was supposed to be natural and instinctive, so how hard could it be? I'd seen movies, but real life was different. We walked to a spot hidden from the road, just out of sight. She turned to me, her face close, mouth slightly open. Her lips approached mine. They opened further. Then, softly, instinctively, I let out a small roar. Holly pulled back slightly puzzled. I thought she was playing around. I was just as confused.

Oh, oh, that was not what she expected.

Her older sister had obviously prepared her for a kiss much better than my brothers had prepared me. We continued on our way talking and holding hands like nothing strange had happened. Holly and I remained close throughout the summer, neither one of us speaking of the kiss. I worried my mistake would spread around the school, a reputation I'd never live down. I was relieved when it didn't. Figuring out girls wasn't going to be easy.

Church offered a different kind of puzzle. My group was finishing our confirmation classes. These were classes that would allow us to join the congregation as members. There were eight of us, and I was chosen to predict the future. Based on our time at church together, we assigned a potential occupation to each person in the group. I only remember two predictions.

The first memorable prediction was for a girl I didn't know well and who rarely came to Sunday school. Not knowing what to choose, I said she was going to be a housewife. It was meant to be a compliment, since my own mother stayed home until I entered junior high, and she was one of the kindest people I knew. When this was announced, the girl looked up with a blank stare. Afterwards, I was told she wasn't happy with the prediction. I looked for her to explain, but she had already left. With school out, I didn't see much of her after that day, but I will always remember the confusion I felt at her reaction. I realized that girls aspired to more than just raising a family. I still had a lot to learn.

The second memorable prediction was for me. It was as a clown. *A clown?* Sure, I liked being funny, but didn't always succeed. I dismissed the thought. Being a clown wasn't part of my path in life.

My next lesson about growing up came during the summer, and this one didn't involve girls or clowns. The last time I went to camp was at the end of junior high. Camp was a yearly event, and I was now old enough to do more than paddle a canoe or shoot a bow and arrow. My group was scheduled to go on a long hike that ended in a white-water rafting trip. While getting ready for the hike, some kids in my cabin decided to have a little fun. After dark, they snuck out and tampered with our counselor's car in a particularly juvenile way. I didn't join in, but I also didn't tell the other boys to stop. The next morning, the counselor became suspicious when his car wouldn't start. It didn't take long to figure out the campers were involved. By the end of the day, the local police were brought in, and the boys who had instigated the act of vandalism were identified and sent home. As for the rest of us, they said we were guilty by association.

Guilty by association?

Except for silence, I hadn't done anything wrong. I silently contained my frustration at being labeled guilty without causing trouble. The punishment was having to pay for the car repair. We still went hiking and white-water rafting, but the counselor carried a grudge for the entire trip. At one point, when he lost his keys, he accused us of stealing them. The keys were found in his sleeping bag, but not before he subjected the whole cabin to a strip search. Camp had shown me the importance of speaking up, how unfair justice could be, and how easily power could be abused.

Around the same time, subtle changes began in how I saw my father. Proximity seemed to shape what benefits his two different families received. It started with small trips to the Country Club.

After climbing out of the pool, and as I stood dripping beside one of his stepdaughters, she asked if I wanted something to eat. I glanced around for an adult, wondering how that would even work. "Don't worry," she said, seeing the surprised look on my face. "We can charge it to the account."

Charge it to the account?

That was a line I only heard on TV or in a movie. My mother clipped coupons. She circled generic brands in grocery flyers. Here at this pool, in this version of the world, having something was as easy as asking for it. I stood in awe as I realized my father's other family enjoyed privileges my family could only dream about. That awareness cast a new light on the occasions when I was invited into his world. It started opening my eyes about what my father could provide, when he chose, and also who he chose to provide things for. These weren't signs of closeness. They were moments of choice.

After my father had divorced wife number two, his visits practically disappeared. Now that he was married to wife number three, invitations to the Country Club started becoming more frequent.

Around the same time, Kathy and I were given an opportunity to join him in his plane on a trip to Niagara Falls. Even now, the details of Niagara Falls are mostly lost to time, except for Kathy getting airsick and the hum of the engine. A connection with my father was trying to take shape, but it was still not fully there. That trip didn't bring us closer, but it didn't push us apart either. He kept trying to reach out, in his own way.

Before ninth grade began, my father and I flew to Hilton Head Island on a golf outing. This was a trip where the only breadcrumbs I could find were a picture of his plane on the runway, one with me in the copilot seat wearing headphones, and a note from my mother.

"Over the Labor Day weekend, Dan took a trip with his father to Hilton Head Island."

Baby Book 1979

No mention was made of either Rick or Kathy. My memories of the trip aren't strong, but a feeling is. I don't know if it happened in the plane or on the fairway, but somehow, somewhere during that trip, we clicked.

John and Mike were at college, Rick was acting aloof, and my father didn't know what to do with Kathy. During the summer before ninth grade started, he offered me a job at his animal hospital. There had been a void in my father's life that his third wife and three stepdaughters couldn't fill. That void would be unknowingly filled by me.

CHAPTER 4

HIGH SCHOOL

Right before eleventh grade started, my father took me on a dream trip to the Caribbean. He bought me a top-of-the-line 35mm pocket camera to capture the journey. I kept a short diary on the back of the pictures.

One passage summed up the attitude I carried during high school. My father and his third wife were out for the evening, and dinner was on my own. I wrote:

"After dinner, I walked over to the bar and ordered a glass of white wine. Didn't like it but I didn't care. Still no worries. Nobody to tell me no. Think I did it to rebel. Don't know why but it was fun. Glad to know somewhere in the world a person is trusted like this. To be able to do what you want. Control yourself by yourself not others."

July 1981

Having one glass of wine when I was younger than twenty-one wasn't about being reckless. In Saint Martin, it wasn't even illegal. It was about seeing what having a choice felt like. My years in high school were about testing the limits of trust, and how much freedom I was ready to hold.

Work, Buckets, and Band (9th Grade)

My father's animal hospital started as a small, converted home on a busy street. Two decades later it exploded into one of the largest practices in the Pittsburgh area, teeming with eight veterinarians and over a dozen other support staff.

John and Mike spent time working there when they were in high school, but Rick did not. This was my turn. Whether it was a rite of passage or a way to instill discipline, I didn't care. I was ready. This was a chance to get closer to my father.

Getting to the animal hospital after school involved walking over three miles along busy streets and winding trolley tracks. I loved balancing on a single rail while progressing down the line. There was never any risk of being hit. With their loud clickity-clack sounds echoing down the tracks, the trolleys could be heard coming from a mile away.

I usually arrived at work early. My father's office was located in the upstairs, and outside of his office was an empty desk. The desk was a great place to catch up on my homework and study. The demands of ninth grade were much greater than junior high, and having disciplined quiet time away from home helped me focus.

Work provided a chance to get to know my father better. Up to that point, we hadn't spent much quality time together. On the first day, he welcomed me. I proudly showed him a black and white portrait my mother had given me years earlier. It showed a younger version of him in his military uniform. Surprised to see it, he asked for the picture and promised to return it to me after he died. I didn't want to hand it over, but saying no felt wrong. I didn't realize it then, but that day I traded a memory of my father for the man himself.

The animal hospital also taught me about punch clocks. On the wall, a card with my name awaited. When the shift started, I placed my card in the slot, listened to the loud thunk of a time stamp being registered in ink, and returned my card to its place on the wall. My responsibilities included removing trash from the parking lot, cleaning cages, ushering people into the exam rooms, and reuniting boarded pets with their owners. The tasks weren't exciting, but they came with a level of trust I wasn't going to squander. In time, those responsibilities would grow to identifying parasites under a microscope, administering subcutaneous fluids, and giving the animals intramuscular shots. I loved learning about this new world and made sure my work reflected it.

There was another bonus. After punching out, my father would give me a ride home. We spoke of school, work at the animal hospital, and just about anything else that came to mind. Sometimes, he would stop at the grocery store and buy a favorite treat from his younger days. Kathy might have wielded power with her control of M&M's, but I had something better: Rocky Road cookies and chocolate milk. I was finally connecting with my father, getting treats that were considered decadent in our home, and earning a paycheck. I was in heaven, but there was more.

At the animal hospital, there was someone else who seemed to understand my father. Roxanne, a tri-colored collie mix, had been abandoned right after outgrowing puppyhood and was being kept temporarily as a blood donor. She was beautiful, alert, and highly obedient, but only with my father. Everyone said she responded to his voice in a way no one else could. That changed the first time I met her. Roxanne also responded to me.

From that moment on, she followed my voice. I took her on walks without a leash. She'd sit, heel, and wag like we'd known each other forever. The others said it must've been something in my tone, something that reminded her of my father. I liked that thought. After a year, she was adopted into a new home. I would've loved to have kept her, but we already had a dog. Still, for that stretch of time, she was one more thing I had come to love about working at the animal hospital.

Roxanne reminded me how closely connected I was to my father, but there were also times that made me question how well I really knew him. One afternoon, while sitting in my father's office, he slipped off his jacket. Beneath it was a gun, strapped tight across his chest.

A gun? My father?

I thought guns were for good guys and bad guys on TV, not quiet veterinarians who bought Rocky Road cookies and chocolate milk for their kids. He noticed my reaction and explained, matter-of-factly, that his second wife had once pointed a gun at him, and it had made him feel helpless.

I was stunned. Why would anyone want to hurt my father? Picturing him with a gun was something I never could've imagined. For a brief instant, the man in front of me felt unfamiliar.

I don't know if it was the shock he saw on my face or not, but after that day, I never saw the gun again, and the most hazardous thing I saw him carrying was a racquetball racquet.

Down the road from the animal hospital was a private health club. My father had been learning to play racquetball and needed a partner. I was given my own card to practice, and became competitive after a few lessons. We both darted about the court chasing the fast-moving ball. Occasionally, his shot would accidentally hit me in the back. The pain of the ball, or who won the game wasn't important. All that mattered was being there with my father.

Years earlier, during one of our stiff weekend visits, he told me: "I'm not a Brady Bunch kind of father." No concerts. No baseball games. That was the bar. Yet here we were, sweating through racquetball matches, talking about school in the car, chasing chocolate milk and cookies. He may not have wanted the part, but he was playing it anyway.

At school, making friends followed different rules. By the time a student entered high school, their place in the social hierarchy was set. Our school sorted people into buckets. Freaks hung out in the smoking area and usually didn't get good grades. Nerds focused on academics. Jocks played sports. Band buddies were in the marching band. If you didn't fit cleanly into a bucket, your friends usually did, and that was enough to classify you. It was possible to have a foot in two buckets, but most kids clonked around in only one.

I didn't like buckets, and didn't like being told what kind of kid I was. Rick tried to get me to smoke, but I hated the smell and wasn't a freak. My grades were decent, but not nerd-level. I was athletic, but after-school practices conflicted with work. Marching band met early in the morning, and since my older brothers had all been in it, joining wasn't a choice. I didn't mind the early mornings or the dorky hat. I minded being told it made me something I wasn't.

Marching band was a voluntary after-school activity, like sports. Symphonic band was for only the best musicians. In ninth grade, I was given a great honor. I was the only freshman placed in the symphonic band. It wasn't the first time I'd been placed ahead of my age, but unlike playing on the seventh grade All Star team, this time, I didn't duck. I held my place. I belonged, but there's a difference between belonging through talent and belonging through maturity.

My French horn was a school instrument, and there were a few dents in its shiny brass bell. One of the other French horn players was a grade ahead of me, and he thought it was funny how the bell of my horn could be bent. I also thought this was funny. It started by occasionally bending the brass edges. He folded it inward. I bent it back. By the end of the year, the bell looked more like a crumpled piece of aluminum foil than a musical instrument.

The music teacher was furious, and when he became angry, the veins in his neck would pop and his face would turn red. I knew I'd crossed a line, but how had he not seen this coming? The French horn section was in the middle of the band room directly in front of him. Plus, he saw me in the marching band.

My mother was called and threatened with having to pay for the repairs. That was the worst part. I knew the family didn't have the money. The thought of creating more stress hurt. I don't know what my mother said, but we didn't have to pay. After being bombarded with many stern words, I was given a new French horn that I promised to protect with my life, which I did. As for the older student, he didn't even get scolded.

At home, I was beginning to see something else, something we joked about, but not without evidence. It went like this: troublemaker, golden child, troublemaker, golden child. John had struggled with school and once broke his jaw in a fight. Mike followed, a drum major, an Ivy League college, a shining light. Rick was next. Pulled into the bad-boy smoking area crowd, he was once caught shoplifting. Then came me. Except for that French horn incident, I had good grades, a part-time job, and a cheery disposition. Besides, I identified with my old Smuckers Jelly shirt which said, *"With a name like Danny, I had to be good."* Kathy was the lone girl at the bottom of the sibling totem pole. Her grades were strong and she had a clean record. Kathy showed signs of breaking the pattern, but she was still a wildcard.

Money and a Dream Vacation (10th Grade)

By the start of tenth grade, I was noticing more about my father. He had a natural manner that made people around him feel comfortable. His charm extended to employees, pet owners, and strangers in stores. He didn't turn it off and on, it was always on. I had coaches and teachers who yelled, but my father did not. He didn't even raise his voice.

That image didn't match what I'd heard from my mother and older brothers. They told me he had a volatile temper when he lived at our house. The man I saw was nothing like that. He was gentle, charismatic, and controlled. It wasn't that I didn't believe my mother or my older brothers, but something didn't add up, and I'd become someone who needed things to add up. Even as I tried to make sense of what I'd been told, I wasn't comfortable asking my parents. The Bible said to *"Honor Thy Father and Mother,"* not question them.

Sometimes, I learned things about my father I didn't really want to know. One day at the animal hospital while I was assisting in the X-ray room, he said, "You know son, I never cheated on your mother."

That statement bothered me. I remembered he'd left my mother while she was pregnant. The next thing I knew, he was married to another woman. He went on to explain why he wasn't wearing any shielding while the X-rays were being taken. "I don't ever plan on having more children. I've had a vasectomy."

It was nice knowing he wasn't thinking about more kids, but this was way more information than I cared to hear. Maybe something was bothering him, and he felt an urgent need to explain. I didn't know. I didn't want to know.

Then there were things I didn't question, but probably should have. Direct communication between my parents was rare. Any time I heard him speak to my mother, it was with an edge that felt undeserved, like she was the problem he couldn't fix. Every now and then, before driving me home, my father would walk over to the cash register, pull out a few hundred-dollar bills, and slip in an IOU so his accountant would know what he did. He told me to give the money to my mother. I wasn't just the messenger. I was the buffer.

John and Mike had told me stories of how they used to bring envelopes of money home, but if my father was having problems with his business or a new wife, the envelopes stopped. They told me stories of how my mother never signed any divorce papers when my father walked away from the family. There was no formal child support agreement. Maybe it wasn't that I couldn't believe it, maybe I simply didn't want to.

While I was trying to make sense of my father, financial tension at home was getting harder to ignore. My mother was doing everything she could to convince the school to give her as much work as possible. Each morning, if a substitute teacher was needed, a call would come in from the school telling her where to go. I remember a feeling of nervousness sitting around the breakfast table. If there was no call, or when a ringing phone was someone other than the school district, disappointment set in. No call meant no money, and our family's needs were growing.

John didn't finish college in four years, which meant another year of tuition. Bills for car repairs, utilities, groceries, and even taking me out to buy clothes showed the stress on my mother's face. She buried every emotion, whether happiness, fear, worry, or pain. She didn't know it, but I was watching and learning about managing both money and feelings.

While working at the animal hospital alongside my father, and living with my mother, a realization grew. I was straddling two different worlds. With my father it was gym memberships, country clubs, island vacations, and golf lessons. With my mother it was hand-me-downs, overdue bills, and powdered milk. I resigned myself to the reality of living two lives, existing in two worlds with two people I loved.

The animal hospital wasn't only about work and the relationship with my father, sometimes it intersected with school, and girls. One day a new employee showed up. Kim was in my grade, but we barely knew each other. Getting to know her felt like a gift. For several months we worked side by side, joked, and laughed. I was determined not to screw this up the way I had with Holly and my first kiss.

Then one afternoon, while we were teasing each other, Kim gave me a small, harmless punch in the arm. It wasn't out of character for her. I playfully returned the gesture. She did it again. I responded with equal force, but this time her face went blank. The next week, Kim didn't show up for work. I didn't have her phone number, and we shared no classes. Just like that, she was gone.

Whatever moment passed between us, I never had the chance to ask. All I knew was, it felt like a test I didn't know I was taking until I'd already failed it. I was beginning to learn how easily someone could vanish without a single goodbye.

In tenth grade, the French horn section needed more musicians, so the two girls from junior high joined me in the symphonic band. Although we were no longer dating, Holly and I had remained close. I'd been born with a large purple birthmark covering most of my right leg. I was a little self-conscious about it. Holly had known about my birthmark, so it wasn't a mystery to her.

A few of my friends thought it would be funny to tell Holly the birthmark was cancer. I didn't think they'd follow through, or that she'd fall for it. I ignored them. A few days later, Holly approached me in tears and asked why I hadn't told her. She'd believed them!

Their joke had landed hard. I reassured her I was healthy, and that it wasn't true. My friend's attempt at a joke was only stupidity pretending to be funny. Holly wasn't laughing. She looked at me not with hurt, but with betrayal. We were close, so how could I have let her be tricked like that? Sadness swept through me. So did guilt. In her eyes, by my not forcefully stopping the prank, I'd broken trust. She was right. There were no excuses. Our friendship didn't end, but it never felt quite the same. That moment stayed with me.

My grades continued to lean towards more A's than B's as my interests started gravitating toward certain subjects. Math was all about rules and how to apply them. It had a logic and structure that resonated with me. French had a similar appeal, but with a twist. Our teacher was nicknamed The Sargeant, and not following her rules struck fear into students' hearts. I was never afraid, and enjoyed how by following the rules, words could be brought to life.

Other classes did not connect in the same manner. In English, we read stories and wrote poetry that were interesting, but I never found Shakespeare or *Moby Dick* inspiring. Biology and chemistry had rules, but the teachers could never find a way to make me relate. History felt like rote memorization. People from the past didn't step off the pages or pull up a chair to explain why any of it mattered now. My grades were still good in English, science, and history, but my heart was in math and French.

As the school year wrapped up, the benefits of working at the animal hospital kept coming. My father bought baseball tickets for the office. When nobody wanted the tickets, they were given away. John was home from college and had put his grumpiness aside. Mike preferred being at school rather than at home. Rick was caught up with his own friends after graduating high school, and Kathy was too young to take to a game by myself. Working at the animal hospital meant I got first dibs on tickets, and John was always up for going to a game, and that summer, we became closer. Sitting across from first base at field level, we joked about knowing the players by their first names. Even though my brothers had drifted away after leaving high school, when they wandered back, moments like these reminded me how strong our family ties still were.

Around that same time I discovered my more caring side. A baby robin had fallen from a tree beside the house, barely a few days old and featherless. It was going to die without help. I found a shoebox and gently placed the bird inside.

For the next two months, I nursed it with a syringe filled with dog food, and as it grew, I dug up worms. I whistled to it, my version of a robin's lullaby, and kept it close. The shoebox sat beside my bed at night, and was carried with me on the long walk back and forth to work. During baseball games, my mother acted as the official babysitter. Not understanding how birds learned by instinct, I even pecked at the ground with my nose, trying to show the little robin how to hunt. When it looked ready to fly, I released it in the backyard. The robin fluttered to a nearby branch, then it was gone. Or so I thought.

The next day, I heard that some neighborhood kids had found a friendly bird, and were starting to play with it. Worried I hadn't prepared my little robin to live in the wild, I rushed over and brought it home. That night, my mother drove us to a remote spot, far from houses and children. We released it together, feeling a strange mix of sadness and hope. For years afterward, whenever I spotted a robin in the yard, I'd whistle, just in case it remembered me. Life moved on, and I carried a love of birds with me.

Later that summer, while working in the lower level of the animal hospital, my father casually asked if I was busy during the upcoming weekend. I wasn't. He wanted to know if I could join him on a trip to the Caribbean. My heart jumped. Permission from my mother was needed, and granted without hesitation. She knew this was a dream vacation for me.

My father said we'd be traveling to the French-speaking island of Saint Martin. On the way down, while lounging in my seat, I felt on top of the world. That's when my father made a strange request. His third wife and her daughters were already on the island, and I wasn't allowed to tell them we were flying First-Class. I agreed to the request, but didn't understand why treating himself and me should feel like a dirty little secret.

Along the back of the resort, a long uninhabited beach connected to a private cove. I had my own room that looked through swaying palms, toward the azure-blue sea. My father showed me around the island, and took me into town to visit his favorite shops. At one store, he started telling me about the jewelry he had bought there for his third wife.

Why is he bragging about giving a woman who was not my mother a piece of jewelry? Had he forgotten who he was with?

Those thoughts didn't last long. I was on a Caribbean island with my father, and could now practice speaking French. Nothing was going to spoil those moments.

One evening while my father was out, dinner was on my own. I walked into the open-air restaurant and, to my surprise, saw Leslie, the same girl from my father's other family who had so nonchalantly ordered food at the Country Club swimming pool. She was sitting at a table and invited me to join her. By now, I knew about charging things to an account and charging meals to the room. It felt quite worldly. Being bold, I ordered a glass of wine. As we started to talk, Leslie said something that made me pause. In a calm and collected tone she said my father should get as far away from her mother as he could, and that she wasn't a nice person.

It struck me as a strange way to talk about one's mother. However, this wasn't a conversation I was comfortable having with my father. We finished our meal and went about enjoying the rest of the time on the island. I was starting to connect dots about trouble brewing in my father's third marriage.

Heroes, Fires, and Victories (11th Grade)

The French horn has the smallest mouthpiece in the brass family and is in the treble clef. The sousaphone has the largest mouthpiece and is in bass clef. At the start of eleventh grade, there weren't enough sousaphone players in the marching band. The director knew I came from a family of musicians, and challenged me with a request to switch instruments. He said I'd still be able to play French horn in the symphonic band. I knew music, memorization, and how to adapt. His challenge was accepted. I never bothered learning how to read bass clef, and instead, I relied on instinct. That fall, my instincts would also be tested outside of music.

With enough money saved from the animal hospital, I wanted to sign up for karate lessons at a studio not associated with school. My mother initially didn't like the idea, but there were circumstances working in my favor. Over the years, she had been worn down by John's and Rick's problems, and I knew some of us were more golden than others. I told her that two years of good grades and solid work should earn me more trust. Surprisingly, she agreed. The next week, I joined the karate classes and started my lessons.

French class were just as demanding. My third-year French teacher, Mr. Kazerowski, was one of the best I ever had because he knew how to push his students. He went by Mr. K, which was a strange coincidence. With his thick hair and mustache, he looked like a French-speaking version of Gabe Kaplan's character from the 1970s sitcom *Welcome Back, Kotter*.

Even though everyone had a limited vocabulary, there were some days when Mr. K taught the class using only the French we knew. Questions asked in French had to be answered in French. That year, class was about expanding our vocabulary and speaking up. During class, Mr. K frequently walked up and down the aisles with a ruler in hand. If any student dared to stop paying attention, the ruler would slap down loudly on the student's desk, bringing the entire class into a highly attentive and slightly amused state. The most important lesson I took away from those classes was about learning to use what little knowledge I had with confidence. Later in life, those lessons would continue to be valuable.

Outside the classroom, the lessons were harder, and not always fair. The relationship with my father continued to grow, but the stars in my eyes were starting to fade. One afternoon at the animal hospital, a veterinary technician taught me something new. An animal had come out of surgery and needed physical therapy for its hip and leg. After showing me what to do, the technician asked me to explain the technique to the owner. I followed her instructions exactly, carefully explaining everything she had shown me.

A few days later, the owner returned to the hospital concerned that their pet wasn't using its leg. After some quick consultations, the other animal hospital technicians concluded I had provided incorrect instructions. Not only were they upset that I told the owner something wrong, but they were also upset that I was doing their job. The technician who had taught me the technique and asked me to talk with the client remained silent.

That evening, my father called me into his office. Without asking for my side of the story, he told me I could no longer explain physical therapy to clients. He might not have thought he was judging my actions, but it sure felt like it. I knew my father needed to keep the peace in his office. I understood. What bothered me was the feeling that he didn't care about what I had to say. There was no consoling, no empathy, no having my back.

Around the same time, I started hearing whispers in the animal hospital about being the boss's son.

The boss's son?

I knew it was technically true, but I didn't think I ever received special treatment. I was cleaning cages and doing whatever was asked of me, enthusiastically and without complaint. It was my first taste of office politics, and I didn't like it.

If working at the animal hospital made me question my place in his world, there were times I started questioning his place in mine. Around this time, my father asked if I could have my mother sign some papers. The request seemed innocent enough and I was happy to comply. What he didn't tell me was that those papers were about the mortgage. After years of inconsistent child support, he was now saddling my mother with a mortgage she couldn't afford. She didn't seem to understand what she was signing, only that my father wanted her to sign it. My mother was very trusting. She was too trusting.

John saw what my father was doing, but it was too late. He couldn't stop my mother. John wasn't mad at me for bringing the papers home. When he explained what those papers meant, I felt anger at being manipulated, and confusion about why my father was acting this way.

The next time we saw each other, I respectfully asked him about it. He claimed that when he left the family, they agreed the house would be jointly owned, and he was now calling in his half.

Calling in his half?

There was still a family living in that house, and that family included me. I started seeing things differently. My father was awesome to be around, but some of his behaviors were undermining the trust we had built.

While I struggled to understand what my father had done, John was stepping into a new role. The days of his yelling at my mother were replaced by someone who, as the oldest boy, believed it was his duty to look after the family. The Rambler couldn't last much longer and was being held together with masking tape, paper clips, and rubber bands. In the year to come, a new car showed up for my mother, courtesy of John. He even convinced her to let him take over the mortgage. Without his support in the background, I'm not sure what my life would have looked like. My older brother sure could have had moments of heroism.

There were other ways my sometimes grumpy older brother showed his better side. When John's job brought him home for a weekend or a holiday, he would bring a stack of comics with him. To me, they were literary gold. *Superman, Spider-Man, The Incredible Hulk, Thor, The Avengers,* he brought them all and more. Rick and I would anxiously wait until he finished reading, and then we'd get our turn. I became well-versed in the world of superheroes and evil villains. John's small kindnesses, like sharing those comics, prepared me well for the future. I had no idea there'd one day be an explosion of superhero shows and movies, and I'd be able to share that world with my wife.

At times, John tried hiding his nice nature behind a rough exterior. If you asked him a question, you were just as likely to get a grunt or a "bah" as a real answer. It seemed like he had his own language. Sometimes, bah meant, "Go away." Other times, it meant, "Let me explain." At Christmas, his gifts didn't come wrapped in shiny paper. They came in brown paper bags that weren't handed to me, they were tossed. His rough nature didn't bother me, it was just his way of showing he cared.

Just after Christmas, the glow of the holiday had barely faded when disaster struck. A late-night call upended everything. My father's animal hospital was on fire! The place that had served as my second home for three years was burning. With Mike at college, Rick out with friends, and Kathy too young, John and I immediately sprang into action. We drove to the animal hospital and saw a burnt-out shell where much of the building once stood. Although the firefighters had just finished extinguishing the flames, work remained.

Some animals were still in their cages in the lower level, others were being carried to the parking lot. John and I identified who we were, and started transferring animals to other nearby hospitals.

As we carefully lifted the animals from their cages, I sadly looked around and saw familiar hallways that were now filled standing water and the smell of smoke. We loaded the car with as best as we could, and then transported them down the road. Our makeshift ambulance made over a dozen trips.

During one transport, a policeman pulled us over. This wasn't a TV show where the cops were helpful. He didn't offer to clear the way, or help transfer sick pets. Instead, he threatened my brother with a speeding ticket. John muttered something sharp about saving lives and not slowing down. The officer didn't seem to care about the animals. He gave John a stern warning and turned to walk away, but my brother wasn't done. For an instant, his grumpy side escaped, and it was directed at the officer. He shot another comment out the window. I didn't catch the exact words, but I knew they were very disrespectful. The policeman stopped for a moment, glared back, and then continued toward his car.

I was surprised at John. Maybe he couldn't control the rougher edges. Maybe his heroic moments weren't always wrapped in niceness, but when the better part of him broke through, it spoke louder than words.

We later learned how the fire started. Instead of being at the animal hospital, the employee covering nightshift had snuck out with his girlfriend. My father would have sued him if he'd had anything to take.

He spent the next year figuring out how to pick up the pieces without me. On one fiery night, I lost both a job, and easy access to my father.

***

My karate lessons proceeded well, and by summer I was finally good enough to enter a tournament. The instructor drove our group on a four-hour ride across Pennsylvania to participate. Teams in colorful uniforms filled the gym, practicing moves far more advanced than anything I'd ever seen. It looked like a scene right out of *The Karate Kid*. I watched in awe as participants swept arms and legs in artistic motions. Their uniforms had fierce-looking dragons curled in a circle on the back. I had trained hard, but these students looked like pros.

The first of my two competitions was fighting. The bigger and stronger opponent didn't worry me. I knew skill mattered more. We approached the center circle and began. I scored first by striking his chest with a solid kick. He struggled to make any contact, and then a turning point occurred. I saw an opening and landed several punches to his chest, driving him out of bounds. No points were awarded.

No points? How could that be?

Still thinking about the missed points, I lost focus. On the next exchange, his foot stopped within inches of my head. His controlled kick tied the match. I attacked again, this time with even more punches. No points again. Frustration set in. Moments later, his foot landed directly in my chest. It was over. Departing the mat, I knew the unfairness had been a distraction.

My disappointment didn't last long. Next up was the forms competition, and this time the results were different. I tried capturing the emotion of every move, some with sharp intensity, and some with flowing grace. When the results were tallied, the competition was tied. I would have to perform a different set of forms as a part of the tiebreaker. I hadn't practiced a different set of forms, but remembered a lesson from my French class that applied to a lot more than French.

Don't be afraid to put yourself out there and make mistakes. Use what you know.

I chose a set of advanced forms I'd practiced, though they weren't polished. As the results were announced, I didn't think I had a chance of winning, but when first place was announced, my name was called! A large, two-foot-high trophy was awarded. Back home, this trophy found a place beside the 1974 Little League trophy Rick and I had earned together.

At the end of summer, I had a big decision to make. After careful saving, I had a healthy amount of money in the bank. Torn between my childhood dream of becoming a millionaire and the urge to live a little, I decided some spending was okay. Two possibilities arose and there wasn't enough money for both. I could buy a car, or take a trip to Europe.

Many students in school had their own car. A car was more than transportation. It was status, freedom, responsibility. A car came with a downside. I pictured the loud arguments my mother and John used to have about his car and the constant costs of gas and insurance. I pictured how our trusty Rambler had slowly fallen apart, and the money needed for maintenance. Plus, with the animal hospital burned down and no part-time job, money wasn't flowing into my bank account anymore. I hadn't yet figured out a new source of income.

The prior year, my French teacher, Mr. K., spoke about how our school sponsored an annual trip to Europe, visiting exotic places like London, Paris, Switzerland, and Rome. The trip was chaperoned by a teacher and was a chance for students to use some of their newfound language skills. I carefully weighed the choice between buying a car and taking a trip. The choice quickly became obvious. I was going to Europe. I didn't know what to expect, only that it would be unlike anything I'd ever done.

Our group consisted of four girls, two boys, and the school's Latin teacher. I didn't know any of them. The journey began with a mix of nerves, excitement, and the thrill of the unknown. In London, during a free afternoon, I visited the brother of someone who lived across the street from us in Pittsburgh. He took me to an English pub, bought me a pint, and explained how *Guinness* was life itself. After rejoining my group, our tour began. We roamed the streets of London, strolled along the Seine in Paris, and studied Lord Byron's poetry while passing by Le Château de Chillon in the Swiss Alps.

Rome was one of the last stops, and it had one tiny lesson to teach me. Navigating the foreign countries had been easy so far. The English spoke English, several in our group, including me, spoke French well enough to make France and Switzerland a breeze, and we had a Latin teacher to help get by in Italy, or so we thought. One afternoon in Rome, we got lost and couldn't find our bus. Directions were needed, and our teacher proudly rose to the occasion. She walked up to a local, and in a clear voice said,

"Where-o, is-o, the bus-o?"

Everybody in our group looked puzzled at first, and then did their best not to laugh. The Latin teacher, our glorious leader, wasn't speaking Italian. Heck, she wasn't even speaking Latin. I still laugh when thinking of her today. It was the first time I realized, just because someone is in charge doesn't mean they know what they're doing.

Europe was everything I'd dreamed of, and unexpectedly, a few girls from our group had taken an interest in me. My track record with girls hadn't been smooth, yet traveling with them showed me there might be hope. By the time we headed home, I knew there was.

Mischief, Girls, and Reality Checks (12th Grade)

Senior year came with a new sense of responsibility. My classmates and I were at the top of the totem pole now. We were expected to act more maturely and be a shining example for the lower grades.

The feeling of responsibility reached beyond school. My older brothers no longer lived in the house. John worked in another state. Mike pursued a graduate degree at college. Rick played small bars in central Pennsylvania, trying his hand at being a rock star. For the second year in a row, only Kathy and I remained. A quiet camaraderie took root between us. Her teasing stayed playful, never meant to wound. After school, we played cards and watched *The Muppets*, imitating their silly voices in a language only we understood.

I enjoyed the quieter house. As long as a wayward brother didn't show up on a holiday, my job was to carve the turkey, read the Bible, and sit at the head of the table. I was ready to responsibly carry on the tradition.

Responsibly carrying on tradition didn't just apply at home. During one marching band performance, I noticed my sousaphone mouthpiece was missing. I told a freshman to give me his mouthpiece so that I, as the more experienced player, could perform. He refused.

An underclass musician refusing a senior was unheard of. In our world, seniors had status. You didn't question them, especially not on the field. It was an unwritten code, and breaking it was like stepping out of line in a military drill. I punched him in the arm, not so hard as to cause a bruise, but firmly enough to show my displeasure. Then something unexpected happened. He looked up and said, "You can hit me again, but it won't be any worse than how hard my mother hits me."

I felt a combination of sympathy and surprise. Parents weren't supposed to hit their children. As his words sunk in, I realized I didn't like how I was behaving. My older brother Mike had bullied me, but this wasn't who I wanted to be. I shook my head in disapproval, not at him, but at myself, and entered into formation. I decided it was better to perform without playing, than to act like a bully.

Performing extended beyond halftime shows. Each year the marching band took a trip outside the state to participate in a festival, a competition, or a parade. Everything about the senior trip was ordinary, except the first night. The hotel we stayed at separated the girls from the boys. The boys were on the third floor and the girls were directly below them. Chaperones patrolled the halls to ensure no boy or girl crossed paths once the lights went out. The chaperones forgot one thing, that if teenagers want to find a way to get together, they will.

Once the lights went out and the doors were locked, it felt like we were prisoners on Alcatraz. Not wanting to be denied our freedom, my roommates and I studied the surroundings. We quickly spotted our chance. The hotel windows were large enough for a person to slip through, the girls were located directly below our room, and the screws securing our window were loose. The girls' window had no screws and opened directly to the outside. Our room had bed sheets to spare. All the pieces were there.

My partners in crime went to work. A phone call was made to the girls' room letting them know what to expect. Our window was disassembled. Bed sheets were tied around my waist and secured to a bedpost. I recall thinking the knot-tying from my Boy Scout days was really coming in handy. When all was ready, my friends firmly gripped the bed sheets and carefully lowered me down to the second floor. Once in the room below, I stared at the girls. They stared back at me.

Now what?

We hadn't thought that part out. The proverbial dog had caught the car, and now we had no idea what to do next.

About the time another of my roommates was preparing for his descent, somebody outside discovered our escape. The jig was up. It was only a matter of time before the strong arm of the law would come down on us. Only one hope remained. I opened the door to the hall and walked out, casually greeting the chaperone who stood guard. The shocked look on their face almost made me break into laughter, but I knew that would not help my situation. The girls also played innocent, insisting they had no idea how I got in. I rolled my eyes in disbelief, and was firmly marched back to my cell.

We knew there would be consequences. Red-faced chaperones, an irate band director, and a fuming hotel manager all filled the room. Stern words were spoken about vandalizing property, sleeping in the hall, and suspensions from school. We all looked as remorseful as possible, nodding our heads and acknowledging how we knew our actions were wrong. None of us were too concerned. We didn't think taking out a few easily replaceable screws qualified as a serious crime. Our mischief had hurt nobody, except the pride of the adults watching over us. After the scolding, we awaited our fate.

The hotel window had been resecured in minutes, exactly like we knew it would, so there were no consequences from the hotel. One of my roommates was the drum major. Not wanting to lose his drum major from the performance, our band director decided we could all still participate in the festival. He deferred our punishment to the school principal. In the end, there were no consequences for the band.

Back at school, the principal called us into his office. We were allowed to explain what we did, how we did it, and why. He laughed, and then told us to promise never to do anything like that again. There were no more scheduled band trips, and we had no intention of climbing out our classroom windows. Promises were made, and just like that, we were fully off the hook.

Since the hotel, band, and school didn't hand down any punishment, my mother was okay with it. She said she still trusted my judgment, even if it was a bit sketchy at times. As for my reputation in school, it was elevated, with some talking about the day Spider-Man scaled a hotel wall to visit some girls.

Of course, band wasn't always about climbing out windows and giving the band director gray hair. The last home game of the football season brought one final unique halftime show. The performance honored graduating seniors, and I was chosen for a special part. A picture of Pac-Man covered the large bell of my sousaphone. The band then formed the outline of a maze on the field, and as they played the Pac-Man video game song, my sousaphone and I raced through the maze, all while being chased by three girls dressed as Pac-Man ghosts. The crowd applauded with delight, and at the end of the show, parents joined their seniors on the field. My mother was there with me on that day, the person who had been with me for the entire tumultuous ride through my high school days. She was showing up for me, again. That night on the field was a finale for my marching band career.

Before that curtain call, something else had already begun. There were two girls I'd met and liked while on the trip to Europe, and they were sisters. I remember standing in the kitchen, nervously staring at the phone.

Should I or shouldn't I make the call? Who should I ask for?

We had a rotary phone in our home. There was no texting, no swiping, no hiding behind a screen. With every number dialed, the wheel slowly clicked back into place. I hoped the voice on the other end would remember the fun we had traveling together, and that she wouldn't crush me. I asked if Eileen was home, and she was. After she agreed to see me for a date, my heart skipped a beat. I did it! I called a girl and asked her out. This was nothing like junior high when asking a girl out seemed more casual. That one phone call triggered a relationship that lasted seven years. However, there were still a lot of mistakes yet to be made, and a lot to learn.

What stands out most from our first date wasn't where we went or what we said. It was what I learned afterward. Eileen was only a sophomore. Her sister Paula was in my grade. I never cared to ask what grade the sisters were in. I liked them both, but Eileen demonstrated more interest in me. I had to decide to either break the relationship with Eileen, or trust my heart and plow forward. I plowed forward.

Paula didn't seem to mind my choice, and if any friends noticed, I didn't care. I was in my own world. It didn't take long before I was invited over for dinner to meet her family. Her parents had been high school sweethearts. Her father was tall and imposing, her mother prim and classy. Besides Paula, Eileen had two older siblings, a brother and a sister that were close in age to John and Mike. As we sat around the table, I noticed how polite everybody was. There was no teasing like in my family. Either they were all on their best behavior, or this was a very different family. Over time, I came to learn this was *a very different family.*

Future dinners at Eileen's home continued to have the polite formality, but there was a small shift. I started feeling acceptance. When she came to our house for my birthday dinner, my mother made her feel just as comfortable. She liked the smaller, less formal, slightly chaotic feel of my home. I liked the more formal, less teasing feel of hers. We were learning about each other's worlds, one dinner table at a time.

Exploring extended beyond food. We also visited each other's church. One Sunday she had a chance to visit my Presbyterian church, and was not impressed with the smaller sanctuary and choir of meekly singing children. On another Sunday I visited her church and was not impressed by the priest. With a booming voice, he declared over and over that *all non-Catholics were going to hell.*

During lunch at school, Eileen noticed the contents of my brown paper bag. A cheese and jelly sandwich on white bread, a mushy Red Delicious apple, and a few store-bought cookies. I never gave much thought to my lunch, but she did. The next day she arrived with an extra sandwich and handed it to me. A sandwich piled with deli roast beef, fresh lettuce and tomato, all on a kaiser roll. Prior to that day, the fanciest meat I'd ever had for a school lunch was bologna. Her action reminded me of my father's country club, but this time, the luxury came with kindness.

I never went hungry at home, but in those days, my stomach always had room for one more sandwich. Every day during my senior year, despite my never asking, a fresh bonus sandwich would arrive. She liked bringing me the food, and who was I to disappoint her? That free fancy sandwich created an awakening.

There's a saying that money can't buy happiness. Back then, I wasn't so sure. My father belonged to a country club and Eileen's father had once been its president. My father owned a business and liked to show it. Eileen's family owned an entire city block in downtown Pittsburgh, and never felt the need to say so. My father was new money, loud and proud. Eileen's family was old money, quiet and polished.

At home, I wore hand-me-downs from my brothers. Eileen didn't even know what a hand-me-down was. Her house had gleaming wood floors and furniture that looked like it had never been touched. Ours had stained carpets, bedsheet-covered couches, and ceilings with watermarks from leaky plumbing. I wasn't ashamed, but I was uncomfortably aware.

When I stepped into Eileen's world, it felt like all those years with my father had prepared me. I knew how to carry myself and blend in. Enjoying the benefits of entitlement wasn't hard. I felt like I belonged, but I also felt poor. That was the realization. I was both lucky and lacking. I was comfortable, and I wasn't.

Looking back, I know I wasn't poor. Not even close. I didn't have what Eileen had, or what my classmates had, or what my father flashed around, but what I had was more than enough. At the time, though, it didn't feel that way. I watched my mother stretch every dollar while Eileen's family moved through life with ease. I watched my father spend freely, while offering sporadic child support. It made me feel like at home, we were barely holding things together. I didn't talk about it, but I felt it. It was in things like the car my family drove, the clothes I wore, and the brown paper bag lunch I took to school. That comparison lived in the background of everything.

***

At the start of my senior year, I found a new job. An usher was needed at the movie theater located a 10-minute walk from home. A friend across the street had just quit and gave me a heads-up. It was a lucky break, but I still had to walk in and apply. Nobody cared about my last name. I wasn't the boss's son. It was simply a job, and that was exactly what I needed.

The theater was a place from another time. It had one large screen centered on an old vaudeville style stage, complete with empty sockets where floor lights once shined. Behind the screen and up long metal stairs were dressing rooms with a hand-sized star on the door, a memory of actors and actresses from long ago. The other people working in the theater were all from a rival school district, but I didn't care, the job was money. My responsibility as an usher was to keep the lobby clean, take people to their seats, change the marquee sign, watch over the audience, and make sure everybody left when the movie ended. The cast of characters in the theater included two girls behind the concession stand, an adult projectionist, and other ushers. The ushers weren't trusted to sell tickets. That would have meant handling money.

Wait. The girls at the concession stand could handle money, but not the ushers?

That logic bothered me, and I came to realize something about myself. The less trust somebody placed in me, the less I felt the need to behave.

Working in the theater was a wonderful experience. This wasn't hard work like cleaning cages. It was easy money. We could eat all the free popcorn we wanted, mix our own special soda concoctions of half Coke and half Sprite, and watch the movies for free. It did get boring watching the same movies over and over, but we had a way to deal with that. After the last customer left, we would look for unfinished buckets of popcorn and punt them into the air, watching the leftover popcorn scatter in all directions. We knew it was immature and would mean more cleanup, but for us, it was maximum fun with minimal guilt.

Outside of school, the combination of a new job, a new girlfriend, and school studies started limiting my free time. Something had to give, and the choice wasn't hard. The karate studio required a monthly payment plus even more fees every time I advanced a level. Giving up karate meant more money for dates, and that felt like the better investment. My priorities had changed. Karate had to go.

Inside of school, my classes remained steady, and as the school year came to a close, one subject was coming to a crescendo. There was only one remaining symphonic band concert. All year, the music kept the French horns in the background. In one of the final pieces, there was a challenging passage that included a brief solo. I sat first chair in the French horn section and my friend Holly sat next to me. As first chair, the conductor expected me to take the lead, but I had different thoughts.

Playing the French horn had always come easily to me. Most of my playing happened in the band room, yet even with little practice and no private lessons, I still held first chair. Holly was different. She practiced for hours at home, took regular lessons, and treated each piece like it deserved her full attention. When the conductor looked to me for the solo, I knew that as first chair the part was mine, but I wanted to give it to Holly. Even though it went against his wishes, the conductor deferred to my judgement. I asked Holly if she was willing to take the part. With a little encouragement, she agreed.

That night, as her solo rang out across the auditorium, I felt like something between us had been repaired. Was my giving her the part really because I recognized Holly's hard work, or did it have to do with the long-buried guilt of the birthmark prank my friends played on her? I didn't really know. I still don't, but it didn't matter. What mattered was how well she played, and how good that felt for both of us.

Graduation came and went with speeches, caps, and relief. I was already looking to my next adventure.

That summer, my father invited me on a special trip. Over the past year and a half, he had navigated both divorcing his third wife and rebuilding his business after the animal hospital fire. He was once again ready to take a more active role and rekindle our relationship. I still had lingering issues related to how he manipulated me into having my mother sign the mortgage papers, and how his financial support to our family came and went, but he was my father and despite those lingering thoughts, I was glad to have him back. We hopped in his plane and took off for Kiawah Island.

The trip to Kiawah was all about golf. By this time, I had used some of my hard-earned money to take golf lessons and was able to hold my own on the course. My father introduced me to golf on our trip to Hilton Head Island. He taught me proper golf etiquette, like the importance of being quiet when somebody is swinging at a ball. We were back together again, on a championship-level course. My father was in a fun-loving casual mood, simply enjoying our time together. It was a wonderful feeling.

That day we were paired with a couple who took their golf extremely seriously. The woman stepped up to the tee. My father, who had always shown proper golf etiquette in the past, wandered off to the left of the tee box. As the woman's golf club rose over her head, he loudly called out,

"Hey son, look, baby alligators!"

She froze, stunned that somebody would yell mid swing. I could see her partner's face turning red. They glared at him as he waved me over. I buried my face in my hand, quietly amused. He had broken a sacred rule of golf.

After the match, my father said the couple was too serious. I hadn't seen this side of him before. He taught me about golf etiquette, then broke it so loudly I couldn't help but laugh. It wasn't the first time he'd caught me off guard, just the most ridiculous.

Upon returning home, excitement started to build. College was in my future. In the spring, I had applied to three universities and was accepted at all three. My choice hadn't been hard. Pitt was my parents' alma mater, and I had fond memories of ushering at football games, but it was too close to home. Following in their parents' footsteps is not the way a young man forges his own path.

Roanoke, with its small classes and scenic campus, was appealing, but the out-of-state tuition cost made it an unlikely choice. Penn State, three hours away, had a strong reputation and offered me a spot on the main campus. It was a rival school to Pitt, but I hoped my parents would get over it. It wasn't simply a school, it was a line in the sand. A way of saying:

This is my life now, and I'm mature enough to make my own decisions.

My mind was made up. I was going to Penn State. The cost of college still weighed on me, but I was going, even if it took grants or joining ROTC. My mother helped me apply for state and federal aid. The grants covered tuition, plus my room and board. In addition, I still had savings from my high school jobs. That meant short-term finances were covered.

That summer, Mike got married in New Jersey. While driving home from the wedding, my mother and I stopped at the Penn State campus for a one-day student orientation. The stage was set. I was ready to fledge the nest.

CHAPTER 5

FLEDGING THE NEST

When a bird fledges, it's also a rite of passage. Like generations before it, the young bird leaves the nest and takes flight, but its education is not yet complete.

In some species, like the mighty bald eagle, eaglets may return to the nest after that first flight. They remain nearby, learning how to find food, how to avoid predators, and how to survive.

By the fall of 1983, I was ready to take that leap, not so far from home that I couldn't return for a homemade meal or clean laundry, but just far enough to get my first real glimpse at independence.

Penn State Freshman Year

When Penn State accepted me, I told my parents one thing for certain: I wasn't going to get a part-time job. I'd already worked every year through high school. College was different. The stakes were higher, and succeeding would take my full attention. I didn't mention wanting time for a social life, since I figured they knew that. Thankfully, there were no objections.

My mother had come with me to freshman orientation earlier that summer, and she was there again when I moved into the dorms. We packed the car with everything I'd need: clothes, toiletries, notebooks, a pillow, a bike, and a couple of posters. I felt more excited than ever to explore this new world.

Starting off right meant changing my name. In high school, I had been Danny. At Penn State, I became Dan. The name felt older, more grounded, more in line with how I saw myself. It also matched how other guys introduced themselves. They were Jim, not Jimmy; Tim, not Timmy; Fred, not Freddy. The childhood version of ourselves was fading. My family still called me Danny, but here, at Penn State, I was Dan. This was something I could control.

What I couldn't control was having to share my space, or the lack of privacy. For the past five years at home, I'd had my own room. Those days were over. My grants barely covered the basics, so getting a private suite wasn't an option. The dorm room looked spartan. It had light blue cinderblock walls, no phone, no TV, no microwave, no mini fridge. There was just a single bed, a desk, and a small closet on each side. Communal showers were down the hall and around the corner. After we unloaded everything from the car, I watched my mother pull away. It felt like the end of an era, and in many ways it was. I'm glad that feeling didn't last long. I still had a roommate to meet.

When assigning rooms, the university matched students based on shared interests. Background and status didn't matter like in high school. We were all on a level playing field. Penn State sent a brief profile in advance, so everyone knew something about who they would be living with for the next year. My roommate and I both enjoyed sports and travel, but there was a difference. He'd been a big fish in a little pond. His small high school let him play on every sports team. I was a little fish in a big pond, and I had played in the band.

When we first met, Tom came across as arrogant. He started by making fun of the picture that had been included with my profile, and then went on to brag about his accomplishments. My brother Mike loved telling people he was better than everybody else. I didn't need that energy to start college, and I didn't want Tom's attitude to dampen the excitement I felt about Penn State. Instead of confronting it, I decided to let my academics and actions speak for themselves. I wasn't going to let anyone put me in a bucket the way high school had done.

Tom and I weren't close, but a few memorable conversations stuck with me. One afternoon, he mentioned a friend who had become a Civil Engineer and traveled the world. I didn't give it much thought. I hadn't even chosen a major yet, but that offhand comment pointed toward the path I would eventually take.

Around the same time, Tom returned from his first ROTC meeting with a stack of materials. I had once considered ROTC as a way to pay for college. Flipping through the booklets gave an immediate impression of blind, unquestioning patriotism with little room for independent thought. I thought college was meant to be a place of freedom, not indoctrination. Even with the offer of a free education, ROTC didn't feel like the right path. Tom gave it a week before reaching the same conclusion. Neither of us found a fit there, and the right path still remained unclear.

When Penn State initially accepted my application, I had to choose a starting point. Telling them my childhood dream of becoming "a millionaire" wasn't going to cut it anymore. Universities aren't built for vague ambitions. The Department of Undergraduate Studies offered two years to explore different fields before committing to a major. Students were pushed into courses that leaned toward either the sciences, business, or the arts. I hadn't really liked science in high school, but it promised the widest range of career options, making it the most appealing. Still, my search for a subject that truly sparked interest continued.

After traveling through Europe and discovering how enjoyable learning French was, I briefly considered a career in diplomatic relations. A political science course let me explore that possibility. The class was small and filled with mostly older students. Nobody cared about who was a freshman or who was a senior. These classes were all about learning, not labels. We were divided into study groups to discuss our upcoming term papers. I researched the material carefully, notating references exactly as I'd learned in high school. When the paper came back, a C was written at the top. I'd never received a C in high school. For a split second, I wondered if I was in over my head. Then I saw the comment, written in red ink:

"I know what the books say. Tell me what you think."

No one had ever asked me to do that in high school English. There, it was all about technical correctness, not original thought. I loved the idea of being asked to express myself, and was even more relieved when the professor announced we could resubmit the paper for a new grade. My second attempt earned a higher mark, and with my confidence restored, I completed the course with a respectable B.

The political science class was fun, but writing didn't come easily. It demanded more time than I was willing to give. I don't remember the professor's name or even what my paper was about, but I never forgot his lesson on formulating my own opinions.

As the semester progressed, other subjects created greater interest. I had loved math in high school, but my Advanced Placement math score wasn't high enough to skip college calculus, so I enrolled in the entry-level course. Repeating it was disappointing, but I knew building a strong foundation would be worth it.

The class was held in a round building with rooms shaped like pie slices. The seats were auditorium-style and descended steeply toward a small stage where the professor stood behind a podium. A giant projector screen towered behind her. She spoke with a heavy Chinese accent, and her lectures were just reciting completed homework problems. Most students couldn't understand the professor's words, but I didn't need to because the material was familiar. Before long, I was sleeping through lectures and tutoring others in the dorm.

By the end of freshman year, only a few students had earned an A in both freshman calculus courses, and my name was among them. The math department even sent a letter urging me to consider a math major, but the only career path anyone mentioned was teaching. I respected my mother's work in the classroom, yet I knew that life wasn't for me.

Other subjects weren't as friendly. To stay on track for the most rigorous career paths, I had to take a certain number of science courses. Some of them were known as "weed out" classes, designed to separate those who could handle the pressure from those who couldn't. During the second semester, I received a C in Physics. I hated getting a C, and hated thinking of myself as average. It didn't weed me out, but it was enough to close the door on Physics as a major.

While science dragged me down, other subjects were lifting me up. There were gym classes in racquetball and bowling. Taking those classes wasn't just about earning easy credits, it was a way of bringing pieces of home into my new life. In Pittsburgh, I had played racquetball with my dad, and had gone bowling with my mom. My parents had given me a strong foundation, not only in academics, but in the kinds of activities that made life fuller.

Students in my classes during those first two years rarely interacted with each other. The school was so big that I didn't share classes with people in my dorm. I helped some with math homework, but it often felt like we were all in our own bubbles. If there was to be any social life, it had to come outside the classroom.

At mealtimes, a hungry student would wander the halls yelling out that they were headed over to the dining hall, and asking if anybody else wanted to go. People would poke their heads out of their room like a prairie dog and call out, "I'm in."

The cafeteria today has changed to pay-as-you-go for each item, but when I was at Penn State, it was all-you-can-eat, and we could eat a lot. As endless glasses of milk, portions of meat, and containers of ice cream were consumed, talk of racquetball games and weekend parties filled the air.

There were girls in the cafeteria swirling about, but there never seemed to be much interaction between them and the boys. I didn't notice or care. I had a girlfriend back home, and I wasn't about to break the trust she placed in me. Promises mattered. Staying loyal kept me steady, but it also kept me at a distance from other girls. Without girls as a distraction, focusing on my grades was easier.

To let off steam, Tom and I started testing each other. He tried his hand at racquetball in our dorm floor competitions, but was never able to beat me. At other times, when a group of us were playfully horsing around, he would try to pin me down. With my old wrestling skills, he failed at that, too. His attitude of superiority slowly faded, and we came to have a mutual respect for each other. When the time came to decide on second year housing, we chose to room together again. We had seen roommates fighting and had already established our own kind of truce. The evil we knew was better than the evil we didn't.

Although Tom and I had developed an understanding, we weren't friends. Real connections were hard to come by. I was constantly surrounded by people in class, in the dorms, at the cafeteria, at parties, and on the sports courts. Among all those crowds, there was loneliness. It didn't help that many of my outlets for stress were solitary. I biked off campus, swam, and ran laps on the indoor track, but always alone. Staying loyal to my girlfriend might have looked noble, but it also became a form of self-imposed isolation.

Still, campus life kept trying to pull me in and make me feel welcome. Nowhere was that stronger than at Beaver Stadium. Penn State football games were much louder and rowdier than anything I had experienced in the past. Before the game there was almost always a tailgate party, loaded with hotdogs, hamburgers and beer. During the game we cheered, sang, swayed, and jumped up and down as wave after wave rolled around the stadium. The energy of those football games was contagious. Everyone seemed to be finding their place.

Outside the stadium, some found their place in Greek life and I wondered if I might too. Curious, I decided to explore that world myself. One weekend, I remember visiting Phi Kappa Tau. It was a local chapter of the fraternity my brother Mike belonged to. Mike may have been rough towards me in younger days, but that still didn't keep me from trying to make a connection. I thought maybe if we shared the fraternity, it would create some common ground.

I was invited to a dinner, given a tour of reference libraries full of old class tests, and told stories about the close bonds members shared. Two things bothered me. The first was the fraternity was nicknamed *Phi Stabba Tau*, because one of the fraternity brothers had stabbed a fellow member. That did not sound like a close bond. Second, I found out the fraternity still actively hazed its new pledges, and the concept of hazing bothered me. If someone was going to be your lifelong friend, they wouldn't spend a year demeaning you. Joining might have been tempting, but after giving it some careful thought, it was a decisive no.

It might have been a struggle to find "my people" at Penn State, but at least I still had my family in Pittsburgh. Getting mail in the dorms was always a treat. My mother would prepare care packages filled with homemade cookies and a letter, keeping me updated about family matters. I loved getting those packages, and always made sure she knew it.

About once a month, I'd head home for the weekend. That was the great thing about Penn State. It was far enough away to feel independent, but not so far that I couldn't go running home. One of the ways I let my mother know how much I appreciated her was by letting her do my laundry. However, getting home could be a challenge. Sometimes it was a ride share, sometimes it was a bus, and sometimes my father picked me up. We hadn't seen as much of each other since the animal hospital burned down. I'd hoped the three-hour drive would be a great way to catch up, but being in the car together didn't seem as smooth as it once was. I remember one trip, when the excitement of my experiences had me talking a mile a minute. My father looked over and said:

"Son, you don't need to fill every minute with talking."

Taking subtle hints wasn't one of my strengths, but it sounded like he was politely telling me to shut up. Inside, I was exploding with excitement, and those rides were our chance to discuss my classes, share his philosophy on life, and catch up with each other. With my bubble slightly burst, we continued on in silence.

The relationship with my father was changing and I wasn't sure if the cause was him, me, or maybe both of us. Like so much else in college, I needed to figure that out on my own.

Once spring semester finished, it was time to relax. That summer had many happy memories, and one was unexpected. The importance of family had been drilled into me, and I was still trying to find a way to connect with my brother Mike. He was living just outside of the big city of New York. I'd never been to New York City and asked if he would mind my using his place as a base to explore from. To my surprise, Mike said it was no problem, and that he would love to have a guest. He'd only been married for a year, and had just graduated with a doctorate degree, so he was in love and optimistic. I hoped those two things would thaw what had previously been tense.

I purchased a Michelin guide and headed on my way. Mike and his wife were wonderful to visit with. They had to work during the day, but in the evening, we discussed my life at Penn State. Once the weekend came, they took me to a play one night and a movie premiere another. It was the best time I'd ever had with Mike. There was no teasing or attitude of superiority. We just had fun.

Penn State Sophomore Year

In my sophomore year, I developed a love-hate relationship with math. The course I loved was Differential Equations, one of the more advanced classes. Each assignment felt like a puzzle waiting to be solved, and I loved puzzles.

In high school, I'd spend hours at the formal dining room table, staring at jigsaw pieces scattered across its surface. I looked first for the edges, then the pieces with similar colors or shapes. My mother, knowing how much I loved a challenge, once gave me a puzzle of a mirror. She even gave me a puzzle of a puzzle. I developed the patience and organizational skills to conquer them all. Differential Equations was no different. When the professor offered extra credit problems, I enthusiastically conquered them.

Every one of my math grades had been an A, but that streak was about to end. The hate part of my love-hate relationship was Statistics. Statistics was less about elegant theory and more about grinding through long strings of basic arithmetic by hand. Speed and accuracy mattered more than careful analysis. If you made a mistake in step one, you were marked down for all the steps that followed. The theory wasn't hard, but I almost always made a small error early on the tests. At the end of the semester, I received a C, and my request for re-evaluating the exams was denied.

For comfort, I tried convincing myself that statistics wasn't really math, but it didn't help. My perfect record of A's was broken. The professor graded how he graded, and there was nothing I could do except hope the universe might hear my plea for justice.

The next year, the professor didn't return to the university. He'd gone hiking in the mountains of South America and disappeared. Rumor had it, he was kidnapped and killed by revolutionaries. I knew I'd wished for justice, but this seemed a bit extreme. Still, he was the one who had tainted my perfect record, so I accepted the universe's verdict and moved on.

As I was struggling with Statistics, an old nemesis arose, a nemesis that continued to cast a long shadow over my transcript. I had taken basic physics in high school. It shouldn't have been so difficult in college, but the clarity that I found in math didn't exist in physics. Physics felt heavier and more stubborn. It dragged. Like the second semester of my freshman year, both semesters of my sophomore year were plagued by a C. My only solace was knowing there were no more physics classes required.

Gym helped me work off the stress of those awful C's, and in my sophomore year I learned several unexpected lessons. Squash is a close cousin to racquetball, and I figured it would be an easy A. The game used a longer racquet, a smaller ball, and seemed to require faster reflexes, or so I thought. Our instructor must have been over sixty years old and walked with a slight limp. Every student was faster, stronger, and had greater endurance, but he always seemed to win. Youthful exuberance was no match for his strategic positioning and accurate shots. By the end of the semester, he had taught us more than squash. We learned never to underestimate an opponent, to approach what we do with humility, and that strategy and experience can beat speed and power. Both on and off the court, I never forgot those lessons.

Meanwhile, I had my own decisions to finalize. Two years in the Department of Undergraduate Studies had passed, and I needed to declare a major. After much thought, I settled on Civil Engineering. It offered more career paths than any other engineering field. Civil engineers could be surveyors, traffic engineers, hydrologists, environmental engineers, or structural engineers. It challenged my drive for knowledge, promised a sound career, and allowed me to keep delaying the decision about what I truly wanted to do with my life. That spring, the School of Engineering accepted my request.

Around the same time, I was facing a different type of challenge, one I couldn't solve with strategy or reflexes. Eileen was graduating high school and trying to pick a college. I would've loved for her to come to Penn State, but I knew pushing her would be wrong. She needed to decide based on what was best for her, not what she thought I wanted. She made her decision, and it wasn't Penn State. I was happy for her, but my heart took a hit. We continued dating through the summer and were as happy as ever, but our relationship was changing. I simply didn't want to admit it yet.

As sophomore year ended, students in the dorm were discussing who to room with the next year. Tom had taken up bodybuilding and was self-injecting steroids. His behavior had become more volatile, and keeping our housing arrangement no longer seemed like a good idea. There was no drama, and no need to discuss why we were going our separate ways. We both knew it was the right choice.

After leaving the dorms, I saw Tom only once more, standing outside a bar. We exchanged polite greetings before he mentioned being in a bit of trouble. While working as a bouncer, he had removed a patron a little too forcefully. Knowing this was connected to steroid use affirmed my decision not to room with him again. We wished each other well and went our separate ways. I never saw Tom again.

For the next year, a few students in the dorm were moving off-campus and asked me to join them. With sophomore year behind me and a new apartment lined up for the fall, I headed back to Pittsburgh, where my brother Rick was still trying to find himself. He needed help running a small authentic, Italian pizza shop that he dreamed of owning one day. Working there sounded like fun and I enthusiastically agreed to help.

The smell greeted you from the sidewalk. It was a mix of pepperoni, sausage, oregano, and freshly baked bread all mixed together. My job was to deliver pizzas. It sounded simple, but I had to learn things like never speeding around corners. When that happened, the cheese would slide and bunch up in the box. Customers never tipped well when their pizza was a cheesy mess.

The best part about working in the pizza shop was that we could make anything we wanted to eat. As a college student with an insatiable hunger, that was too good to pass up. My job at the theater had treated me well with free popcorn, movies, and drinks. Now it was free pizza and meatball sandwiches.

The food perks were great, but the thing I loved the most was that it was only Rick and myself. He taught me how to twirl the dough and then gently toss it into the air. There we were, the Little League champions from long ago, on a different kind of field, tossing pizzas instead of a ball. Those ordinary moments of working together were shaping the person I was becoming.

As my time in the pizza shop ended, my father called. The animal hospital had fully recovered from the fire and was thriving once again. He had learned his lesson about having a reliable employee working nightshift, and turned to me.

I was happy to help, but didn't like how the request was framed. If I wanted any money for the upcoming school year, working the night shift for the next two weeks was required. It wasn't presented politely or as an option. He might have had other problems in his life, but there was no reason for him to have taken that approach with me. This was a new side of my father I was dealing with, and I didn't like it.

Those two weeks ended up being miserable. Late night mopping and cleaning cages were enough to keep me awake until 2AM, but when the next few hours rolled around, I turned into an exhausted zombie. My father told me it was okay to rest my head on a desk and sleep as long as the phone was beside me. Two or three times a night, a piercing sound rang through the halls, shaking me from my haze. It was the phone, and at the other end of the call was a frantic pet owner. Fluffy had a tummy ache, or Fido wasn't acting quite right. It was my job to calm the owner down and determine if a calm voice and basic first aid would suffice, or if a consultation with the doctor on call was needed.

Waking a sleeping veterinarian in the middle of the night was rarely met with joy, especially if the emergency wasn't an actual emergency. My prior work experience at the animal hospital proved invaluable, and it was rare I called a doctor unless there was a true need. By the end of the two weeks, my nerves were frazzled from being jerked from a state of half-asleep to a state of full consciousness. It might have helped train me for crisis management many decades later, but I haven't ever been able to hear the same piercing ring without jumping.

There was another awakening that summer, one just as unpleasant. While working those late-night shifts, there were no timecards or paychecks, only a few token dollars handed over to me for spending money. Then I realized he was treating me the same way he had treated my mother after their divorce. With her it had been a verbal agreement followed by sporadic envelopes full of cash. With me, it was a verbal agreement, followed by a few meager bucks from the cash register. My father still hadn't lost my trust, but it had been eroded a little bit further.

Penn State Junior Year

The new apartment was both off campus and away from town. Those were the least costly apartments, and we were all trying to keep expenses down. Gone were the days of all-you-can-eat cafeteria meals that pretended to be nutritious. We survived on a steady diet of macaroni and cheese, spaghetti, Campbell's soup, and ramen noodles, and clean dishes no longer effortlessly materialized. In the dorm cafeteria, dishes were placed on a rack and magically whisked away, only to appear clean and ready for use the next day. Now, a dirty pot left in the sink for more than a week would start growing fur, and nobody wanted to eat out of a furry pot. Off-campus life was going to be very different.

I quickly found that except for the meal situation, living off-campus came with an improvement in living arrangements. My roommate was a senior, and as much as Tom was volatile, Joe was laid back. I hadn't known him in the dorms, but when it came time to try making wine in a plastic tub, Joe was all for it. I can't say our experiment succeeded, but I was studying engineering, not food science. When the time came to imbibe in the fruits of our labor, nobody seemed to mind the subtle notes of an old bicycle tire. After Tom, this felt like an upgrade.

There were other adjustments that had to be made. There was no nightlife around the apartment complex. Fun was no longer right outside our door. Social life in the dorms had been a constant buzz of activity. During parties, fifteen to twenty underage students would cram into a postage-stamp-sized room, all crowded around a keg. Twice that many waited in the hall, eager for their turn to shuffle in and grab a beer. The whole scene looked less like a party and more like a clown car, students piling in and out, laughter spilling into the corridor.

To find nightlife now, we had to make our way into town. As for bars in State College, they weren't all that different from the dorm rooms. The streets were lined with every kind of bar: a beach bar, a sing-along bar, a yuppie bar, you name it. On Saturday nights, they looked like dorm parties, only bigger and louder. The crowds were still there, only this time, the students were lined up along the sidewalk instead of in a hall.

As fun as the social scene could be, life off campus came with its own lessons. Everything required more planning, and a lot more patience. Instead of a fifteen-minute walk to classes, I had to take a fifteen-minute bus ride. No longer could I return to a dorm to quickly exchange books or take a nap. Bus schedules controlled my life. I had to haul twice the number of books and find sleep in whatever corner of the campus I could find.

I wasn't the only student with this predicament. There were hundreds of others snoozing away on floors, couches, chairs, and any other place where rest could be had. Some common areas looked like oversized kindergarten nap time, but these weren't children. These were seriously exhausted college students trying to survive, and I was one of them.

Survival was what some of my classes felt like, and there was one much worse than the others. When sophomore year had ended, I celebrated never again having to see my arch enemy, Physics. Little did I know its evil cousin, Thermodynamics, was waiting in the wings.

There was no avoiding Thermodynamics. It was a prerequisite for civil engineers. Someone thought students needed a well-rounded curriculum that included this awful subject. They thought wrong. From the first day, I knew I was in trouble. Nothing the professor said made any sense, and I couldn't tie the lectures back to anything in the materials. At one point I wondered if I had the correct textbook. Then came one of the worst decisions of my college career. Reading *Garfield* comics made more sense than anything being presented. Garfield the cat loved spaghetti and squishing spiders. I could relate.

If that's what the tests had been on, I would've aced them. Unfortunately, they were about things like heat transfer. By week eight of the twelve-week semester, I was staring at an F. Getting an F in the course meant having to retake the class, and I didn't want to suffer through it again. The cartoon cat was put away, and I made a greater effort.

When the final test landed on my desk, I stared blankly at the problems. They still didn't make any sense. My mind raced in circles, spinning faster with each passing second. For the first time, I just wanted to run. Every thought shouted that I couldn't do this, that I was completely unprepared. I forced myself to take a deep breath and dove in, writing down my best attempt at each problem, not knowing if a single answer was even close. Somehow, I got a B on the test. That wasn't great, but it was enough to lift me from an F to a D. This was my only D in college, and I felt shame, but the shame was nothing compared to the relief I felt about not having to take Thermodynamics again. That same anxiety would visit me again in other exams, but now that I had faced it, I knew how to survive.

French helped balance out Thermodynamics. By my junior year, I remembered how much I enjoyed learning the language, and decided to try a course at the college level. I had a strong foundation from high school, but wasn't ready to write papers on French literature, so I enrolled in an intermediate-level course. I loved practicing in the language lab, and was well on my way to an easy A. Minoring in French even briefly crossed my mind, but there were a few things standing in my way.

French was an elective, and beyond my junior year I didn't have room in my schedule for it. Continuing with French would mean I wouldn't graduate in four years. There was already enough financial stress at home and I didn't want to add to it. Also, reading French literature was challenging. I was swamped with my engineering curriculum. Stretching myself further wasn't realistic. Finally, to succeed at French takes practice speaking, and the professor encouraged students to sit in a coffee shop or restaurant with classmates and chat. I didn't really know anybody in the class, nor did I have spare money to spend at coffee shops and restaurants. I earned an A in the course, but another French class would have to wait. As for the part of me that loved learning a foreign language, that never went away.

Even as French lingered in the background, the next decision loomed, which was what engineering specialty to choose. By year's end, I was ready. Structural stood out. My decision was clear. I didn't choose it because I dreamed of bridges or skyscrapers. Structural engineering was grounded, logical, and built on strong organization. That all resonated with me. I wanted a career with both a dependable salary and a stable foundation. I chose structural engineering because it ticked every box.

When meeting with a counselor to schedule my senior year, she had two big concerns. I would have to take more credits per semester, and students didn't typically wait until their final year to take so many tough technical courses.

Tough technical courses? Uh oh.

If the classes were going to be anything like my arch enemies, Physics and Thermodynamics, I was in big trouble.

To address the counselor's concerns, I reduced my workload by registering for summer school. None of the specialty courses were offered, but I could complete my remaining prerequisites. It still left the second concern about my senior year being packed with technical courses, but up till then I had done well in structural engineering courses. I thought I could handle it, so with a cumulative grade point average still comfortably over 3.0, I was ready for the home stretch of my academic career.

However, storm clouds were gathering in more ways than just academics. Pressure was building on all fronts with school, family, and the girlfriend I'd been holding onto since high school. That final year would test more than my intellect.

The Motorcycle Summer

The summer of 1986 didn't begin with academics. My parents were no longer enthusiastic about making the long drive to pick me up, and I didn't really like the bus trips home. Something had to be done. Jim, who also lived in the apartment, knew of my dilemma and had the perfect solution. He suggested I consider buying a motorcycle, or as the cool riders called it, a bike. They were a cheap, low-maintenance form of transportation that looked awesome, especially if one wanted to attract girls. I still had some money in the bank saved from my high school jobs, so the inexpensive part sounded good. I had a girlfriend, so the second part wasn't as important to me, at least not at that point in my life.

Jim owned a motorcycle and offered to teach me how to ride. I jumped at the opportunity. He took me to an open field, dismounted from his bike, and told me to hop on. I swung my leg over the seat like a seasoned pro, but quickly noticed my feet didn't touch the ground. Jim told me not to worry about it, and began patiently explaining how the motorcycle operated. Clutch, accelerate, shift, brake, each hand and foot had a responsibility. Together, they worked in perfect symphony to make the bike go. With excitement building, I pressed the starter, prepared to accelerate, lifted my feet onto the footpegs, and then it happened.

Instead of going forward, the bike started tipping sideways. I tried placing my foot back on the ground to steady the bike, but it was too heavy and continued toward the earth. My first ride ended with the bike on its side. My heart sank. I thought Jim was never going to let me live that down, and that my riding days were through. To my surprise, Jim thought this might happen, and that was exactly why he was teaching me on grass instead of concrete. He helped me pick the motorcycle back up and let me try again. As the bike rolled across the field, I could feel the possibilities unfolding before me. There were open roads and the freedom to go where I wanted, when I wanted. There were just a few small problems to overcome, those being my mother, my father, and my girlfriend.

When I told my mother about the motorcycle, the worried look that had been etched into her face from years of family and financial struggle deepened. She didn't think they were safe. My mother trusted my judgment, but she didn't trust other drivers. My father wasn't much different. For similar reasons, he absolutely did not want me buying a motorcycle. I explained it was a cheap way to get around, and would save him from driving me back and forth from college. He didn't want to hear it. My girlfriend also had concerns. She said motorcycles were death traps. Like my parents, her only reason was fear for my safety.

I listened carefully, weighed the pros and cons, and then did what any self-respecting young adult would do in a similar situation. I bought a motorcycle!

The day I bought my motorcycle was one of the best days of my life, but there were still lingering doubts. The man I bought it from was in his sixties, and was only selling because his wife insisted on it. While turning into his garage the prior week, the tire slipped, and the bike fell on top of him. He caressed the seat while gingerly limping around the bike, his knee in a brace, and sadly handed me the keys. He wasn't simply selling a machine. This was his soulmate. That part about the bike falling on him made me wonder if the advice I'd been given about motorcycles being a death trap was true. I'm glad those doubts didn't stay with me long. The roar of the engine and surge of power was infectious. I was at an age of invincibility. Nothing was going to stop me.

When my mother and girlfriend heard about my purchase, they were disappointed, but they also accepted my decision. When my father heard about it, he reacted very differently. With a tone that told me it wasn't open for discussion, he firmly said if I could afford a motorcycle, I could also afford to pay for my own college expenses.

Pay my own expenses?

State and federal grants already covered most of my tuition and housing, so the money wasn't what bothered me. I knew a bank would loan me the money if needed. What I struggled with was my father's attitude. We'd always been on good terms before this, but threatening to no longer support my senior year felt like he was abandoning me.

This was around the time he was selling the animal hospital. Rick would later tell me the IRS was chasing our father for unpaid taxes, sending him threatening letters, and that an arrest was imminent. An arrest was never made, but the animal hospital was sold, and after his debts were paid, he used the leftover money to start a new practice. At the time, none of this was explained to me. All I knew was that my father cut off all financial support because I bought a used, inexpensive motorcycle against his will.

My father's anger would eventually fade, and I don't know if it was because of him or me, but our relationship would never be the same. The part about him walking away from my mother when I was three years old was always in the background. After adding in his behavior surrounding my motorcycle, I now had experienced enough other parts of my father to start piecing together what kind of man he was. I remembered how he used me to manipulate my mother into signing over the equity in our home. I remembered his unnecessary coercive demand about working nightshift to cover college expenses. These were the things that damaged our relationship. He would always be treated with respect, but they were the sort of behaviors I committed to avoiding.

Even with his questionable behaviors, there were parts of him I wanted to embrace and hold onto. I remembered his generosity, and when at work or out together, how he effortlessly displayed charm with everyone he met. My father had two very distinct sides. In years to come, I would try to recapture the feeling we had from lounging on a tropical island, golf trips in his plane, playing racquetball, and spending time together in the car after a long day at the animal hospital. As for his darker side, I learned to recognize when it emerged, and to always be cautious of it.

My mother saw what was happening and helped me apply for a government loan. With funding secured, I was ready to return to Penn State. In the motorcycle, I had found a new best friend. It didn't judge, didn't argue, didn't withdraw support. It roared to life when I needed it to and carried me where I wanted to go. The motorcycle gave me a sense of freedom I had been craving, but I realized that freedom came at an unexpected cost: I could no longer fully trust my father.

During that summer, Jim and I became better acquainted. He taught me tricks such as placing a newspaper under my coat for extra warmth. The wind didn't cut through newspaper the way it did through denim. And then there was Jim's favorite, which was polishing a leather seat with just the right amount of Armor All to snug a girl passenger up against the rider with a gentle bit of braking.

He might have been a player when it came to girls, but not all his lessons were deliberate. One afternoon, while taking a corner too fast, I watched Jim's bike slide on a patch of gravel. By the time he started regaining control it was too late. His bike wobbled, and then skidded off the road before laying down in a ditch. He wasn't seriously hurt. His hands were raw, but a leather jacket and jeans had prevented further damage to his skin.

From watching Jim's accident, I learned that even the best riders can fall. I also learned to be aware of road conditions, to be extra cautious on gravel, to watch my speed on turns, and to respect the importance of proper riding gear. My lessons were coming fast, and fortunately, were not at my own expense.

That summer was special. There is nothing specific I can point to, but it had a completely different feeling. Classes were more laid back than those in the fall or spring, and the relaxed attitude included the professors. I took an eclectic mix of courses to round out my final prerequisites of theater arts, writing, and basic electrical engineering. On days when the classrooms were too hot, the professor would head outside and teach our course on the grass.

Afterward, we'd wander into town for a beer or two before heading home. There was no stress, no drama, just a sense of ease. Everyone seemed to get along, and I felt a comforting sense of belonging. Had I known summer at Penn State was like this, I would've signed up years earlier.

Penn State Senior Year

Senior year brought another change in living arrangements. Some of my junior-year roommates had graduated and moved on. I had lost touch with everybody from the dorms, and my engineering classmates were only casual acquaintances. I started to doubt the saying that college was about making lifelong friends. Then luck came my way. I reconnected with Aaron, someone a bit sketchy I knew from high school who needed a third roommate to help cover apartment costs. I was in the right place at the right time.

Aaron was a freewheeling communications major who was always up for a good time. Sometimes his good time went too far. One evening, he opened a small packet of white powder and laid it on the coffee table. He carefully used a knife to shape thin rows and invited those of us to join in. He thought snorting lines of cocaine might be a fun experiment. The other roommates and I disagreed. I made my displeasure clear, grabbed my jacket, and headed into town. Singing songs over pitchers of beer at the bar, that was my limit. There were some lines I wouldn't cross. After that night, the only coke I saw in the apartment came in a can.

There was also an unofficial fourth roommate. Aaron's girlfriend, Mary, was around most nights once the fall semester began. She and Aaron could often be found together in the bunk above mine. The living arrangement was uncomfortable, but it came with compensation. Every month she slipped me enough cash to make ignoring the nightly sounds overhead tolerable.

Mary had graduated the year before and worked in the finance department at a local car dealership. Over dinner, she'd brag about convincing naïve buyers to purchase overpriced warranties they couldn't afford. Her stories were proof of the dishonest car-salesperson stereotype, and they made the money she gave me feel dirtier. Still, I took it. Maybe I wasn't as principled as I thought, or maybe that was when I realized how complicated principles become when you're just trying to survive.

One evening, while minding my own business on the apartment balcony, I felt a sharp sting on the side of my head. I reached my hand to my ear and felt some goo. It was an egg. A student about twenty yards away had decided to amuse himself at my expense. My roommates were quite unhappy, as was I. They wanted to go over, bang on the door and cause trouble. The laid-back summer version of me took a different approach.

We marched over to the offending room and firmly knocked on the door. As music blared into the hall, a glassy-eyed person holding a red solo cup full of beer opened the door. He knew we meant business, and we did. "What's with the egg?" I asked. "That was a great throw, but we could really use some beer."

Realizing we weren't there for a fight, he invited us to join the party, and the beer flowed. Diplomacy won the day. The wrong was made right, and the beer made it official.

Living near the bars and off-campus parties sounded like a great idea, but I had forgotten one thing. My hardest courses awaited, and I wasn't ready. For the first four weeks of my senior year, I remained in summer mode. I went to class, took notes, did the homework, and enjoyed the nightlife. My mind was saying summer. My new classes thought differently.

The first tests slapped me back into reality. All six classes hovered around an F. For the first time, I seriously considered dropping out and starting fresh the next semester. Panic set in. I met with each professors. One by one, they saw I understood the material and gave the same advice:

"Stick with it. College is about learning, not the grade. Do not drop out. Regain your focus and keep at it."

I decided I wouldn't run away when things got tough and through that experience something changed in me. My carefree days of playing in the bars faded, and I became more serious.

By semester's end, I had raised my grades to one B and 5 C's. I remember a strong feeling of wanting to leave academia behind and start putting my knowledge to use. This was the semester prospective employers looked at when deciding whether to hire somebody. It was my worst semester. Those C's stood out on an otherwise solid transcript. My professors were proud of how I finished, and told me not to worry. They once again reminded me that the most important thing was learning. Their encouragement kept me focused. My courses during the spring semester all started out strong. Summer was a thing of the distant past, and I focused on learning, just like the professors said.

One type of exam stood out. It had 10 questions, with 10 points for a right answer, 5 for no answer, and 0 for a wrong answer. Tests were graded on a curve, so scoring 60 on an exam could mean an A. In other classes, 60 meant a D. This professor was teaching us how to make calculated risks. A student could leave every question blank, score a 50, and hope to pass. I didn't love the method, but I respected the message: If you don't know the answer, admit it.

Obtaining a license to practice structural engineering took four steps: pass the Engineer in Training test, graduate from an accredited college, work for four years under a licensed engineer, and finally, pass the state professional exam. During the spring of my final year, I took the Engineer in Training test and passed. One step down, three to go. One month later, I received the final semester's grades. I thought I had some A's coming, but each class ended with a B. No problem, I thought. B's are respectable and there are no C's in sight. Graduation was in my future. The second step to becoming a professional engineer was complete.

***

Before graduation day arrived, I was knocked off balance. Eileen had decided it was time for us to go our separate ways. My moment of triumph was suddenly clouded by sadness. Being seven hours apart between her college and mine had left little time to be together. In times of joy or pain, phone calls weren't enough. Neither of us was there for the other. While I was enjoying my summer and battling through the intensity of senior year, she was feeling left behind. She joined a sorority, and like I had been doing for the past four years, she started figuring out who she was and what she wanted.

It wasn't me. We grew apart.

I didn't dwell on it, but the feelings couldn't be easily shaken, either. I didn't want to let personal drama overshadow my parents' joy, and graduation was a moment of pride for them, so I put on a brave face.

My mother and Kathy drove me to graduation. At Penn State, it was a massive affair held in the arena where the basketball team played. My father, my mother, and Kathy were somewhere in the crowd. I looked for them but had no idea where they were sitting. A forgettable speech was given by a forgettable keynote speaker. Then, each engineering discipline stood and was pronounced as having graduated. All the students shifted the tassel on their cap from left to right and sat back down. Diplomas were picked up later, under the bleachers. The ceremony had felt as empty as I felt inside.

My father drove me home that day. Since I had bought the motorcycle, we'd seen less of each other. On graduation day, the only real time we had together was on the drive from the ceremony back to Pittsburgh. During the ride, he handed me a small gift. It was a half mug with a saying printed on the side, *"When soaring to new heights, it's easy to get caught in a tailspin."* A half mug isn't useful, and the message seemed more like a warning than an inspiration. I didn't want to seem shallow or ungrateful, but it felt like he was phoning it in.

The disappointment didn't last long. Throughout my life my father may have missed ballgames, concerts, and performances. He may have undermined my trust with his past actions, but in that moment, he gave me something more important than any gift. When my formal education reached its grand finale, my father showed up. Once we pulled into the driveway, he dropped me off and left. I was ready for my new life, and neither one of us was sure where he fit.

CHAPTER 6

A PROFESSIONAL LIFE

In high school, I wasn't pursuing a career in veterinary medicine or as a professional movie usher. My social life was plenty busy, classes were challenging, and the only purpose for work was to make money.

In college, taking classes was supposed to be about following your passion. There's a saying, *"If you love what you are doing, you will never work a day in your life."* I can't say I loved structural engineering. It was something I understood and that would create a stable, viable career path, but my passion? I chose long-term professional stability over the pursuit of fleeting idealism. My purpose in college was to prepare for a career that was practical.

Finding a job in the real world was my next step, and it would be very different from the animal hospital or the theater. I'd have to get this job on my own merits. As for keeping it, the safety net was gone. There were no family connections to shield me, no dim theater lights to hide behind. It was a sink or swim proposition, and I had no intention of sinking.

A Fork in the Road

In 1987, there were no apps to help with a job search. It was all about scanning help-wanted ads in the newspaper, mailing résumés, and following up with phone calls. I visited the public library and scoured newspapers from across the country. No city was off-limits. By the end of my second week, I had mailed a dozen résumés and was waiting for the responses. That's when my mother surprised me.

While lounging on the couch anxiously waiting for a call, my mother suggested I get a part-time job at the local McDonald's.

McDonald's?

I had nothing against McDonald's, but my professional dreams didn't involve flipping burgers or learning how to properly place a pickle. For a graduation gift, she had given me a briefcase. At the time, it felt like an initiation into the professional world. Now, it started to feel suspiciously like a lunchbox.

I still remembered the days when she scrambled to find any job she could to bring in money for the family. It had only been two weeks. Her suggestion felt like she was giving up on my hopes and dreams. Taking a part-time job would have made me feel like I was giving up, too. My motivation to make follow-up calls grew.

As the days passed, I began getting nervous. The thought of working at McDonald's like my mother suggested started feeling like a real possibility. Then, a fork in the road appeared. One path led to an engineering job at a wastewater plant in Kansas City. It wasn't structural engineering, but I had a well-rounded education in other Civil disciplines, and my skills were adaptable. It was better than McDonald's, but not what I was hoping for.

The second path led to a small, local engineering company in downtown Pittsburgh. My courses in college were mostly about designing highway bridges, not buildings. Neither offer was perfect, but this one seemed the best. Besides, a job in my own backyard was appealing. I could live at home, pay off my college loan, and save money for a car or an apartment. An interview was scheduled.

I met with the owner of the company in Pittsburgh, Mr. Dotter. He warned me that structural engineering could be miserable and difficult. The work was tedious, stressful, and thankless. It felt like he was doing his best to discourage me from the job. I wasn't deterred. My technical skills were up for the challenge. If I ended up in over my head, college had already taught me how to survive. I knew the owner saw my enthusiasm, but I had no idea what to make of his discouraging words.

The next day, I was hired. There's one final entry in my Baby Book. My mother wrote,

"On June 16th began working for Dotter Engineering in downtown Pgh. Loves it."

– Baby Book 1987

Dotter Engineering

Dotter Engineering was a family-run business located in the heart of downtown Pittsburgh. They specialized in commercial buildings, hospitals, schools, post offices, and hotels. Residential homes, large factories, and bridges weren't part of their focus. I later learned that Mr. Dotter was one of the most respected structural engineers in the city, and working at his firm carried a certain amount of prestige.

On the first day, I dressed in my finest suit, rode the light rail through the tunnels, across the river, and into downtown Pittsburgh, the Steel City. With great anticipation, I walked narrow streets riddled with potholes, breathed in the exhaust from passing traffic, and stared up at tall buildings. Gargoyles with carved stone faces stared back, welcoming me to my new life.

I took an elevator, barely large enough to hold four people, up to the fourth floor, and stepped into the lobby. The receptionist, who was Mr. Dotter's wife, greeted me politely, and made a few quick introductions.

Just beyond the front door, a carpeted hallway lined with small offices for the senior engineers led to a larger room. At the end of the hall sat a spindly desk with a lone computer. It looked out of place, as if someone had put it there as an afterthought. Engineering firms were only beginning to experiment with digital tools, and this computer came with restrictions. Anyone who wanted to use it had to ask for permission. There was no internet, no quick answers. Engineers relied on their education, their experience, and whatever reference books they had managed to collect.

Beyond the computer, a larger room opened up on both sides. Cubicles for the engineers stretched along the windows to my right, while a row of drafting tables filled the space to my left. Across from my desk was a floor-to-ceiling glass partition. Inside, the head draftsman puffed furiously on a cigarette while shuffling 8½ x 11 pages with standard engineering details across a vellum sheet.

At the far end of the room stood the reference library, a wall of knowledge that stretched across generations. The oldest books were musty, their covers torn and spines frayed. They were filled with guidance on concrete, masonry, wood, and steel. Mixed among them were volumes on modern structures, codes, and specifications.

I was in awe. The library felt like a cathedral of engineering memory, a place where long hidden knowledge was waiting to be rediscovered. I couldn't wait to start working on something, anything.

One of the first people I met was a young engineer named Tony, and he casually shared a story about how I got the job. He told me that when the position opened, there were two candidates under review. Every engineer in the office got a vote. Tony was a Penn State alum, and once he saw where I went to school, the choice was easy. We quickly became good friends.

Later that morning, one of the senior engineers asked me to make some simple calculations. In college, we had focused on basic engineering principles. Now, I had to figure out how to apply that knowledge in the real world, and adapt it to buildings. I went straight to work. Two hours later, he returned to review my progress. Everything was organized and checked exactly as I'd been taught. This was when I learned my first real lessons. The kindly engineer pointed to the calculations and said,

"Everything looks good." I felt a wave of pride.

"But…"

But? Gulp.

"You're not in college anymore. This is not how we do things here."

He carefully explained how calculations were done outside the classroom. He showed me the differences between academic theory and professional practice, detailing how rules of thumb and specialized knowledge were applied for efficiency. I listened closely, and then realized something important. I was being accepted into the secret world of structural engineers. That evening, I went home happier than I'd ever been.

There were other lessons too, not about design, but about how to deal with clients. I remember a phone call from a demanding architect. The call was placed on speakerphone while one of the senior engineers listened in. The first time the architect asked a question, I didn't know the answer and stayed quiet. The senior engineer stepped in and answered for me. When the next question came, I tried again. My answer was correct, but it still wasn't good enough. There had been hesitation in my voice.

After the call, the senior engineer gave me some advice. He told me never to answer too slowly or too quickly. If I didn't know the answer, I should simply say, "Let me think about that and get back to you." If I did know the answer, I shouldn't respond too quickly. He said the architects needed to feel their questions were important. Answering too fast makes it seem like you're not taking them seriously.

Another time, while working on a project for the state, Mr. Dotter accompanied me to the review. I had confidence in my design but was intimidated by the process. Mr. Dotter calmly told me not to worry, just be myself. He brought along every page we had. When I asked why, he said, "Once the state sees a big pile of paper, they'll believe you worked hard and will trust you. They probably won't even look at your calculations."

When we arrived, I nervously sat down across from the state engineer. His desk was buried in papers, and boxes were stacked around the room. He glanced at the pile of papers we brought, looked at me, and asked, "Where did you go to college?" "Penn State," I said.

That was it. From there, we launched into a warm conversation about his son, who was currently a student at Penn State. There were no questions about the project. None. As we left the office, I swear I saw Mr. Dotter give the faintest smile. He didn't say a word, but I could almost hear him whisper: "Told you so." I had learned my second lesson in client management. These skills would prove invaluable years later, when I became a manager myself.

A few months into the job, I started wondering about how many vacation days we got. Tony didn't have the answer. With a sly grin, he pointed me toward Mr. Dotter's office. I couldn't tell if he was being helpful or setting me up. I stepped into the office, and in my most respectful voice, asked about vacation time. He looked at me, tilted his head in deep thought, and said, "I'll get back to you." Back at my desk, I smiled. A senior engineer had already taught me what those words meant: Mr. Dotter didn't know the answer.

The next day, I found out no one had ever asked that question before. There were no time sheets and no clocks to punch. It was a casually run, small family business. If someone needed time off, they simply took it. No one kept track because it was based on trust. As the company grew, Mr. Dotter realized it was time to set a standard. He said, "The most I've ever taken is one week, so that's what you get." While I still thought Tony treated me like a guinea pig, getting the same deal as the owner sounded more than fair to me.

Back at home, I still had some adjusting to do. With my siblings all out in the world, it was just my mother and me. At college, I had the freedom to eat, clean, and be merry, however and whenever I liked. At home, those freedoms were gone, and I was back to respectfully living on my mother's schedule.

Home-cooked meals were a clear upgrade from college fare. My mother didn't ask for any help with groceries or cooking. All I had to do was show up at mealtimes and food automatically appeared. She liked cooking for me, and I liked eating. The hardest part was doing the dishes, and that wasn't very hard.

As long as my clothes were placed in the proper hamper and not tossed around a room, I didn't have to worry about laundry anymore. That part didn't bother me at all.

There was no church at college. I was a hedonistic pagan, staying out late on Saturday nights and singing and swaying at the bars. Sunday morning was for rest and recovery. Back home, church returned to my life. I sat beside my mother every Sunday in the same pew we'd occupied when I was a child.

In college, nobody cared what time a roommate wandered back after a night out. At home, if I stayed out late, my mother would be up with the light on, waiting for me. To avoid keeping her up, I limited my late nights out.

Holidays were quieter now. Mike and Kathy were living in faraway states. John and Rick were nearby, but there was always an excuse not to come over. By then, most of our older relatives were either too frail or already gone to join us. It was just the two of us. I didn't mind it too much, but the house felt empty. Still, I loved spending time with my mother and was glad she wasn't alone in the house, especially for holidays.

Sometimes, we did simple things together. I remember donating blood with her, the two of us sitting side by side. She was still setting a good example about giving, and I was doing my part as a responsible son. Those moments were special then and the memory is still special now.

Great Expectations

Outside of work, life was shifting as well. Eileen and I were still in touch, and I wasn't ready to give up on us. By that point, my father had been married four times. I didn't want to be like him, treating relationships with women like a revolving door. After some convincing, I asked Eileen about trying to get back together again. We knew that once summer ended, she would have to return to college. When she agreed to give our relationship another chance, my heart skipped a beat.

Dating again didn't mean all was well. Near the end of summer, I remember Eileen proudly showing off a new haircut. Family and friends were all telling her how wonderful it was, but I thought differently. In the back and on the sides, her hair was shaved like a crew cut. On top, it was arranged in curls that stuck up just enough to provide body. Maybe the blouse didn't help, as it had a high collar that encircled her neck just below the chin and flared out like a vase.

Her new hairdo looked comical, but I couldn't tell her that. My unwillingness to say something should have been a hint that things weren't right between the two of us, but telling a woman her hair looks bad when everyone else is being supportive is not a road any man wants to go down. I may have been clueless about women, but I was not suicidal. I politely told her that it was nice.

By the end of the summer, she returned to college for her final two years. Once again, we were back in a long-distance relationship. I felt a mix of joy that we were still a couple, and concern that nothing had really changed.

Work continued going well into the fall of 1987, and I absorbed everything I could, eager to prove myself to the company. Progress didn't come with complete independence, and like all new engineers, my calculations continued to be carefully checked. The senior engineer assigned to review my calculations was a meticulous man who spoke with a mild Indian accent. Mr. Shah would return my pages covered in red marks, explaining the corrections he wanted to see. It wasn't that my conclusions were wrong, he just had a very specific way he wanted the numbers organized and the logic presented. Tony had prepared me for this. His words of advice were simple: "Don't argue. Just make the changes. You're getting paid either way."

I wasn't used to having my work nitpicked, but I had much to learn and wanted to make a good impression. Taking a deep breath, I thanked Mr. Shah for his comments and went back to my desk.

After a few weeks, frustration turned into curiosity. When Mr. Shah returned a page covered in red, I started asking him to explain any part that didn't make sense. In a professor-like manner, he would calmly walk me through the logic. Under his mentorship, my knowledge and discipline grew quickly.

One of the most exciting moments early on was a trip outside the office with a different senior engineer to visit a project site. It was an old, abandoned brewery in a run-down part of the city, slated to be converted into office space. My job was to take photos, gather measurements, and then assist with the design.

We got to work immediately, stepping over fallen debris and weaving through dim, nondescript hallways. Crumbling walls leaned inward. The air was thick with dust and the scent of mildew. Then we reached a room that stopped us in our tracks, not because of any structural significance, but because of what was inside and how it felt.

The room was frozen in time. A thick layer of debris blanketed a desk in the corner. The sun filtered through holes in the ceiling, catching dust in its golden shafts of light. A brick wall bowed inward, as if the building itself had exhaled and never recovered. In one corner lay an old fedora hat. In another, an empty safe, tipped on its side, the door flung open. Scattered across the floor were canceled dividend checks, as if someone had opened the safe, tossed them into the air, and walked away. It felt like a scene from an old gangster movie.

With permission, I pocketed one of the checks as a souvenir. It became a kind of talisman that reminded me how vibrant the place had once been. As we continued snapping photos and taking notes, I looked up and noticed a brick-vaulted ceiling. The engineer explained that this type of construction was no longer used as it was too expensive, too labor-intensive. To me, it felt like discovering ancient ruins. I wasn't just documenting decay, I was helping to resurrect it.

Indiana Jones had nothing on me.

I was going to help tie this building's past to its future, to turn something forgotten into something vibrant and new. For the first time, I felt it *clearly*: the work I was doing had purpose.

Back in the office, daily routines settled in. Tony showed me the best lunch spots. When Mr. Shah joined us, he would calculate how much everyone owed. Nobody ever had exact change, so the bill was always rounded. If he thought he still owed someone, you could count on finding nickels, dimes, and pennies on your desk with a handwritten note of thanks. Mr. Shah was a very exacting man.

Of all the lunches, one stood out. As our group was finishing up at a nearby McDonald's, my mind wandered. While casually looking around the restaurant, a tall, thin police officer approached our table.

"What are you looking at?" he barked. "How would you like to be thrown in the wagon and locked up?"

"No sir," I squeaked.

The other engineers looked as confused as I was. The officer returned to his much shorter, much rounder partner, and the two left the restaurant. I hadn't been paying attention before, but I was now. The two officers looked exactly like Laurel and Hardy.

Had I unknowingly been staring? I didn't think so.

The others were baffled. We were structural engineers. We didn't cause trouble. They knew my only crime was eating too slowly.

There was plenty of teasing back at the office, but the encounter stuck with me. Until then, I hadn't given much thought to police officers. They were the good guys, authority figures who kept the peace. After that day, I wasn't so sure.

After work, life was lighter. I went to baseball and hockey games, and sometimes tagged along with colleagues for free happy-hour appetizers. Pittsburgh's premier downtown health club offered a discount to adults in their twenties. I swam laps, ran the indoor track, pedaled the stationary bikes, and played squash. My skills at squash had improved enough that I started entering tournaments. With each win, I felt stronger.

During one of the tournaments, someone stole a credit card from my locker. The thief enjoyed a nice meal, shopped for electronics, bought some clothes, and then disappeared. Fortunately, I noticed the card was missing quickly, reported it, and wasn't responsible for any charges. Like my encounter with the police, I went from feeling secure to feeling vulnerable. Even with my challenges during lunch and at the club, the city was sharpening me with each passing day.

As 1987 came to a close, so did another chapter. My grandmother, the last of my grandparents, had passed away the prior year and her estate had finally settled. At the time, the whole family traveled to Florida for the funeral, and we all helped my mother navigate the airports.

What I remember most from the trip is that I never saw my mother cry. She focused more on whether her children were okay than on her own grief. I don't remember her ever crying when growing up, except for that one time when I was still a toddler. Just as I'd learned from her, emotions weren't shown during my grandmother's service. It would take years to unlearn that habit.

Now that the estate had closed, my mother wanted to pass along the strong sense of family she still carried. She gave each of her children small keepsakes to remember my grandmother, but there was more. Though my grandfather had died six years before I was born, she also wanted me to have a way to remember him. Among my grandmother's things was a small gold tie clip. It wasn't real gold or designer-made, but that didn't matter. The memory of him did, and when she gave it to me, I held it as if it had magical powers. The tie clip was a bridge to a past I'd never known. Ever since, I've worn the tie clip to family weddings and funerals, not as a flashy accessory, but as a subtle remembrance honoring the past.

The time had come for another ending. While one connection to the past had been placed in my hands, another piece of my past was about to be let go. My old college motorcycle had been spending more time in the repair shop than on the road. One of Tony's friends had a car for sale, and by chance, I needed one. A whirlwind of activity followed. I bought the car, sold the motorcycle, and as I did, I could almost hear distant sighs of relief from my mother, my father, and my girlfriend.

The car, a black, fully loaded Chevy Cavalier Sport Edition, looked more at home on a NASCAR track than a suburban street. I still had a couple of friends in the neighborhood, and the day the car appeared, they performed the expected ritual. They each slowly circled the car, examined the wide, studded tires, and admired the electronic dashboard. Finally, they stared over at me, then at the car, then back at me. I waited. A subtle nod confirmed their approval. My car had passed the test.

Buying the car felt like another step into adulthood, but as my second year at Dotter Engineering ended, the road ahead at work, at home, and in my heart was about to get more complicated.

Shake-Ups

As the next year progressed, Dotter Engineering added two more engineers and the place had become a bustling center of activity. The company was growing fast. My job hadn't really changed. It was exactly as described during my initial interview. Structural engineering could be tedious, stressful, and thankless. It still didn't bother me. The excitement of learning and friendships in the office made it all worthwhile.

In the fall of 1988, Mr. Dotter made the unexpected announcement that he was selling his business. Three of the senior engineers were buying the company and assured everyone that nothing in the day-to-day routine would change. Under Mr. Dotter, the office had felt like an extended family, with a steady stream of client visits and chances to connect outside the drafting tables. However, that changed quickly. When an architect called with an invitation to attend the grand opening of their new office, the new owners coolly declined. Mr. Dotter never would have turned down an opportunity to strengthen ties with a client. One of the younger engineers offered to go, but the new owners wouldn't let him. I couldn't shake the feeling that the family atmosphere was slipping away.

Tony was the first to go, taking a job designing glass block. He didn't vanish completely, but he was no longer in the trenches watching my back. When word spread that the new owners had no intention of ever offering partnership to the other professionals, the two engineers hired after me left as well. By spring of 1989, work had slowed. The three people who had left were replaced by a single engineer who was only a few years older than me. The cracks in the company's foundation were widening, and the pace of change was uncomfortably fast.

By spring of 1989, Eileen was nearing the end of her senior year and still didn't know what to do with her liberal arts degree. She went to college for four years without ever really thinking about where it would lead. She asked me what kind of job she should get. I said I didn't want to be responsible for her choice of a career. It wasn't my place to tell her what to do. She must not have appreciated my lack of advice, because the rest of the conversation turned cold.

There was another time I remembered her going cold. Earlier in our relationship, she mentioned something about a prenuptial agreement. Her family wanted to protect her wealth, but it caught me off guard. Eileen had often told me how much she disliked the way her mother controlled the family's money, and how that control hung over her father like a shadow. Her request felt out of character. This was the sort of thing the parents would ask for, not her. Her family's wealth wasn't important to me, and I wasn't willing to formalize our relationship with a document built on a power imbalance. This wasn't the middle ages.

I was offended, but didn't want to let it show. I told her the only document I'd sign would be one that said she could have everything I owned. After my response, the topic never came up again. The mention of a prenuptial agreement felt like we were close to an engagement, but there were clues that suggested I might have been wrong.

Paying attention to the clues wasn't my strong suit. I had a well-paying, steady career and couldn't wait to no longer have a long-distance relationship. We would finally be in the same city and could start a future together.

A few weeks before graduation, Eileen told me she didn't think we should see each other anymore. I was blindsided. This was the same thing that had happened right before I graduated, and here we were again. She said our relationship had been nothing more than puppy love, and that it wasn't real.

Puppy love?

My heart sank. The past seven years had felt pretty real to me, but she had made up her mind and said it would be too painful to discuss anything further. We had been here two years earlier. We were here again. Last time I'd felt there was still a chance, but this time, the fight to stay together had left me. There was nothing left to do but respect her decision.

For the next several weeks I was in a haze. Our parents, co-workers, and friends could not believe we were no longer a couple. At first, they thought I was joking. Then, they saw the sadness that surrounded my every move. I don't remember much about that time, but anger wasn't one of the emotions I felt. It was simply a time of sadness, wrapped in pain, wrapped in more sadness.

***

While a door had closed in my life, a window started to open. John had been working as a civilian engineer on a Navy ship, testing weapons systems. The long deployments were too stressful and he resigned, with the hope of finding a job back in Pittsburgh. When he came home in summer 1989, it felt like he brought a sense of relief along with him, and it felt the same for me. We both needed a distraction, and we filled the void together by going to baseball games, hockey games, and playing one-on-one basketball. It was like the world was trying to right itself.

John used money from his vacation time payout to buy a Suzuki Samurai, a convertible similar to a small jeep. That is when he taught me how to drive a stick shift, although I already understood the concept of a stick shift from my motorcycle days. John was a great teacher. Even when the ear-shattering sound of grinding gears could be heard as I stalled and started on hills, he remained calm. I loved having John at home.

Around the same time, Rick started occasionally showing up at home again. When his pizza shop dream didn't pan out, he began singing in a rock band in central Pennsylvania. The standard greeting when seeing Rick was, *Get a haircut, ya hippie.* Rick would look over, flash a smile, and then give a flip of his long, dishwater blond hair. The house was alive with energy once again.

The energy within the house wasn't always good. To tide John over until he could find an engineering position, he found a job as a bartender in a small neighborhood establishment, except he did more than work at the bar. He started drinking there, too.

Rick had struggled with drinking and had overcome it, but when he stopped by the house, I sensed a disdain in the way he looked at John. It was almost as if he was saying, *You're not better than me.* As for John, he didn't respect Rick's dreams of being a rock star. He thought the "hippie" wannabe-rock star was irresponsible. There was something quietly bubbling under the surface between John and Rick.

One night, as I was trying to sleep, the doorbell rang. My mother answered it and was surprised to find a policeman. There had been an accident. A car had hit a nearby mailbox, and a trail of oil led straight to our house. I heard Rick's voice at the door. He told the officer that John had been drinking too much and was upstairs.

Rick and John hadn't gone out together. Why was he getting involved?

By the time I dragged myself out of bed, John was gone. He'd been arrested for a DUI.

Did Rick just hand John over to the cops?

I couldn't believe it. I later found out he had. It permanently damaged the relationship between the two brothers I was closest to.

Looking back now, Rick believed he was doing the right thing. He just hadn't thought through the consequences to John or to their relationship. Or maybe he did, and didn't care. The small fissures between John and Rick expanded. They didn't even want to be in the same room together. Our family had weathered turbulence before, but it never felt fractured like this.

Life at home was no longer as peaceful as it once was. There was now tension in the air. John had refused a breathalyzer, which guaranteed a guilty verdict. His sentence included classes, a fine, and the cost of the damaged mailbox. On top of that, his Suzuki Samurai was totaled, and insurance wasn't about to foot the repairs. DUIs didn't come with sympathy. Even with no job and a DUI conviction, he didn't learn his lesson. John still worked at the bar, and still drank too much. In addition, he was becoming more distant.

As things at home were heating up, my mother asked me to start contributing to the household expenses. I knew it was fair, but it also felt like a gentle nudge to leave.

All of the pieces were falling into place. After two years living rent-free at home, my old college loan had been paid off. I had a good job, a car, and enough saved for a first month's rent. When an apartment about two miles away opened up, I didn't hesitate.

It was time for me to fly.

CHAPTER 7

IDC

As much as I loved my family, the desire for a peaceful sanctuary of my own had grown strong. It wasn't only about getting some distance from the underlying tension at home. I needed more freedom, and the choice didn't happen impulsively. It was planned. I found a small one-bedroom corner unit on the top floor of a modest complex. Fewer neighbors, no footsteps overhead, no toilets flushing above me. The apartment sat along a bus line, which meant I could avoid the daily grind of rush hour traffic and the steep cost of downtown parking. It was practical, efficient, and exactly what I needed.

During those first two years at Dotter Engineering, I remained firmly tethered to home. After moving to my first apartment at the end of 1989, the ties were still there, but that was about to change. Unknown forces were pulling me in a different direction, and one by one, the ties were beginning to unravel.

Independence

Living away from home gave me the chance to experiment with cooking. In college, dinner usually meant boxed macaroni and cheese or a can of Campbell's soup. The meals were quick and forgettable. In my new apartment, I had shelves fully stocked with every spice. My mother had given me a three-ring, loose-leaf Betty Crocker cookbook as a housewarming gift. It was filled with basic recipes and simple advice. There was nothing elaborate, just the raw material to build upon. I recognized some of those recipes as dishes my mother cooked. Meals like meatloaf, Swiss steak, and beef stroganoff were tried first. I even attempted my own versions of meals I had never seen written down, like baked spaghetti. The results were uneven, but they gave me the confidence to experiment even when there was no recipe. The cookbook still sits in my kitchen and each time I pull it from the shelf, I think of her and give thanks.

Owning an apartment didn't mean the ties to Lovingston Drive were severed. Sundays were still spent in the usual pew beside my mother, and the sound of the mower at her house remained my responsibility. Independence was a work in progress.

With cash in hand and an apartment to fill, I stepped into the furniture store. I stood in the front lobby while a flurry of activity buzzed around me. Salesmen swarmed customers the moment they walked through the door. I paused, looking left, and then right. My clothes were respectable, my hair neatly combed, yet nobody approached. I wandered through the store and chose a nice black lacquer bedroom set, a living room set, a kitchen table with four chairs, and a few pieces of art for the walls. Still, no one came over or paid any attention to me. Eventually, I walked over to a desk and asked for help. The salesman looked up slightly confused. It was as if my cloak of invisibility had suddenly vanished. The sale took only minutes to complete, and as I left, I still couldn't figure out why I'd been ignored.

It wasn't the first time something like this had happened. I remember standing at an outdoor food cart, only to have the vendor look over my head and serve the person behind me. Before the person behind me could order, I politely but firmly let the vendor know I was next. He apologized profusely and took my order. I knew that to be seen, I had to speak up, but sometimes speaking up isn't enough. I needed to learn how to be more visible and really stand out.

I only stood out on the squash court, and it came naturally. The game rewarded instinct and risk. I fought relentlessly for every point and kept winning tournaments. Work wasn't about winning. There, I was quiet and serious, shaped by the routines at Dotter Engineering. I didn't see the gap between those two sides of me yet. If I was going to succeed, the part of me that thrived on the court would have to find its way into the rest of my life.

In early 1990, as I neared the end of my third year at Dotter Engineering, the buzz that once filled the office had begun to fade. I didn't worry too much at that point. Mr. Shah's red marks had nearly vanished, and I was gaining more confidence in my abilities every day. That confidence came with growing ambition. When the engineer hired to replace the younger staff needed help on a project, I jumped in. His feedback wasn't like Mr. Shah's. These weren't thoughtful corrections or lessons in logic. They were arbitrary demands. Entire pages needed to be reworked, not because they were wrong, but because he said so.

I remembered Tony's advice about just doing what the senior engineer said. Senior engineers held the licenses and carried the liability. I was still a year away from mine and was still expected to comply without question, but I also knew how the business needed to make money. Reworking pages for no apparent reason was inefficient. I brought my concern to one of the principals. He sat in his office, puffing on a cigar as the smoke curled around his head in a halo of indifference.

"Just do whatever the new engineer says."

There was no discussion, and no curiosity. There was only compliance ordered. I nodded, walked out, and started updating the calculations. As the numbers were changed, my mind drifted. Being readily dismissed and ordered to follow directions didn't sit well with me. I was in a company where making partner wasn't possible. Younger engineers were leaving for better opportunities while I was stuck unnecessarily doing busywork. The time had come to start thinking about a different future.

Tony and I still kept in touch. He'd found a new job he wasn't interested in, but he thought it might be right for me. He had opened the door for me once before. Now, he was doing it again. If I was going to break away from the depressing environment that now enveloped the office, I was going to have to trust my instincts and take a risk. My mind was made up and I scheduled an interview.

The interview at IDC was nothing like the one I had with Mr. Dotter. I was ushered into a room and introduced to four people. They took turns peppering me with their own questions. My answers were provided with confidence. I thought the interview was as much about me interviewing them. When the Human Resources director asked if I could design concrete in a semiconductor factory, I responded without thinking:

"Yes sir, I can. Concrete doesn't know what building it's in."

The engineer beside him exhaled slowly and shook his head. I couldn't tell what it meant. When I left, I had no idea how it had gone. Two anxious days passed, but then the call came. IDC wanted me to start as soon as possible.

The next morning at Dotter Engineering, I walked into the principal's office and gave my notice. He leaned back, puffed on his cigar, and said,

"Good luck."

That was it. There was no, *We'll miss you.* There was no, *You did good work.* There was only silence.

As for the rest of the office, it wasn't much different. There was no acknowledgment from the people I'd shared an office with for three years. Their lives were going on, as was mine. However, leaving without a ripple was a strange feeling. That silence was the clearest sign of all that I was absolutely ready for something more. Two weeks later, I took the elevator down from the fourth floor for the last time.

On my first day at IDC, I was still thinking about the interview with the engineer who had shaken his head at my response. I wondered if I'd come off as being too flippant. As it turned out, he was the office manager. The first thing he did was apologize for the person who had questioned if I could design concrete in their buildings.

"That was a stupid question," he said. "You shouldn't have had to answer it."

I hadn't even started working yet, and by answering a silly question with confidence, I had already passed my first test.

That phone call from Tony about an opportunity changed everything. Dotter Engineering had been a local firm rooted in Pittsburgh. IDC was a multinational company. My professional landscape was expanding. Through mergers and buyouts, I would stay with that company for the next thirty years, and it wouldn't always be as a structural engineer.

Settling In

In July 1990, around the same time I was figuring out my new job, an unexpected call reminded me about family obligations. When the phone rang, Mike explained that John could no longer cover our mother's mortgage, and that he planned to take it over. Neither Rick nor Kathy were in a position to chip in, so Mike asked if I could help. I agreed without hesitation.

After that, every month, like clockwork, I sent a check to Mike. I never mentioned it to my other siblings. About a year later, Mike called and said the checks weren't needed anymore. He gave no explanation, just a simple, abrupt statement. I later found out he'd taken over the full payments himself. I never really knew why, but always suspected he regretted asking his younger brother for help, and simply wanted full control. Even as he assumed control, I couldn't shake the feeling that I'd done something wrong.

While I tried to make sense of things with Mike, IDC was teaching me its own lessons about control. My new employer was based in Portland, Oregon. The Pittsburgh office wasn't created to serve local clients. It was a strategic outpost, planted within 500 miles of over half the U.S. population. The company focused on massive industrial factories, not the schools, post offices, or hotels I was used to. In fact, IDC didn't do any business in Pittsburgh at all. There was no overlap with Dotter Engineering, no competition. It was a completely different world.

During those first days, a few differences were immediately apparent. IDC was a bigger, faster, and far less forgiving company. Gone were the casual conversations about policy and handwritten notes. In their place were employee manuals, timekeeping systems, and a chain of command I didn't yet understand.

For designing a commercial building, an owner hires an architect who then hires all of the different types of engineers. At Dotter Engineering, I had always answered to the architect. In my new world, there was a different hierarchy. An owner hired IDC, who assigned a project manager, who assembled a team of engineers and architects. The architects didn't run the show and weren't considered exceptional, they were just another group on the team.

These large factories cared more about chemicals and air, so the process and mechanical engineers carried more weight. Structural engineers were at the bottom of the company totem pole, and we were expected to support whatever the other technical disciplines needed. I didn't care very much about the hierarchy. I was there to work the numbers, not the people.

As I was shown to my desk, I glanced over at the library. The sleek metal bookcases were half empty. Easy access to old, musty books with their wealth of knowledge was gone. I would also miss something more important, though, and that was I no longer had easy access to other structural engineers.

Within a week of being hired, the only other structural engineer was fired. The office manager saw my concern and told me not to worry. A few days later, his replacement arrived from Texas. This person was nothing like anyone I'd worked with before.

Roger stood over six feet tall and had a neatly trimmed blond mustache and beard. He strutted into the office with the confidence of someone who already owned the place. His loud talking, cowboy-boot-wearing persona didn't fit the quiet, conservatively dressed structural engineer mold. For the past five years, his work had taken him into a field unrelated to structural engineering, leaving his technical skills rusty. Returning to the profession was not his goal. He only wanted to move back to Pittsburgh. Since he was licensed, supporting him became my responsibility.

The engineers at Dotter Engineering were like a straight line, precise and impossible to misinterpret. Roger was more like a bowl of wet spaghetti hurled against a wall. He was disorderly, slippery, and oddly resistant to sticking with a plan. His calculations were impossible to decipher, and there was no substance to his technical explanations. I'd come to IDC hoping for growth. Instead, I was spending my days untangling Roger's messes. It wasn't just inefficient, it was demoralizing.

Fortunately, there was the occasional distraction to remind me that working at IDC could be fun. My first project was for a client in Virginia. After spending several months grinding out calculations, I was asked to join the engineering team on a trip to the site. At Dotter Engineering, travel meant a short drive across town. Now I was boarding a plane and spending a few nights away from home.

I don't recall much about the job itself, but one dinner sticks out. The company was paying for the meal, and I didn't want to be wasteful. I planned to order something simple, like a hamburger and a glass of water. My restraint didn't match the mood of my colleagues. I watched as pre-dinner drinks and appetizers filled the table. It felt like country club living on the company's dime.

Maybe it was okay for engineers to live a little?

With small pangs of guilt, I cautiously joined in, sharing in the appetizers and adding bacon to my burger. After dinner, Roger, who was also on the trip, suggested we stop by the Manassas battlefield. A little history sounded good to me, so off we went. Roger wasn't thinking very much about history. He'd had a few too many drinks at dinner and decided it would be more fun to stage a re-enactment. With arms flailing, we ran across the battlefield and shouted orders to imaginary troops. Structural engineers can't always be serious, and I needed some ridiculousness in my life.

When we returned to the office later that week, it was as if nothing had happened. The battlefield was behind us. The serious work resumed. As the trip faded from memory, an uneasy feeling about Roger lingered, which I didn't understand quite yet, but I would.

Oregon, First Contact

My mother always hosted Christmas dinner at the house on Lovingston Drive, and 1990 was no different. My brother John had invited a girl I didn't recognize. He sat at the head of the table as was the eldest son's right, and I took my place along the side. The food was the same, the company polite, but something felt off.

Since John's DUI, I could see an unmistakable chip on his shoulder starting to grow. He was still nice to me, but an air of grumpiness was returning. It was as if he resented the burden of being the oldest son and not being able to find an engineering job in Pittsburgh. John was spending more time at the bar, and we weren't hanging out as much.

I glanced across the table at the girl who had been invited. She looked overweight. *No, not overweight. Pregnant, maybe?* We'd been watching hockey games in town a few weeks earlier, and he hadn't said a word. I couldn't very well ask a question like this since that seemed rude. I pushed the thought aside and went back to enjoying the holiday.

A short time later, my suspicions from Christmas were confirmed. John married the girl he had brought to Christmas dinner. Within a month, he became the father of a baby girl named after my mother. The wedding had been organized quickly, and I could understand why.

I was disappointed not to have been invited, but more than that, I was surprised by how little I knew about my brother's new life in Pittsburgh. As his life-changing events were happening, I was on the other side of the country chasing something new.

In January 1991, IDC sent me to Portland, Oregon for an assignment that would eventually stretch to five months. Portland felt like home from the start. The city was surrounded by hills, with a river running through its heart. Long steel bridges spanned the water, just like in Pittsburgh. It felt familiar. It felt right. My hotel was directly beside the downtown office, which meant no rush-hour traffic to battle and no buses to wait for. If I needed a car, a company vehicle could be signed out. Best of all was that living on an expense account let me sample new restaurants and explore as much of the Pacific Northwest as I could.

The home office buzzed with activity on every floor. I was free from Roger's chaos back in Pittsburgh and back in a world of structure and discipline. My questions were no longer brushed aside or met with a shrug. The structural engineers in Portland reminded me of the ones at Dotter Engineering when I was first employed. They were precise, thoughtful, and serious about their craft.

One of the things I noticed right away in Portland was how different the culture was from Pittsburgh. The team in Pittsburgh had developed a close, tight-knit feel. If someone received a speeding ticket, or had a sick pet, everybody knew about it. When asked how you were doing, it wasn't just a casual greeting. They actually seemed to care. There was a nice balance between friendliness and maintaining professionalism.

In Portland, people kept more to themselves. It was still friendly, but only on the surface. If someone asked how you were doing, they didn't really want to know, they were just saying hello. The Portland office was still professional, but it felt cold.

I also noticed a bit of friendly tension between the two offices. In Pittsburgh, I'd been told that West Coast people speak too slowly, and because of that, they never get anything done. When I arrived in Portland, I heard the other side of the story. East Coast people speak too fast and never think things through properly, and because of that, they never get anything done. I felt caught in the middle. I loved both cities. Something inside told me to steer clear of what seemed like harmless teasing, just in case it wasn't so harmless.

One of the structural engineers who avoided those conversations entirely was Lee. He was sharp, diplomatic, and careful not to make waves. Lee could amicably take any side of a discussion. If he disagreed with you, he'd start by agreeing, then gently steer the conversation toward his way of thinking. In the end, you'd be convinced his idea was yours all along.

Lee joined IDC one month before I did. He moved to Oregon after working at a prestigious firm in California. His outgoing, friendly nature and my more personal approach bumped up against the reserved culture in Portland. We recognized each other as fellow outsiders, and hit it off immediately. I soon found myself on the Oregon Coast watching him dive for fish and crabs.

Lee was more than a friend though. From the day he arrived, Lee was considered one of the brightest minds in the company, especially in earthquake analysis. He spoke with an endearingly heavy Polish accent and had more energy than anyone I'd ever met. Whenever I had a question, Lee was there, not just with an answer, but with an explanation. He broke down complex theory in a way that made it feel simple, even exciting. His enthusiasm was contagious. After talking with him, I couldn't wait to get back to work.

A few months in, Lee was overloaded and needed help with a project. I gladly volunteered. Many late evenings were spent creating page after page of calculations. They were long days, but I loved what I was doing, and who I was doing it with. All of those extra hours grinding out numbers ended up being the perfect preparation for my upcoming Professional Engineering exam that fall.

When I accepted the assignment in Oregon, I didn't know what I was looking for. Surrounded by hard-working engineers, new experiences fueled by an expense account, and people like Lee, I felt like I might be getting closer.

Weddings, Tests, and Loans

As the project wound down, I returned to my apartment in Pittsburgh. Mike had married back in 1983, and John had married in January. Rick and Kathy's weddings were just around the corner. I hadn't been dating much since my breakup with Eileen, and was about to become the only unmarried sibling. That was a lonely feeling, one that would stick with me for years.

In May 1991, Rick was married just outside Pittsburgh. Still upset about being turned in for a DUI, John did not attend. His best man was an old high school friend he wasn't really in touch with anymore. Rick asked me to be an usher. That decision stung. He was the brother I'd played baseball with, the one I'd tossed pizzas with. I thought we were close.

Maybe we weren't?

The night before his wedding removed all of my doubts. Rick asked if I wanted to grab a drink. He didn't want a bachelor party or a night out with his best man, he only wanted the two of us. He didn't want to drink before the wedding so we went to a nearby bar and ordered Cokes. There was no loud music and nothing to distract. We just talked. Rick shared a few personal stories about singing in his rock band, and some of the struggles he overcame. He had a more serious maturity about him that I hadn't seen before. The closeness I shared with my brother hadn't disappeared, it had just evolved.

Kathy's wedding was held later that year in a mountain canyon far from Pittsburgh. After high school, she had left for college in Colorado and graduated in just three years. We didn't see much of each other during that time, just the occasional call and a few letters.

Kathy planned the wedding herself and was a whirlwind of energy and organization. On her wedding day, she wore a western-style gown.

After the ceremony, the happy couple took off in their RV, hoping it wouldn't break down. I followed in my car to make sure they made it to their campsite. For years afterward, I'd get teased about being on the honeymoon with her. That day was the last time there would be a photo of my mother, my father, and all of my siblings in the same frame.

***

Long ago, I'd excelled at wrestling, won trophies in karate, been accepted into two college honorary societies, and landed a good job. Through it all, my mother would always say, *Don't get a big head now.* She said it so often that eventually, I could hear her voice in my head. I usually ignored the advice because I thrived more on encouragement than caution, and my confidence was growing every day.

Four years had passed since college graduation, and I was finally ready to take Pennsylvania's Professional Engineering exam. This was what I had worked so hard for.

How hard could the exam be?

The test had around fifteen questions, and each engineer could choose any five. Each response required detailed calculations, code references, and clear logic. The questions weren't all structural, and they varied in difficulty. Although others had advised me to focus on the easiest ones, regardless of the subject, my pride took over. I was a structural engineer and wanted to prove it!

On test day, I could hear my mother whispering, *Don't get a big head now.* I ignored the voice echoing in my head and thought I knew better. Only the structural engineering questions were attempted. When the results came back, my score fell just short of passing.

I failed? I shook my big head in disappointment.

The failure to pass the test didn't affect my salary and it didn't close any doors. It only bruised my ego. I'd have another chance to take the test in six months. On my second attempt, I wouldn't make the same mistake twice and ignore the little voice in my head.

While I dealt with the crushing emotional aftermath of the first exam, my brothers were struggling in their own ways. John wasn't making enough at the bar where he was working, and Rick's car was giving out. I had a steady income and only myself to take care of. They needed help and I was there.

John, his wife, and new baby daughter had moved in with my mother. His wife told me they needed money and asked for a small loan. I let John know of her request and after he acknowledged it, I provided the cash. A few months later, I saw John with a new video camera and a brand-new VCR. These were hardly necessities. I cautiously asked when he planned to pay me back. His response surprised me.

"Talk to my wife," he said.

I'd given the loan to her, with his knowledge. When I asked her, she said they were broke, and that I should talk to John. Their deflection caught me off guard. After having paid my mother's mortgage and bought her a car, I thought he was a responsible brother. Maybe I thought wrong. He had slowly been changing since the DUI conviction. His star was fading. Neither John nor his wife made any attempt to ever pay me back. I wasn't angry at them, but my understanding of family obligations was beginning to change.

When Rick needed help, his request was different. He had a low-paying customer service job with AT&T that required a one-hour commute each way. His car was giving out and after only two years of marriage, he had three small children to support. He needed a much larger amount. A brother in need couldn't be turned down, so I wrote him a check. Rick didn't want to feel like a beggar receiving charity, so at his insistence, we made the transaction official. We agreed on a monthly payment he could comfortably afford. I drafted a simple document offering zero interest and a fixed duration. A book of numbered coupons accompanied the loan papers. Rick knew he wasn't good with money and appreciated the structure. For the first few months, payments came regularly. Then they stopped.

I asked if everything was okay and was told yes. I offered to adjust the terms, letting him know that even a dollar a month was fine by me, but he declined. He said a full payment was coming, but it never did. As his birthday approached, I sent him a special card. Inside, were the words, "Happy Birthday. The loan is forgiven." When Rick opened the card, he stood silent and just stared. A look of happiness spread across his face unlike anything anyone had seen before. It felt good knowing he no longer carried that burden. Beneath the paperwork and payments, I'd just wanted to help him out and preserve his dignity in doing so. His continuing to miss payments, even if only a dollar per month, wasn't preserving anything.

Through the instances with my brothers, I learned that despite my beliefs about family obligation, I was not a bank and had my limits. Future loans would not come so easily.

A Small Success in a Sea of Chaos

In early 1992, things became more interesting at work. Unfortunately, interesting didn't mean better. IDC was awarded a large project in Massachusetts, and the Pittsburgh office was chosen as the main design center. It was the biggest job the office had ever taken on, and we needed more people. Some people came from branch offices, others were new hires. Roger, although still his same chaotic self, was starting to demonstrate some even more concerning behaviors. He was hiding behind the work of others, and using charm to mask his technical shortcomings.

I had seen this before when Roger visited Oregon and first met Lee. These two charismatic engineers were engaged in a technical conversation. At first, Lee was impressed by Roger's big-picture thinking. I pulled him aside and told him to look a little closer. When he did, he discovered what I already knew. Roger couldn't back up his talk with pencil and paper. His calculations looked like scribbles in a two-year-old's coloring book, and made just as much sense. Still, as the most senior engineer in Pittsburgh, he was chosen to lead the structural effort. I knew challenges were coming with Roger. What wasn't expected were challenges with some of the new people.

The first to join our group was Pedro, a senior designer, or at least that's what we thought. Roger assigned him tasks suited for his role, but after a few weeks, I noticed he spent more time complaining than working. I knew Roger's organizational skills were lacking, but this felt different. Tension grew between them and that's when I learned what bad management really looked like. Roger, unable to clearly explain his concepts to Pedro, unexpectedly reassigned him to me. I knew this wasn't going to end well.

After a few more weeks of slow progress, it became clear that he wasn't cut out for the job. I reported my assessment. Instead of acknowledging the hiring mistake, Roger decided to play games. He ignored the fact that Pedro wasn't qualified, and started blaming me for the project's lack of progress. Fortunately, the office manager had been watching. He saw what was happening and pulled me aside. "Don't worry about Roger's games," he said. I was grateful someone had my back. With that reassurance, I pushed the office politics out of my mind, and put my focus back where it belonged, on the job.

A few months later, I received a phone call from Mr. Shah. Work at Dotter Engineering had slowed, and he was looking for a new position. He asked if I'd mind if he joined IDC.

Mind?

He would be a life preserver in a stormy sea. He would bring order to chaos. I told him I'd be honored to have him as a colleague again. A short time later Mr. Shah was hired, and I hoped his presence would be a stabilizing force.

By the time April rolled around, I took the Professional Engineering exam for the second time. I wasn't going to make the same mistake of answering only structural engineering questions. My big head had been reduced to normal size. Instead, I chose a transportation question, a water flow question, and the three easiest structural questions. I passed with ease. My journey to becoming a licensed professional engineer was complete.

I had always operated by a certain set of principles, but the license made those ethics a legal reality. My signature now carried a weight that went beyond the office, and violating it could mean a stiff fine or the loss of my career. The code covered areas such as:

– *Act as a faithful agent for clients and employers.*
– *Do not injure another engineer's reputation maliciously.*
– *Respect the work of engineers who came before you.*
– *Charge fair compensation for services rendered.*
– *Avoid anything that undermines the dignity of the profession.*
– *Practice only in areas where you are qualified.*

– *Use your professional seal responsibly.*
– *Never assist in unlicensed practice.*

I took these principles to heart. As long as I was a licensed professional engineer, I committed myself to them, professionally and personally. Others in my sphere, like Roger, didn't always follow those same principles.

Strangely, passing my test should have been a moment of celebration, surrounded by friends, family, and colleagues, but the memory is blank. There were no party horns or marching bands, only the next day's work. Maybe part of growing up was realizing some milestones pass without fanfare.

Around that same time, my father invited me on a trip to Kiawah Island, South Carolina. Since starting my professional career, we'd seen much less of each other. I was busy with work and he was busy running his new animal hospital. The trip felt like a chance to reconnect. It would be a father-son golf outing where I could show him how far I'd come.

I booked a rental car, a Ford Mustang convertible. It felt like the perfect way to make an impression. In my mind, I pictured the two of us strolling down the fairway, talking about the good times we shared when I worked at his original practice.

When I arrived in South Carolina, things didn't go as planned. The rental agency didn't have a Mustang convertible available and they offered a cheaper model with none of the same flair. I sighed and took the keys. It wasn't ideal, but I wasn't going to let it ruin the trip.

I pulled up to the front of the condo. Standing at the door was his fifth wife, along with her two young daughters. My father hadn't mentioned they would be joining us. Things only got worse. He and his wife had one bedroom, and the teenage daughter had brought a friend so they took the second. That left me sharing the third bedroom with a ten-year-old little girl. This was not the trip I'd imagined.

That evening, we all went out for a late dinner. Afterward, I stayed behind at the restaurant to watch a game on TV. Upon returning to the condo, the front door was locked. It was past midnight, and waking everyone by knocking felt rude. I crawled into the back seat of my car and went to sleep. Early the next morning, I heard a sound. The older daughter had come outside to smoke. She looked surprised to see me climbing out of the car. I asked her not to say anything, and she agreed.

My father and I did spend some time on the golf course that day, but it didn't feel special. After I bought a motorcycle in college, the closeness we'd once shared never fully returned. That awkward trip didn't rekindle it. Whether he felt the distance or not, I did.

***

Nearly four years had passed since the breakup with Eileen. I wasn't seeing anyone, and felt no need to. One night, I was out for drinks with a few engineers and went up to the bar to order another round. Without thinking, I said hello to a woman watching nearby. She raised an eyebrow and said, "If you want to talk, you'll have to buy me a drink."

Paying for a conversation didn't sit right with me, so I headed back to the table. One of the older engineers saw what had happened and asked why I hadn't stayed at the bar. "Why would anyone pay just to talk to somebody," I said. "I'm happy with work, sports, golf, and beer."

That was my life back then. While shaking his head slowly, he said I was beyond hope, and doomed to the life of a bachelor. That didn't bother me.

My sheltered world was about to change. Rick's wife knew I was single and decided to get involved. She introduced me to one of her friends. We dated off and on for a few months and enjoyed each other's company, but something didn't feel right. The only other person I'd dated for more than a few months was Eileen. Maybe I didn't even know what "right" was supposed to feel like. The relationship didn't last beyond six months. There were no arguments or dramatic endings, just a realization that I still didn't trust myself to make a serious commitment. At least, not with her.

At work, things were supposed to be clearer. Client reviews were a routine part of every project, but routine didn't guarantee stability, especially when Roger was involved. As lead engineer, he was expected to come prepared to every client meeting. Before each meeting, I made sure to review my calculations with him. My presence was simple. I would provide backup and support if requested.

It didn't take long to realize that wasn't why I was in the room. Once the meeting began, Roger would act like he'd never seen my work before. He asked basic questions, like he was the client. Instead of instilling confidence, he stirred doubt. Any frustration with the work was directed at me.

I was stunned. By cutting me down in front of the client, he was violating the very engineering principles I had committed myself to uphold.

His behavior didn't stop at client meetings. It also crept into performance reviews. During my first year at IDC, the office manager, project managers, and the senior staff all wrote about my strong work effort and technical excellence. When Roger was responsible for my review, things changed. There were no negative comments about my work ethic or technical ability, but there was one comment that threw me off. A new engineer had come to help with the big project, and he always dressed impeccably. His silk ties and well-tailored suits impressed Roger. A comment on my review said I should dress more professionally.

Dress more professionally?

I didn't look like someone who had just crawled out of the city dump. It was deeply insulting. There were times I wore a colorful or playful tie, but my clothes were never an issue at Dotter Engineering, and certainly not by anyone who cared how well I did my job. They were no worse than my peers, but Roger wasn't reviewing the other people in the office. He was reviewing me.

I wasn't confrontational. There was a big project in the office, and the group needed to get along. The office manager who was mentoring me shook his head at the comment and told me it meant nothing, and not to worry about it. I took a deep breath, upgraded my wardrobe to more closely match the engineer Roger admired, and focused on the work at hand.

Even with my wonderful experience in Oregon, and Mr. Shah's steadying presence, Roger's behavior made me start to wonder if it was worth staying at IDC. A few painful months passed, and then, an opportunity appeared. A structural engineer was needed on the construction site in Massachusetts. I didn't know what Massachusetts would bring, only that I needed a change.

CHAPTER 8

BREAKING OUT

Travel had always stirred a sense of adventure in me. I'd tasted it on my high school trip to Europe, and again when my father took me to the Caribbean. The assignment in Oregon reawakened that feeling.

At first, Massachusetts offered a way to escape Roger's chaos. Over time, it changed me. Opportunities started appearing that forced me to rethink the meaning of the word "home." Travel became a way of life. I still had an office, but it wasn't important anymore. What counted was mobilizing at a moment's notice and surviving whatever came next.

Massachusetts

My time in Oregon wasn't meant to last long. The assignment started as a few weeks and kept stretching out. There was no formal travel letter, only standard company guidelines. Massachusetts came with new terms. This time, the company wanted me away from home for up to a year. A formal travel letter would be required.

At the start of any assignment, it was common to ask about the package: per diem, lodging, rental car, return flights. I was still new to long-term travel, and was still learning that company policy was negotiable.

Before the new assignment began, I'd already made a smart move by offering to drive my own car to Massachusetts, skipping rental cars and flights home. It wasn't part of any negotiation; I was just doing what made sense. Having my own car spared me from arranging someone to watch it in Pittsburgh, and the project manager appreciated the cost savings.

The compensation covered all living expenses while leaving my regular salary untouched. When I saw what the company was paying for, I accepted the one-year relocation without a second thought. I just wanted to get away from Roger, and would have agreed to anything.

The project manager was a lively man with a round face and a voice that barked more than it spoke. He looked exactly like Mr. Spacely from *The Jetsons*, and carried the same impatient energy. He told me I'd be reporting to IDC's onsite Construction Manager, Bill Steadman.

In the summer of 1992, when first arriving in Massachusetts, I snapped a few photos, and jotted down my first impressions on the back of one. I wrote,

"I continued on to Hudson and met Mr. Steadman. He made what I believe will be a lasting impression on my life."

Whatever Mr. Steadman did to earn my respect so quickly is lost to time, but it was likely nothing more than being himself. Bill was quiet and methodical, working long hours without complaint. He didn't raise his voice or throw his weight around. Decisions were made with logic, not ego, and there was a calm precision to the way he operated. After months of Roger's chaos, it felt like stepping into a better world.

I no longer worked in a formal office. Our new headquarters sat in a single-wide trailer parked right next to the action. From the moment I arrived, the message was clear: this wasn't a desk job. Paperwork still needed handling, but I spent most days on site watching the construction, documenting what I saw, and staying close to the work.

Wanting to make a good impression, I started arriving around the same time Bill did, usually by seven in the morning, and often stayed twelve to fourteen hours. I don't remember recording any overtime, and I didn't care. Getting the work done and earning respect mattered more to me, and there was always something that needed doing.

With code books and drawings in hand, I walked the site with a sense of purpose. Watching my designs take shape in the real world was exhilarating. Although I wasn't allowed to direct the contractors, my observations carried weight. If the work being installed didn't match the drawings or specifications, it had to be corrected. The owner made it clear that my word mattered.

It was my first time on an active construction site, and I must have driven the general contractor crazy. Other engineers might have known where the rules could bend and where they couldn't but I didn't, so I followed everything by the book. The owner, Bill, the project manager, and the engineers back in Pittsburgh were all pleased with my approach. The general contractor, not so much.

I loved working on the construction site, and seeing the way plans on paper came to life. Everything about my new job energized me. I couldn't get enough of watching fresh concrete being placed, or the sight of steel dangling from a crane. I walked with a bounce in my step and listened closely as concrete and steel inspectors questioned the contractor's work. Those conversations were more than background noise, they were lessons. While the general contractor might have quietly growled at me, the concrete and steel subcontractors were generous with their knowledge. Every observation became a chance to learn.

The learning didn't stop at the edge of the site. In the office, drawings and specifications were created. Now I could see what happened when those documents hit the field. I saw how they were managed, how they were stored, and how field issues were communicated. If a dispute arose, it was critical to find clear, accurate information fast. Bill often used a saying I already knew:

"He who is most organized wins."

It took a few months for me to see how that concept applied to the world of construction, but when it did, it left a deep impression.

Organization came naturally to me, but that wasn't the case for everyone. Semiconductor projects are highly dynamic and often involve frequent changes. It's critical the team be thoughtful, strategic, and highly organized. That described how Bill looked after the work in our trailer. It did not apply to how Roger looked after the design back in Pittsburgh.

Mr. Shah had done his best to bring logic and stability to the Massachusetts design, but Mr. Shah was not in charge. Roger was in charge and he didn't have the organizational skills needed to guide the project properly. Having Roger in charge was like handing the keys of a Ferrari to a 3-year-old. Revisions were being issued so frequently that the contractors were struggling to keep up with them. To restore order, Bill called in reinforcements from IDC's construction group.

One day, I looked out the trailer window and saw three men approaching. They didn't wear suits or carry laptops. They wore scuffed boots, sun-faded jeans, and expressions that said they'd seen worse. They moved like hired guns heading into a saloon, rough around the edges but unmistakably in charge. After a few quick introductions, each man grabbed a stack of papers and attacked the change orders like they were hunting for something. There was no small talk and no hesitation, just the sound of pages flipping and problems being dismantled.

Over time, I got to know these men. They didn't ask where I came from or what I knew, they just watched how I worked. Eventually, I was invited to join them at their card game after hours. I didn't normally drink whiskey or play poker, but there I was sitting at the table, elbow-to-elbow between rough-and-tumble construction managers, doing my best to fit in. They were road warriors who traveled from site to site, putting out fires and leaving behind order. As cards were dealt and my money disappeared, stories of past projects surfaced like old war wounds.

Though new to site work, I listened, learned, and stayed late. Slowly, they accepted me as one of their own. One of those late-night stories stayed with me. It went like this:

An employee was called out to a construction project on an emergency basis. While rushing toward the trailers, a wind gust caught his new cowboy hat. He watched as the hat sailed through the air and landed on a gravel road. Just then, a bulldozer came by and flattened the hat. Unshaken, the employee gathered his crumpled hat, dusted it off, and immediately went to work.

Later that week, the employee filled out his expense report. He made sure to carefully record each item, including the cost of the flattened hat. When accounting saw the expense report, the line item for the hat was rejected. The employee tried to explain how the hat had been damaged on the construction site.

His pleas fell on deaf ears. The manual had rules for situations like this. He was told to take personal responsibility. It wasn't the company's problem. The employee stared at the accountant, took a deep breath, and went to rework the expense report. Within minutes, the report was resubmitted. Although the line item for the hat no longer appeared, the total remained exactly the same. As the employee handed in the updated expense report, he simply said, "Find the hat."

Outside of the trailers, I was still trying to find common ground with my father. We hadn't found common ground on Kiawah Island, but that didn't mean I was ready to give up. He often talked about his love of flying, and there was a small airport near my apartment. I decided to sign up for flying lessons in a single-engine plane.

The checklists and procedures that came with learning how to fly felt familiar and manageable. Takeoffs and landings, though, were a different challenge. At five foot six, seeing over the front of the plane required effort. It was like being a kid at the dinner table, stretching toward a plate just out of reach. Sitting on phone books wasn't an option in the cockpit, so I had to adapt. To orient on the runway, a quick glance out the side window provided the reference point.

Just when I started to feel comfortable, my instructor introduced a new challenge. One day, after we reached altitude, he turned to me and said he was going to shut off the engine.

"Shut off the engine?"

"Yes," he said. Then he did.

There were no airbags dropping from the ceiling and no screaming passengers. The plane didn't fall from the sky. Instead, he calmly showed me how to adjust the controls, glide the plane, and scan the ground for a safe place to land. Before we got close to the ground, he restarted the engine, and we resumed the flight. My tests in college had taught me how not to panic in a crisis. Having the engine turned off was teaching the same lesson in a different way. Those lessons would continue to prove valuable throughout my career.

Flying offered a way to feel closer to something my father loved, but by the time Massachusetts was behind me, it was clear that becoming a good pilot meant owning a plane. Maintenance, hangar fees, insurance, and fuel costs added up quickly, and a plane wasn't practical for commuting. The appeal had always been rooted in learning, not logistics. Continuing the lessons no longer felt realistic, and when I moved back to Pittsburgh, my wings were grounded. What began as an attempt to connect with my father ended as a reminder of how differently we viewed life, including our views on money.

Flying wasn't my only chance to reconnect with family, there was also Mike. My brother and his wife lived in Massachusetts, about an hour from the construction site. We hadn't been in touch for a while, but I remembered how kind he had been when visiting years earlier. Back then, he was newly married and had recently earned his doctorate. What I hadn't considered was that he now had a three-year-old son and was trying to get a new business off the ground. Without realizing it, I'd stepped into the middle of his storm.

When I arrived at his home, everything seemed fine. He'd gained a lot of weight and joked about it by saying it was a sign of prosperity. I brought a bottle of wine with a Penn State label on it and presented it to Mike and his wife. I thought it was a fun, light-hearted gift. They used it not to tease the wine, but to tease me. Their demeaning comments took me off guard. I dismissed it as my brother simply returning to his old behaviors. I didn't realize it was just the warm-up act.

The next morning, I was treated to a pleasant breakfast with generous portions of bacon. Mike needed help at a new workspace he'd rented and asked if I'd come along. The second we walked through the door, his attitude changed. He moved around a large piece of equipment, barking orders with growing intensity. I followed his instructions attentively, but each additional request came with a barrage of yelling and cutting remarks. This version of my brother reminded me of how he behaved when we were growing up, but now it was worse. He was louder, meaner and more personal.

On the construction site, dealing with forceful personalities was nothing new. Confrontations happened, but even then, respect was part of the exchange. After about fifteen minutes, I stepped aside and firmly reminded Mike that I was his brother, not a colleague. I told him I didn't deserve to be treated so poorly, and an apology was owed. He cursed, told me to shut up, and went back to work. Not willing to tolerate his abuse, I calmly walked to a nearby abandoned chair and took a seat.

On the drive back to his house, we didn't speak. At dinner that night, he had a friend over. I thought he might be ready to apologize, but instead, he doubled down, mocking me in front of his guest. I finished the meal politely and left. Mike had created a rift. I would remain civil because he was family, but without an apology, he would not be forgiven.

The visit with Mike wouldn't be the only drama I faced that year. My role on the construction site with the contractors was making me stand out. I was no longer invisible the way I had been with the furniture store salesmen back in Pittsburgh. My visibility was increasing, and that wasn't always a good thing.

The Accident

I was working at my desk when, suddenly, it happened.

A loud crash.

Large sections of concrete and steel had collapsed to the ground. I wasn't permitted to leave the trailers. Waiting in the trailers for any news was nerve-racking. Thoughts raced through my mind:

When structural engineers make mistakes, people die.

In the first few hours, Bill assessed the situation and made a few phone calls. After most of the people had gone from the site, he turned to me and said, "Get out there. Take the video camera and record what you can."

I anxiously crawled over and around the pile of construction debris filming everything I could reasonably get to. The once organized area of the construction site was in ruin.

After returning to the trailers and dropping off the camera, Bill provided more directions. "Go back to your apartment. Avoid the media. Keep a low profile." He kept me informed as the investigation began. Early indications pointed to a formwork failure, which was the contractor's responsibility. Although the news gave me some relief, I knew that as the onsite structural engineer, every part of my work was about to be scrutinized.

That evening, I turned on the television. One of my documents had been obtained by a local reporter and my name was flashing across the screen. As my mind processed what I was seeing, a lump grew in my throat.

I remembered what Mr. Dotter once told me: "A good engineer is one who stays out of the news." The media took my document out of context and sensationalized the story. Claims were made that I knew were false. The experience permanently changed how I viewed journalists.

Over the next few days, OSHA investigators and a few lawyers came to speak with me. The advice I was given was simple: "Don't guess, just tell the truth." It took weeks to clean up the site and resume work. Some of the workers didn't return to the site, and would carry injuries for the rest of their lives.

As for my role, the official reports would eventually clear our company of responsibility. I hadn't observed the specific cause of the collapse. I had, however, raised concerns about other conditions on site. Those issues could have led to serious accidents if left unaddressed. The general contractor had reviewed my reports. They were often treated as optional reading. He might have been technically within his rights to dismiss my concerns, but to me, it felt like something deeper. It felt like he didn't take engineers seriously.

The investigation found that the general contractor didn't have his paperwork in order. The concrete contractor had failed to install the formwork correctly and tried to cover up the mistake. The formwork subcontractor hadn't even done proper calculations. The fines would be steep. Once cause was identified, the focus shifted away from me, and the site returned to normal.

Joining the Construction Group

In the summer of 1993, as the project began to wind down, Bill pulled me aside. My work ethic, organization, rapport with people, and attention to cost stood out. He noticed I was constantly on the move and rarely sat still. To him, that restless energy was a strength. Bill knew working with Roger hadn't been a highlight of my career. He asked if I'd ever considered a future in construction.

"Joining the construction group would mean three things," he said. "More money, more responsibility, and you can live anywhere in the world you want." It was a tempting offer.

How could I justify changing careers?

More money would mean a faster path to reaching my financial dreams. Greater responsibility would satisfy my rapidly growing ambition. As for living anywhere in the world I wanted, to advance in the company, I needed to be closer to both the home office and the influential managers who worked there. For someone looking to get ahead, Portland was where the action was. Staying in Pittsburgh meant stability, but it also meant being out of view.

Structural engineering had originally been about having a stable career for starting my own family. The family part hadn't worked out. Throwing caution to the wind by putting my engineering degree aside and chasing my own ambitions felt selfish.

What would my parents think?

Would I be a disappointment, like when John turned to bartending?

Still, the three things Bill mentioned were hard to ignore. I was at a crossroads. An answer wasn't needed immediately. That was helpful, because choosing which path to follow required careful thought.

Once the job in Massachusetts ended, the company sent me to Portland for a three-month project. During that time, there was an opportunity to improve my living situation. I found a short-term furnished apartment on an upper floor, with a view of Mt. Hood, a solitary snow-covered peak rising beyond the city. In the mornings, it appeared as a silhouette against a fiery orange sunrise. The view took my breath away, and despite a love of sleeping in, I found myself getting up early to watch the mountain emerge from the darkness.

The apartment required a hefty upfront payment that needed the project manager's approval. I put together a short presentation justifying why the apartment was better for the project than my staying in a hotel. There would be reduced travel and food costs, less time lost to cross-country flights, and most importantly, a happier, more productive employee. The project manager looked back and forth between the presentation and me, then said, "Sure."

A manager who listened and agreed with my logic?

It definitely wasn't anything I'd experienced with Roger in the Pittsburgh office. More importantly, my time in Massachusetts taught me skills I hadn't even realized I'd learned. I now knew how to communicate effectively with management. The time had come to continue applying those skills.

Being in Portland gave me the perfect chance to sit with the head of the structural department. I scheduled a meeting, explained the construction group's proposal, and then listened carefully.

"Dan, you're at a difficult part of a structural engineer's career. The first ten years are stressful. You're constantly learning and never really know what you're doing. The second ten years, you're scrambling to apply everything you learned. It's only during the third ten years that you start to enjoy and appreciate the work." He paused and waited for a reaction, as the wheels spun in my head.

Wait. I have to wait another thirteen and a half years before my job becomes fun?

The conversation hadn't really gone as I expected. His speech was about as inspirational as Mr. Dotter's discouraging words when I was first hired out of college. I hadn't taken Mr. Dotter seriously, and now another senior engineer was telling me that structural engineering was a miserable career path. That would've been helpful to know when choosing my major. What changed everything wasn't what he had just said, but what came next.

"I can't give you more money. If you stay with the structural group, you'll be behind both Roger and Mr. Shah, so I can't give you more responsibility. In addition, our department doesn't have the budget to relocate you. You'll have to stay in Pittsburgh."

There was nothing more to discuss. I showed no reaction, respectfully thanked him for his time and returned to my desk. By offering nothing, not even words of encouragement, it sounded like he didn't care if I stayed with his department or not.

If he didn't care, why should I stay?

Besides, if changing careers didn't work out, I figured my professional license wasn't going away. It would always be possible to return to engineering, even if that meant joining a different company. Professionally, leaving Pittsburgh and joining the construction group felt like it came with minimal risk.

There were also personal reasons for leaving Pittsburgh. The city came with plenty of baggage. There were the ghosts of girlfriends past, and a family that still saw me as the four-year-old child who spilled his milk on the floor. With both personal and professional motives aligned, the final decision was easy. My mind was made up. I submitted a formal request to join the construction group, and although the approval did not come right away, I was confident it would. Portland was going to be my new home even if I had to will it into being. That confidence showed up in different ways.

Lee needed a dive buddy, and my sitting on the rocks as he submerged didn't count. Before coming to the U.S., he had served in the Polish Navy, where they taught him how to dive. He loved it and wanted to share the excitement of exploring his world beneath the waves. The Oregon coast was less than ninety minutes away and had dive sites challenging enough to energize him, but he needed a partner. I started taking scuba diving lessons, as if the approval were already on its way.

By December, the request was approved. I was set to join the construction group and move to Portland. Excitement and nervousness took a victory lap in my head. I remember telling my family about the move. My father was proud to see me chasing a dream. John and Rick were busy working through things in their own lives, so their response was basically a meh. My mother was excited for me, but sad I'd be leaving Pittsburgh. She was the only one who made me feel like someone would miss me. That was exactly what I needed.

The construction group gave me a two-week house-hunting trip, and during that time, I found a condo about thirty minutes from the home office. As 1993 came to a close, I loaded up my Chevy Cavalier and started the long drive from Pittsburgh, Pennsylvania to Portland, Oregon. The excitement of the future overrode any sadness of leaving the only place I had truly considered home.

When I left, I didn't look back.

Oregon – Go West Young Man

Upon arriving in Oregon, I was filled with hope, and wanted everything to go smoothly. Wanting something, though, doesn't make it so. The first rough patch came when the older couple selling their condo told me they hadn't moved out and closing would be delayed a few days. I had to find somewhere else to stay. My budget was already stretched thin, but I managed to find a cheap, run-down motel halfway between the office and my new home. It would have to do.

When I finally got the keys to the condo, my excitement started to grow. I had moved to a new city, bought my own home, and started a new career. It was time to receive my first assignment in the construction department.

IDC wasn't a general contractor, and they didn't have a license to be one. They were a group of construction managers. There's an important difference between the two. A construction manager advises and represents the owner, helping ensure quality, budget, and schedule stay aligned. A general contractor builds the project, manages subcontractors, and gets the work done in the field. Occasionally, IDC would lend staff to a general contractor who needed help. The company must have thought I needed more experience because for my first project, I was embedded with one of the biggest general contractors in the Portland area. There were no other people from IDC on the job. They threw me into the deep end to either sink or swim.

On my first day, I reported to a highly stressed-out manager. He had no idea what to make of me. All he knew was that his company had handed him someone from an engineering firm to help out. After receiving a few small tasks, I did my best to muddle through. Every time the manager passed by, something felt off.

Was I working too slow? Was I doing it wrong?

He never had time to explain, but tension was starting to build. My approach to the work did not change, and I continued to muddle through.

A few weeks later, he wanted me to consolidate information on the design documents by creating a drawing that showed mechanical, electrical, and plumbing openings in a wall. It was a request more appropriate for a draftsman in an engineering firm. I asked several questions to make sure I knew exactly what he wanted, then drew it up and handed him the sketch. He studied it, took a deep breath, and then exploded.

"What is this? This isn't what I asked for. Don't you know what you're doing?" Surprised, I stared back blankly, and then nervously replied. "No, I have no idea what I'm doing. This is my first job as a construction manager."

His eyes rolled to the back of his head. The room went quiet. The yelling stopped. The pressure cooker had blown off steam, and there was nothing left. Frustrated, I returned to whatever I had been doing. Bill had taught me to be calm, methodical, persistent, and organized. Now, however, those traits didn't seem to be working. That night, as I tried to fall asleep, I thought about construction management and wondered what I had gotten myself into.

The next week, the manager who had exploded at me didn't show up for work. I was told someone found him curled up on the floor, gently sobbing. They said not to worry about it.

Was this my future? Gulp.

I did my best to put it out of my head and went back to work. Maybe what Bill taught me was okay after all. I never saw that manager again. A few months later, my work on the project wound down without incident, and I returned to the home office.

Back in the office, there were no new projects waiting. It felt uncomfortable that the construction group had brought me in without knowing what to do with me. To stay busy, I asked if anyone needed help. While making the rounds, a short, balding man looked up from his desk and peered at me over his glasses. His workspace was buried in papers, drawings, and books. The estimating department was overloaded, and I had shown up at just the right time.

Over the next few months, my reputation started to build with the estimators. Material quantities were calculated, pricing strategies absorbed, and every opportunity to learn was taken. The office became a temporary home, back among some of my old best friends. Numbers.

While work was moving forward, so was a new hobby. My friend Lee was excited that my dive certification was finally complete. He gave me more warm congratulations for that achievement than anyone had given me for passing the Professional Engineering exam. I greatly appreciated his enthusiasm. It was time for my first adventure.

The Oregon coast wasn't about warm, clear blue water and gently floating just below the surface. The cold water of the Pacific demanded a wetsuit and hid plenty of dangers. Visibility could vary from twelve inches to twelve feet, and the tides had to be monitored closely. Dive at the wrong time, and you risked being pulled out to sea. Choose a landing site carelessly, and the choppy waters could violently crash you against the rocks. Pick up a crab the wrong way, and it could snap your finger in two. The Oregon Coast was all about planning, hunting, and a bold sense of adventure.

I had carefully paid attention during certification classes, studied the manuals, and bought all new gear. My confidence was high. Lee's wife, however, wasn't so sure. She thought we wouldn't catch anything, and she said there'd be a meal of hot homemade soup awaiting our return, "just in case."

Hot homemade soup? How dare she! We were mighty hunters!

Lee and I loaded up his truck, brimming with confidence and bravado. On the way, he told me tales of past dives and shared valuable advice, like never attempting to shoot a wolf eel. If one was speared, they don't run, they viciously attack the person who shot them.

Survival depended on more than just advice. I was decked out with two regulators, two flashlights, and two knives. These were treacherous waters, and for safety, every piece of gear had a backup. Losing your partner was a real possibility, and those backups were a necessity in case something went wrong.

A Hawaiian sling, crab gauge, and a goody bag sat at my side, patiently waiting for the right moment. The sling used a heavy elastic band to launch a trident-shaped spear toward its prey. I stretched the band down the pole with one hand. When released, the pole snapped forward, pinning my target against the bottom.

We climbed over large rocks on the jetty and prepared to enter the water. A wetsuit keeps the diver warm by trapping a thin layer of water between the suit and the diver's skin. It takes only a few seconds for the water to warm up, but before it does it feels like jumping into a bucket of ice cubes. Lee and I entered the water, endured the ice cubes, gave each other the okay signal, and descended into the murky green water.

On the way down, the only sound I heard was my own steady, rhythmic breathing: *in and out, in and out, in and out.* We could see colorful anemones and sun stars perched on the rocks, but these creatures weren't what we were after. Once on the ocean floor, sixty feet down, the fun began. We moved slowly along the bottom, scouring every stony crevice for ling cod, and every patch of sand for Dungeness crab. By the time we surfaced, our goody bags were full of crabs. There would be no soup that evening. The Mighty Hunters had prevailed! With adrenaline still flowing, we rushed back to the local dive shop, refilled our tanks, and went in for a second dive. It was as successful as the first, and this time it included a few fish. Exhausted, we rinsed our gear, loaded the truck, and headed home to enjoy our bounty.

Back in Portland, Lee showed me how to clean and cook a crab. To make sure his wife's efforts didn't go to waste, we ate our catch with a bowl of her fresh homemade soup. It was a wonderful feeling, and as seemed to be the custom with Lee, the meal ended with a shot of Polish vodka.

We would come to make many more trips like that in the cold Pacific waters. Each time, Lee's wife would make soup in case we came back empty-handed, and each time, we returned loaded with fresh seafood.

The coastal adventures were amazing and my job was going well, so it was time to share. The people in the office had heard stories about all the crabs Lee and I caught on our dive trips. We had more crabs than could be eaten, so I asked if anyone wanted some after our next dive. There were plenty of enthusiastic volunteers to take me up on the offer. I was from Pittsburgh. There were no crabs crawling around in Pittsburgh's rivers. I didn't realize what a valuable commodity a Dungeness crab was in Oregon, especially a free one. After the next dive trip, my abundant catch was shared. I was making friends fast in the Portland office.

With new friends and new hobbies, life was good. Still, I missed family. My mother never had money to spare and didn't like to travel. My father was busy growing his new practice and taking his fifth wife's family on cruises. John was working bar shifts and trying to navigate raising his daughter. After Mike's behavior toward me in Massachusetts, I had no interest in seeing him. Rick still had money problems and was trying to balance work, rock star dreams, and family life. Kathy, too, seemed as broke and averse to travel as her mother. I was lonely and I wanted somebody, anybody, to come visit me and share in the wonders of the Pacific Northwest. My eagerness for a visitor showed up in an unexpected way.

Early one fall morning, while I was still recovering from one drink too many the night before, Rick called. He was coming to Oregon alone.

Coming to Oregon?

Through the fog, the prior night's conversation started to materialize. I had invited him to Oregon and offered to cover his airfare. He also wanted me to cover his wife's airfare, but it was more than I could afford. He couldn't afford her airfare either and was calling to say he'd be coming alone. I was excited about Rick's visit, and we immediately started planning his trip.

I loved having my brother in Oregon, and the visit started perfectly. We began by hiking among waterfalls in the Columbia River Gorge. He pointed up at the trunk of a large tree, and asked, "What's that?" It was a type of fungus shaped like a clamshell. Rick had always loved teasing me growing up. Now it was my turn to have some fun. I placed the serious side of me in a box and said, "In Oregon, the clams grow on trees. It's a tree clam." He picked up on the joke right away, and just like that, the tone of the trip was set.

That night, I took Rick to one of Portland's nicer seafood restaurants. He was delighted. Unfortunately for me, so was the waitress, as she only had eyes for him. It reminded me why going out with my more charming older brother was always a bad idea. I let Rick enjoy the attention.

Hey, he was married. He wasn't supposed to be flirting like that.

A flashback to the furniture store raced through my mind. The way the waitress acted, as if I wasn't even there, echoed that old feeling of being invisible. Even when I asked for a refill, she didn't take her eyes off Rick. Unfortunately for her, she overlooked the simple fact that I was paying the bill. I knew it was petty, but her tip reflected my displeasure.

The next morning, we woke up early. I'd be diving for crabs so Rick could see what a mighty hunter his brother was. Our next stop was the Pacific Coast. We were excited and things were going well, except on the way up from the dive, my goody bag opened, and the crabs escaped. Thankfully, he didn't make fun of my efforts. I wasn't about to let the trip end there. He accompanied me back to the dive shop to refill my tank. I swam back down for a second dive, and this time, the goody bag was firmly secured. I triumphantly brought up several delicious-looking Dungeness crabs. Rick had never seen such large crabs before and was amazed. I cooked and cleaned the crabs, relishing every minute of his visit. Coming to Oregon was a trip neither of us would ever forget.

Countdown

By late 1994, projects in the construction group were beginning to slow down. To stay productive, the company offered training sessions, including weeklong courses in construction management and OSHA safety. It was a chance to prepare for whatever came next. I didn't have to wait long.

Early in 1995, the company sent me to oversee construction in an area that would soon house large semiconductor equipment. I served as a construction manager, not just an assistant to a general contractor. The estimating department was reluctant to give me up, but it was time to put my training to the test.

There were three main areas to monitor. The contracted scope of work had to be complete. The schedule had to be met. The budget had to stay on track. No changes were allowed without a clear change order in place.

The work didn't start smoothly. The contractor's crew moved slowly and was already hinting at extra costs. The procedures were simple. If a problem couldn't be easily solved, it had to be escalated up the chain of command. Managers didn't get in trouble for having problems. They got in trouble for failing to recognize them and escalate them immediately.

The foreman in my area acted cagey and treated me like I'd just fallen off the turnip truck. I escalated the issue immediately. He was removed from the project, and a new foreman took his place. The new foreman didn't fool around. He put the crews straight to work. My judgment had been sound. I followed procedure and passed another critical test. The area was suddenly humming with activity.

As months passed and the construction neared completion, I was told to report to a conference room with one of the client's senior managers. My colleagues had been summoned to meetings like this before, and it never ended well. The manager demanding my presence was an imposing man with the reputation for having an explosive temper. As I walked across the campus, my client counterpart looked at me like I was a condemned man heading to the gallows. Each step felt heavier and heavier as the dread settled in.

What had I done wrong?

We entered the room and quietly took our seats. The manager glared menacingly across the table, and in a measured tone, growled: "Dan, I hope you know why I brought you here today."

I didn't.

"No sir," I said respectfully, hoping my voice didn't squeak. He growled even louder, "I brought you here today because…"

Gulp.

"Your area is one of the best managed areas on the site, and I have an award for you."

What?

Terror and pride are not really best friends, but there they were, hand in hand, swimming around in my head. I could hear both my client counterpart and the manager laughing at the trick they'd played. They handed me a certificate and a check. After giving a tentative smile and receiving much praise, I returned to my desk.

No one at the company had ever received a cash award from this client, so I had to ask Human Resources if it was allowed. It was. I had survived my early trials with the construction department, and wasn't just getting by, I was excelling.

In the summer of 1995, a three-month project in Pittsburgh needed some help. When I told them my mother would house me and save the company the cost of a hotel, it tipped the scales in my favor. My mother was delighted to have her wayward son back home, and I was happy to be there.

Being back in my home town reminded me why I spoke the way I did. My mother had raised me with a sense of polite decorum, but on a job site, that upbringing became a barrier. Engineers spoke with a stiff formality. Contractors spoke in a rougher, more casual way, and didn't warm up easily to outsiders. The construction managers in my group all came from construction, and none of them had been engineers. They all fluently spoke the contractor's language. When I spoke, it was obvious I wasn't one of them. I noticed this in Massachusetts and Oregon, but it didn't seem to matter in those places. In Pittsburgh, it mattered. My speech was formal, too polished. I sounded like an engineer or someone from upper management.

One day, a delivery truck arrived. I wasn't busy, so I asked the subcontractor if he needed help. Surprised, he said sure. For the next two hours, I hauled gypsum board off the truck and into the building. Then I went back to my desk, thinking nothing of it.

At the end of the day, the subcontractor pulled me aside. "Nobody trusted you when you first showed up," he said. "You talk like management. Maybe you're not so bad after all." They saw the way I spoke as a weakness. I saw it as part of who I am. To me, it was a strength, and I wasn't about to change.

After the job in Pittsburgh completed, I returned to Portland. It had been eight years since graduating college, and the only time off I'd taken was for holiday visits with family. Family was great, but I wanted an adult vacation, one that felt like a reward.

Club Med was known for tailoring vacations to single travelers. I booked a package to Martinique, a small Caribbean island famous for its scuba diving. When I arrived, my impression was that it looked like summer camp. There were cabins, communal dining, and counselors orchestrating every move. On the first dive trip, the staff initially refused to let me join in because of a broken flipper strap. I understood their caution, but I was an experienced diver used to the murky, dangerous waters of the Oregon Coast, yet here I was being handled with kid gloves in a warm, clear pond. Eventually, they found a spare set of fins on the boat. The dive almost put me to sleep. It felt like staring out the window of a tour bus.

Evenings weren't any more exciting. Buffet dinners served the same dishes in rotating disguise, each night spiced a little more than the last. During the meal, the counselors performed cheesy shows and encouraged drinking games. Wine flowed freely. At my table, people recounted dating experiences and described their ideal partners. Everyone seemed to have a checklist, and I didn't match a single box. Tall, dark, and handsome? No. Salsa dancing Texan? Definitely not.

When the trip ended, the counselors handed me a diving medal, but it felt hollow. I'd come looking for a grown-up experience, only to find a place designed for people who wanted to be told how to have fun. I was searching for a lifestyle that felt authentic to who I was, but it clearly wasn't waiting at Club Med.

While juggling work and scuba diving adventures, I realized something. There was a part of my life that hadn't fallen into place yet. At 31, I was still clueless about women and their checklists. Dating at work wasn't much of an option. IDC was an office of mostly male engineers and construction managers. I thought it wise to be cautious about mixing work with pleasure.

After living in Portland for over a year, I'd learned to adapt to both construction site and office cultures, and kept my walls up. Walls can protect, but sometimes they need to come down. Some advice I'd received long ago was to meet women in a grocery store, health club, church, or bar. Grocery stores and health clubs were out. People were there for a purpose and didn't want to be bothered. Portland was more secular than Pittsburgh, so I hadn't joined a church. Bars felt wrong, and besides, I'd been told a long time ago that if you want to meet a nice girl, you don't hang out in them.

The mark left when my seven-year relationship with Eileen ended hadn't fully disappeared. When meeting women, my walls were up, and my own checklists were at the ready. A married woman chased after me once, but that was way out of bounds. It felt like every avenue to connect with someone was a dead end. In late 1995, feeling increasingly hopeless, I turned to a dating service.

The first girl they sent my way was 19. Way below my age range and too young to have lived much yet. Nope. The second girl's life revolved around beauty pageants for small children. Watching five-year-olds in makeup, preening like adults, felt creepy. Nope.

The third girl and I dated a few times. She'd recently divorced and said she was only there to make friends. After five or six dates, when things seemed to be going well, I bought her a diamond pendant. Shocked at how expensive it looked, she insisted on giving it back. Embarrassed and emasculated, I convinced her it was costume jewelry. Girl number three. Nope.

The women the dating service offered had been extremely disappointing. Three matches in six months left me wondering if love even existed for me. Despite being a construction manager, I was still an engineer at heart, someone who measured the world, observed it, and explained it in numbers. Romance didn't fit into that framework. It felt mystical, like fortune telling or astrology, a place where logic failed. My life needed a bit of that mystery. I needed something beyond numbers and schedules. There had to be a force out there in the cosmos that guided people together. It wasn't within my control, so I decided to give up trying. If love was going to find me, the universe would have to lend a hand. One more piece had to fall into place before its plan could move forward.

In March 1996, there was once again no work in the office. Even the estimators were slow, and my career looked like it was coming to a dead end. There was also another problem. The Portland office saw me as just one of many construction managers.

A restless feeling started growing in me. I missed the sense of freedom my motorcycle had once given me, so I bought a brand-new 1100cc Virago Special Edition motorcycle. It was a classic cruiser with enough power to either get me into trouble or get me out of it. I bought the accessories to make the bike glitter in the sun and turn heads when

I drove down the street. Serious riders can quote specs and talk pistons. Me? I liked that it went vroom, vroom.

I enjoyed riding through the Oregon countryside and, despite having accepted my fate with women, I bought a second helmet "just in case."

With the motorcycle, the final piece had fallen into place, and the stage was set. Now all I needed was a gentle nudge.

CHAPTER 9

LIFT-OFF

Most imagine lift-off as a spark followed by fire, a force that lifts you from the launch pad and hurls you into the unknown. Mine wasn't like that.

It didn't begin with spectacle. No fireworks, or grand gestures. Only a small spark from a streak of light dancing across the sky, and a voice from a dream. Then silence. I thought the spark had gone. One minute I'm polishing a headlamp and the next, riding toward something that feels both unlikely and already underway. Just as the journey began, a second stage ignited, carrying me deeper into unfamiliar territory.

I didn't feel ready, not for love, not for a launch. Yet, the universe had its own timeline, and it didn't ask permission. There was no way to know the countdown was complete, no flashing green light. There was just the feeling my feet were no longer on the ground.

The Shooting Star

On a warm night in March of 1996, a once-in-a-lifetime event occurred. Comet Hyakutake, its long tail clearly visible, traced a path across the sky. Portland is cloudy and rainy most of the spring, but when the comet came, the sky was clear. The news explained how special it was. The comet had last visited Earth 17,000 years ago and wouldn't return for 70,000 more.

Curious about the hype, I wandered through the condo parking lot, searching for a clear view. It was a long shot. However, the comet wasn't the only thing that caught my eye. A woman was outside doing the same thing, staring up in wonder at the rare, bright streak of light overhead. We greeted each other politely. She hesitated when she heard my voice. I didn't know why.

As we stood there, appreciating the beauty of the night sky, we started talking. Karen lived next door and had noticed my motorcycle. She'd been curious to meet the man who rode it. I asked if she'd like a ride. She said it was tax season and she was too busy. Maybe later. I took it as a polite brush-off and we each returned to our homes.

That night, I picked up the newspaper and found the story about Comet Hyakutake. I pulled out a pair of scissors, cut out the article with care, and tucked the clipping away. The universe provided the spark. The rest would be up to us.

Dating

A couple of weeks passed uneventfully. I spent my time cleaning the motorcycle, riding when I could, and waiting for work to pick up. One afternoon, while wiping away bugs from the headlamp, a voice called out behind me.

"Excuse me, is that offer for a ride still good?"

I turned and was surprised to see Karen. I let her know the offer still stood. There was no discussion about where to go, or for how long. Those were details that didn't seem to matter. I didn't think of it as a date, but it was.

When the day came, every surface on the motorcycle shined. Just as my old college roommate Jim had taught me, the seat was properly buffed with Armor All. As we rode, I lost track of time. Having Karen on the back of the bike, leaning gently into the curves and accelerating on the straightaways, felt effortless. It seemed like we'd barely started when I suddenly realized three hours had passed and we were at the coast. We filled up the tank with gas and headed back.

At the condo, Karen looked tired. I offered to take her out for something to eat, and she agreed. Over dinner, our conversation felt natural, like talking with someone I'd known all my life. That's when Karen admitted she'd been exhausted during the ride and had been holding on for dear life on the way back. I smiled sheepishly. My walls were down.

The ride may have left her worn out, but it hadn't dampened her spirits. When the evening ended, we made plans to see each other again.

Over the next several months, we got to know each other better. There were red flags telling me we shouldn't be together. Karen had been married twice before. I had never been married. She couldn't have children and didn't want any. I'd always pictured having a family. The red flags didn't scare me away.

There were red flags for her, too. I was ambitious, and told her I could be called away on an international assignment at a moment's notice. It didn't help that a girl kept showing up at my condo in cute tennis outfits. I said the girl wasn't interested in me, she just wanted advice on getting a job at my company. Karen looked at me with a raised eyebrow. Her friends and family were all telling her I couldn't be trusted. She blocked out the noise.

Something unexplainable had drawn us together. Karen had encountered many people whose actions didn't match their words. She was skeptical, but when we talked, she said my words made sense to her. We clung to each other like two people tossed in a stormy sea, not out of fear, but as if our touch anchored us to a shared destiny. Amid all the reasons we heard for why we shouldn't be together, we chose to listen only to our hearts.

One afternoon, Karen grew curious about how I ended up in Oregon. While explaining, I pulled out photos from a visit I'd made to Portland five years earlier. Homes in Pittsburgh were typically brick, aluminum siding, or stone. On the Oregon Coast, they were all wood. It struck me as unusual, so I snapped a picture of a random wooden house while driving through one of the towns. When Karen saw it, she was speechless. That house belonged to her cousin, and she had spent a lot of time there. It felt like a "sign."

As we grew closer, she explained her hesitation at the sound of my voice when we first met. Something about me felt familiar even though we'd never met before that night. I suggested maybe she'd overheard me talking in the parking lot when I loaded my dive gear into the car. She didn't buy it. My voice was in her dreams, and it was like destiny gently calling her name.

I still wasn't a well-oiled machine when it came to women. Karen joined me on an early morning dive trip to the Oregon Coast. She was just there to watch. Before submerging, I told her not to worry if I didn't come back up. It just meant the crabs had eaten me and there was nothing anyone could do. She didn't laugh, just stared, as if trying to decide whether I was joking or broken. My offhand comments didn't deter her as she patiently waited for my dives to finish.

Another time, we were talking about work. I told her when people asked about my dating life, I opened my wallet and showed them a picture of the motorcycle. Karen's only reaction was a quiet, scrutinizing gaze. The next time we met, she handed me a picture of herself. The motorcycle picture didn't disappear, but it gained a companion, and that was good enough for her.

That summer was wonderful. It was a season filled with long rides, nice restaurants, baseball games in Seattle, and quiet evenings together. Work had slowed to a crawl. Amid talk of a possible project in Asia, I bought a few books and began learning Chinese. Karen knew I was a traveler. She knew my job could pull me away at any moment, but didn't seem to care. At one point, without saying why, I casually suggested she get a passport. To her, it sounded like a possible vacation to Mexico. To me, I thought an assignment in China was on the horizon. We didn't share the same page yet, choosing instead to focus on the present.

After a few months, things were going so well that it felt like the right time to take the next step. I asked her to accompany me on a weekend in Las Vegas. She agreed without hesitation. Neither of us had been there before, and we both stared at the massive casinos and flashing lights in amazement. I wasn't the type to sip martinis in a tux while playing roulette, and she wasn't going to hang on my arm in a sequined dress. Instead, we made a game of collecting plastic coin cups from as many casinos as possible. When the time came to leave, my mind remained caught in the spectacle, and how exciting it had been to experience it together. With Karen by my side, the world felt right.

While we were taking in Las Vegas, unseen forces were already tugging us apart. The morning after we got home, I received a call. There was a project struggling in Ireland, and my presence was needed as soon as possible. "How fast can you be here?" I looked at Karen. She didn't say a word. I hated the thought of leaving her, and dreaded another long-distance relationship, but the assignment was only supposed to be for a few months. I answered.

"Three days."

An Irish Whirlwind

Karen was in shock. Everything between us suddenly felt uncertain. We controlled what we could, circling around the logistics. There were flight times to reserve, phone calls to make, and time zones to figure out. We didn't speak of the ache. I packed in a mad rush, then covered the condo with Post-it notes, each one a small instruction to keep life running in my absence. Karen smiled at the sight, amused and touched, but also recognizing it was exactly how she would have done it herself. As I looked around, I realized I was leaving more than Karen behind. She would be responsible for everything I owned, including the condo, the car, and the motorcycle. Dating had been one thing, but trusting her with my whole life wasn't something I felt prepared for.

Karen carried a fear of abandonment I didn't fully understand, and her friends and family weren't helping. They said she would never hear from me again. Karen still didn't quite understand where she fit into my life. She wasn't a one-night stand, not to me. I assured her I would call. The airport beckoned. It was time to go.

Shortly after departing Portland, the plane landed in Seattle. I called and playfully asked if she missed me yet. At the next layover in Chicago, I called again. She didn't see my gestures as an annoyance, and without realizing it, I was providing her with a life preserver. The fears her friends and family tried to plant about never seeing me again were fading. She wasn't fully steady yet, but those fears were loosening their grip and were being replaced with trust.

In Ireland, a new adventure awaited. On my first day, I was told I'd be embedded in another company's construction management group. I had been in a similar situation before, and it had been challenging. This job looked no different.

My manager was a hard-working, fun-loving Irishman named Declan. They called him The Tasmanian Devil, and he lived up to the name. From the papers on his desk, to the contractors he spoke with, everything Declan touched stirred up a whirlwind of chaos. Unlike Roger, from the Pittsburgh office, Declan wasn't malicious. The trouble he caused was unintentional and always came with a smile.

Away from the site, he taught me it was never proper to talk business, especially in a pub. Girls, beer and golf were all acceptable, but discussing work was off limits. I liked Declan, but after a month, for my own sanity, I knew I needed to find a way to break free from his whirlwind.

There was still a lot to learn about Ireland. The pub wasn't just a place to socialize and drink. It was also a cultural classroom. One night, while alone in the town of Leixlip, I wandered into a local pub. It was dark. Wood booths with worn cushions lined the walls. A karaoke machine sat in the far corner, and a haze of cigarette smoke filled the air. Each step made a soft, tacky sound, like my soles were peeling off a floor layered with old beer and the ghosts of a few hundred spilled pints. I crossed to the bar, took a seat and placed my order.

There's no such thing as a quick beer in Ireland, and that meant both pouring it and drinking it. Pouring a pint of Guinness is a sight to behold. It is an art. The bartender tips the glass at just the right angle, then gently pulls the tap. At about three-quarters full, he stops and lets it settle for a few minutes. The glass is topped off, and allowed to settle once again. Mesmerized by the tiny bubbles streaming into the foamy head, I paid the bartender and gathered my pint.

To my left, grumbling quietly into his half-filled glass, sat a man with tousled hair and an impish look. He slowly looked up, recognized me as new in town, and decided to impart some wisdom. I listened like every word was gold. Then, as if struck by a hint of mischief, he said, "The Irish are the best liars in the world. Never believe the first truth."

It was a puzzling saying. We kept talking. He offered more pint-fueled wisdom while I listened intently. With our glasses near empty, I waved at the bartender to order another round. By the time I caught his attention and turned to my left, the man was gone. I didn't remember everything we talked about in our brief conversation, but one phrase stuck with me: *"Never believe the first truth."* It only seemed fitting to commemorate the meeting with a poem.

An elf in a pub at his worst,
Said to not trust a truth that's a first,
With a wink and a smile
Meant to charm and beguile
He then vanished, his tale unrehearsed

Still trying to figure out where my new friend had disappeared to, I glanced around the bar. To my right sat a girl who was two sheets to the wind. Seeing I was alone, she cast a lazy glance my way and struck up a conversation. Upon realizing I was American, her focus turned quickly to convincing me to sing Don McLean's *American Pie.* She assumed all Americans knew the words. I politely declined. Seeing that I had not yet fled her side, she then told me how a person could tell the difference between a Protestant and a Catholic, just by looking at them. She treated me like a Catholic brother-in-arms, but missed one small detail. I was not Catholic, I was Presbyterian, a Protestant. Not wanting to disillusion her, I finished my pint and headed back to the hotel.

Getting home in Ireland could be a challenge, especially if you were far away. One weekend, a co-worker invited me into downtown Dublin. We bounced from pub to pub, and ended up at his friend's apartment. When it seemed time to go I looked around, and he was gone. I would need to find a taxi.

As the evening wears on in the city, finding a taxi becomes harder and harder. By the time I reached the taxi office, dozens of people were trying to get home, and the wait was two hours. Instead of passively standing in line on the frigid sidewalk, I started walking. It was about 15-20 miles back to my hotel, so I'm not sure what I was thinking. Maybe it was impatience, and a pint or two of Guinness. Fortunately, after about ninety minutes of walking I came across a gas station. It turned out to be the perfect place to catch a taxi.

Back at work the following Monday, I learned why he'd disappeared. My co-worker had met a girl and completely forgotten about me. His friends in the office laughed and said it wasn't the first time he'd vanished like that. I wasn't upset. The evening opened my eyes to the unpredictability of living overseas, and survival was becoming a fast lesson.

Learning who to trust and who not to trust became easier once I learned my friend Lee was in Ireland working on the same project. One weekend, he suggested renting some gear and scuba diving in western Ireland. It sounded like a great distraction. We arrived at Killary Harbor, ready to explore the cold waters of the Atlantic Ocean. A small motorboat took our party of four to a popular site. Lee and I entered the water first, while the other two divers chain-smoked on the boat. They waved us on, and we descended.

Upon reaching the bottom, singing clams shot out of the sand and made musical clapping noises around our heads. Every time the symphony played, Lee and I laughed. These underwater surroundings felt comfortably familiar, yet very different. After about sixty minutes we surfaced, but didn't see the boat. Colorful words entered my head. I'd been abandoned on land in downtown Dublin, now I was being abandoned at sea. We floated on the surface, blowing our whistles and debating whether to swim for land.

Eventually, the boat returned. The captain explained he wasn't used to divers staying down so long. The two chain-smoking divers were done in fifteen minutes. When he didn't see us right away, he started searching. Lee and I shook our heads and smiled politely. For us, it hadn't been a long dive and we both had the same thought. The captain was an eejit.

Adapting to our surroundings didn't always come with clear answers. On the way home, we passed pastures full of sheep that looked like they'd just finished a paintball battle. Some had red splotches on their sides, others blue, others green. We guessed it was how ranchers identified their free-roaming herds, but it was more fun to imagine sheep shooting each other with paint balls. The rest of the drive was about as serious as sheep fighting in the fields, though an unpleasant surprise still lay ahead.

Theft, and More Big Decisions

Lee dropped me off at my hotel apartment. Approaching the door, I saw that it was slightly ajar. Someone had broken in, grabbed a suitcase, and packed it with my belongings. Everything could be replaced, but the thought of being robbed shook me.

The Garda, Ireland's police, came to take down the details. I expected someone with an athletic build, a neatly pressed uniform, and a gun at their side. Instead, the man who arrived had a portly build, wore a warm, fuzzy sweater, and carried a flashlight in place of a gun. The Garda looked over my place and explained that petty crime was common, and the thief would probably never be found. He then made a surprising suggestion. "Since there's nothing to be done, why don't ye join me at the pub for a pint."

By that point, I'd experienced enough of the country to just go with it. I gladly accepted, enjoyed the pint, and figured the rest could wait until morning.

The next morning, an uneasy feeling surrounded me, and it wasn't about the robbery. Lee lived on the far side of Dublin, about forty minutes away. It was too far away if help was needed. At the hotel, there wasn't anybody I knew or could rely on. My experience in Dublin and on the boat didn't reassure me that anyone would be around if trouble arose. A feeling of isolation grew. Most people on my project found comfort socializing in pubs, or at the bottom of a pint of Guinness. I needed more.

After a few months, the company asked me to return home. Lawsuits from the Massachusetts building collapse were finally making their way through the courts and the lawyers wanted my deposition. The deposition itself would be uneventful, but I looked forward to seeing Karen again.

I'd been calling often, and our phone bill was eating up about thirty percent of my paycheck. The calls felt essential because they kept us from drifting apart. When my assignment was extended by a year, we had a decision to make. My college years had taught me that long-distance relationships don't work, and I didn't want another one. The thought of breaking up didn't sit well with me either.

I invited Karen to Ireland for a three week, all-expense paid visit. With the travel time and jetlag, two weeks wasn't enough. She liked the idea, but needed approval from work. When she approached her boss, he told her that nobody deserved a three-week vacation. He countered by saying she could only have two. When Karen told me his reply, I made a bold suggestion:

"Quit your job. Come live with me."

I offered to take over her mortgage, make her credit card payments, and provide whatever spending money she needed. My expenses in Ireland were already handled by the company, and the money we saved on phone calls would more than cover the rest. She needed time to think. The vision of running away to Ireland sounded like a romance novel, but we had only been dating for seven months. She wasn't comfortable being "beholden" to me, or to any man. It was a big, risky decision.

As December rolled around in Ireland, pressure was building on me. I was a foreigner. An outsider. I was the only IDC employee embedded in the contractor's construction group. Being trapped in The Tasmanian Devil's whirlwind while wondering what Karen would decide raised my stress levels. An overwhelming urge to run away was sweeping through me. These were the same feelings I'd had in college when every test came back with an F. Karen was at home. My friends were at home. Safety was at home. Work wasn't supposed to be this hard. I didn't know where the feelings came from, just that they were there.

The managers onsite noticed a decline in my work, and decided a change was needed. They offered me management of the cleanroom. The move wasn't done only for my benefit. There were two other purposes. It pushed the outsider into a corner they could ignore, and placed someone in charge of a space nobody else wanted.

To the Irish construction managers, the cleanroom was a black box. Working in one required specialized knowledge of all the parts and pieces. Most people avoided entering the area because it meant taking the time to put on gloves, shoe covers, head covers, and a full cleanroom suit. They didn't recognize it, but the cleanroom was the heart and soul of the factory.

From my perspective, I liked the concept of having little management oversight. This was the opportunity to break free from Declan, and out from the shadow of my peers. When the cleanroom was offered, I accepted immediately.

That year, the Christmas season in Ireland brought both pain and joy. While stepping out of the raised tub in my apartment, I slipped and fell, cracked a rib, and gave myself a black eye. At work, people joked that I must have been in a bar fight, and would give a knowing wink when I told them the truth.

After that, a contractor took pity and put me in touch with a housing agent. Within days I was offered a new place. It was a two-story yellow brick duplex with a heating oil tank in the backyard.

Just before the Christmas holiday, I was handed the keys. All my belongings fit into two suitcases, so moving from the hotel apartment was easy enough. I was relieved to be out of the hotel.

In mid-December, Karen let me know her decision. She agreed to quit her job, sell her car, and move to Ireland. She planned to arrive in January, so we would soon be reunited. Just like that, any remnants of my urge to run away disappeared.

As Christmas Day dawned, I sat aching, bruised, and alone. A long list of problems was staring me in the face. A rare snow had fallen and the heating oil tank was empty, the home's phone number hadn't been provided, the VCR was broken, and I couldn't figure out the security alarm. Ireland had shut down for the two-week holiday. None of it could be fixed. None of that mattered. Karen was coming.

By the time the new year rolled around, the long arc of chaos had finally curved toward reunion.

EPILOGUE TO PART 1

My mother sheltered us. She persevered through unimaginable challenges, while teaching love and responsibility by example. The burdens she carried didn't break her spirit, but they wore it down. By the time I understood that, I had already inherited some of the ways she absorbed pain. Her singing and sayings will always be with me.

My father arrived with gifts and a smile. He was generous, attentive, and charming. All of that could disappear quickly. I saw times when he was irresponsible, manipulative, and controlling. It was challenging to try to reconcile those two versions of the man. Both were real. Both were unforgettable.

John carried more than most. Eventually, the burden broke him. He gave up engineering for bartending, was arrested for a DUI, and developed a growing chip on his shoulder. These weren't detours. They were the beginnings of a long descent into resignation, something I swore to avoid. He had shining moments of responsibility and brotherly camaraderie, but his light dimmed too fast.

Mike always thought himself better than the rest of us. His humor was meant to demean others, and improve his standing at their expense. Kindness came at a price. Cruelty was free. For years I kept trying, looking for a connection, and for one brief instant I thought I'd found it. Outside of that brief instant, it was never mutual. When I stopped reaching out, there was nothing. Others saw him differently. Others were not me.

Rick and I remained the closest. He never quite achieved rock star dreams, but he never forgot about his younger brother. He taught me about brotherly love, not in perfect gestures, but in the way he laughed, played ball, tossed pizzas, and joked about tree clams. He even showed love in his own misguided way when he turned John over to the police. His affection was imperfect, but real.

Kathy giggled past discomfort. I brought home stuffed animals on band trips and teased her by turning them upside down, but nothing ever had the drama that surrounded my older brothers. As our lives moved in different directions, we still spoke to each other in our own language, but the calls grew less frequent.

Work began as a job and slowly became a proving ground. I moved from part-time high school shifts to my first structural engineering role, then to a licensed position, and eventually into construction management. Each step was less about title and more about growth. I was learning to be seen, to adapt when foundations shifted, and to trust my instinct that what I was building in my personal life could survive almost anything.

Karen appeared standing under a comet. Though I still had a lot of rough edges, I was finally ready to connect with something beyond work. She accepted who I was, and appeared ready for adventure herself. With Karen by my side, I was confident, ambitious, and ready to take on the world.

Family never disappeared, though its pull weakened over time. My independence grew as I moved to college, to my first apartment, to Oregon, and finally to Ireland. The further I traveled, the more my personality evolved, and in time, I started to generate a pull of my own. By the time Karen prepared to travel to Ireland, my universe was rapidly expanding.

PART 2

PLAYING WITH FIRE

DEDICATION TO PART 2

Only one person has influenced me as deeply as my mother. This person traveled the road with me wherever it led. If doubt crept in or the way forward felt unclear, she stood beside me. Her presence wasn't overbearing. She didn't dictate the what, when, or how of my life, but she provided the balance I lacked. Eventually, that person would become my wife.

In the song *Tightrope* from *The Greatest Showman*, there is a line about choosing uncertainty with someone you trust completely. The main characters move through an unpredictable journey while balancing their commitment to each other. That was our life.

Part 2 is dedicated to my wife Karen, and all the times she stayed with me walking the tightrope.

CHAPTER 10

THE EMERALD ISLE

When people find out I once lived in Ireland, they usually say the same thing.

"I've always wanted to go there."

"Why?" I ask. "The history? Joyce and Yeats?"

"No, I just want to sit in an Irish pub and drink a Guinness."

"There are Irish pubs in the U.S. They all sell Guinness."

That usually kills the conversation. By the time I've explained that corned beef and cabbage is American, shamrocks come from New Zealand, and it's greener in Oregon, I've lost them completely.

Karen doesn't let me talk to strangers about Ireland anymore.

The truth is, I wasn't much better informed myself. In a letter home, I wrote:

I came to Ireland in September 1996 for the purpose of work. My perceptions of the place and people were derived from news reports about Northern Ireland, and American stereotypes such as the Fighting Irish of Notre Dame, corned beef and cabbage on St. Patrick's Day, and that cute little leprechaun on the box of Lucky Charms. Karen came to Ireland not for a vacation, but so that we could be together as a couple. She had even less knowledge of Ireland than I did. We live here, work here, play here, and interact with the people on a daily basis. Ireland is our home, at least for now, for better or for worse.

- Letter from Ireland 1997

A Whole New World

By mid-January, I still hadn't fully settled into the duplex. My mind was consumed with the cleanroom manager role, which demanded everything I had. Days began at 7:30 AM and ended at 7:30 PM. When I wasn't in the construction trailers or on the jobsite, I could usually be found in the pub, networking with clients, contractors, and colleagues. Only work and sleep mattered. That focus was about to be interrupted.

The day Karen arrived, I was bursting with excitement. On the way back to Maynooth from the airport, she said the first thing she needed to do was iron, and if the duplex didn't have an iron we would need to stop and buy one. My wardrobe consisted mostly of jeans and flannel shirts, so I was honestly confused.

"Why do we need that?" I asked, trying to sound reasonable.

"I'm not going to walk around in wrinkly clothes, and neither are you," she said, calm and firm.

Without giving any more thought to the conversation, we headed straight to the store. Details of the purchase didn't stay with me. Something else occupied my mind. I still wasn't used to driving on the left side of the road, and it took my full concentration to stay in the correct lane. A two-word mantra kept repeating in my head: *stay left, stay left, stay left.*

Those first few weeks were bumpy. There weren't big fights, just big adjustments. We'd spoken often on the phone and thought we were on the same page, but she assumed something that wasn't true. When it came to domestic affairs, she thought I had common sense. I didn't.

We stepped through the front door smiling, finally together again. Then the house made its introduction. The heating oil tank was still empty, which meant no heat. There were no bed sheets, no pillows, I didn't know the phone number, the VCR didn't work, and the alarm system was still a mystery. I'd spent the past three weeks sleeping in my coat on a cold, hard mattress breathing in the frosty air. Work had been so busy that I didn't make time to figure out why the oil wasn't delivered, where the shopping mall was, or how to get help. Karen knew me well enough by then, so it wasn't much of a surprise. She took charge quickly. While I was at work, her first days were spent walking around town and learning the lay of the land. It only took a few days for my caveman lifestyle to disappear.

As Karen brought order to our home life, she wanted one final appliance for the kitchen, an electric kettle to boil water. I'd always just boiled water on the stovetop.

"Why do we need that?" I said without thinking.

She patiently explained that waiting fifteen minutes for a pot of water to boil on the stove was inefficient. The kettle could do the same job in three to four minutes. The look on my face told her I still thought having an electric kettle was silly.

Still, a small concern took root. Karen had quit her job and crossed an ocean to join me. She had handled her own finances long before we met. Despite reassurances, she didn't think of my money as "ours" yet. Having to justify every little expense made her uncomfortable. It wasn't that we couldn't afford the kettle. Heck, I didn't think she even needed my approval. Still, being questioned about irons and kettles only fueled her anxiety. We didn't fight or raise our voices, but I could see how uneasy she felt. After we bought the kettle, I stopped questioning her purchases and started encouraging them instead.

By the end of the first week, one issue remained. My late-night socializing had worked when Karen was back in Oregon, but now I wasn't alone. On Friday, while she rested at home recovering from jetlag, my evening was spent at the pub, telling everyone how thrilled I was that she'd arrived. I didn't realize she wasn't thrilled waiting by herself in a strange place while I stayed out. Not being able to contact me only made it worse. After that night, she sat me down and provided a reminder that she hadn't come to Ireland to be left behind.

A little frustration surfaced. Wanting me to be home was fine, but I thought giving her space was considerate. We had already been out together every night since her arrival.

I asked, "Why didn't you tell me?"

She replied, "Don't you know that I always want you home?"

This was new information. It signaled a rapid evolution in our relationship. She needed to tame the wild animal in me, which was okay up to a point. After a short discussion, we agreed on some simple guidelines. I would keep pub nights occasional, limit the pints, and be home by eight. In exchange, she would find ways to stay busy during those evenings.

Getting the house in order hadn't taken very long, and Karen needed something to fill her days besides waiting for me to come home from work. In Oregon, her forty-hour workweek was packed with scheduling, payroll, and phones. People leaned on her constantly. In Ireland, I was the only person she knew. The silence that followed caught her off guard.

A health club sat within walking distance of our home, and it offered an outlet. The club had a pool and it gave her the chance to exercise and take swimming lessons. We both decided to join.

Before we could start, the club handed us each a health survey. One question asked how many pints we drank per week. I wrote three. Karen wrote zero. When we returned the forms, the staff member gave us a look that hovered between suspicion and disbelief. The woman explained that the Ministry of Health sought to limit people to seven pints a week. This sounded less like a health initiative and more like a government-sponsored happy hour. I smiled.

"The Irish government supported raising my weekly pint limit to seven?"

I shouldn't have said that out loud. Karen gently elbowed me. Not having taken the hint, I glanced at her form, then at mine, then back at the staff member.

"Should I change mine?" I asked. "Maybe add a few, just to be safe."

Karen didn't respond. She looked at me, then looked away. She loved my sense of humor, but when it came to pints, I was fast approaching her threshold.

While learning how to survive at home, surviving at work required the same level of attention. Construction report-out meetings carried a fierce intensity. Once a week, fifty or sixty people crowded into a tiny room for a big show. Each area manager had to give a brief report highlighting any problems. If the client learned of a problem before it was reported, the unlucky area manager would be figuratively drawn and quartered in front of everyone in the room.

In one meeting, the new client site manager placed a teddy bear in the middle of the table. He said if things got too tough during the report-out, we could give the teddy bear a hug. He'd used the idea in Arizona and thought it would work in Ireland. It did not.

Ninety percent of the managers on the project were Irish, and they all looked in horror at the cute little teddy bear sitting on the table. No matter how tense the meeting got, nobody dared touch it. I'd been in Ireland three months and knew that foreigners needed to adapt to the local ways. The teddy bear never adapted, and after a few weeks it just disappeared.

As the lone IDC American in the Irish construction manager's organization, I had no choice but to adapt. It helped that my contractor's work hadn't started and the spotlight wasn't on me. Report-outs weren't required yet. My focus stayed on organization, planning, and keeping my head down. I had no desire to disappear like the teddy bear did, so I blended in.

The role of cleanroom manager came with a new client counterpart. Doug was my age and carried himself with a swagger that made it clear he was in charge. His company didn't fully trust the locals, so he'd been sent from Arizona to oversee the work. Like me, he was adjusting to the Irish culture, and that gave us common ground from day one. I knew my path to success went through him, and if he looked good, so would I. Those early weeks were about listening closely to his reporting needs and making sure they were met. We were well prepared when our work on site started. His star was rising, and I quickly earned his trust.

While Doug focused on internal reports, my focus was on the contractor. In the morning, the construction site had limited activity, so it became a time for paperwork. I often said the Irish were the most productive people on the planet, and could prove it. The crews showed up around 8:00 AM and held a leisurely meeting to plan the day. No sooner had they agreed on the plan than they wandered to the dining tent for breakfast. Plates came piled with baked beans, sausages, and soggy steak fries swimming in ketchup. Conversation continued in steady, unhurried tones as the food disappeared.

Once breakfast ended, the crews returned to site. Tools were lifted, adjusted, and admired for several heroic minutes before it was suddenly time for tea. Everyone retreated to the trailer to recover from the strain of starting work. By the time tea was finished, the morning had nearly vanished. A brief effort was made to restart, but almost immediately the lunch bell arrived to save the day. Those morning hours dissolved in a rotation of walking, eating, and joking. I would pass the lunch tent and see men slumped in their chairs, exhausted from the labor of constant breaks. Taking rest in Ireland, I decided, was itself a full-time job.

After the morning passed, a miracle occurred. From 12:00 PM to 5:00 PM, the crews performed a complete day's work. It was a wonder to behold.

By calling the Irish workers the most productive on the planet, I had unknowingly endeared myself to the contractor I managed. Perhaps he missed the sparkle of mischief in my eye when I said it, or perhaps he saw it and chose to appreciate the humor. Some American managers blamed the slow starts on hangovers, which would have required a continuous stream of nightly pub visits. Knowing these lads, it wasn't entirely out of the question. I didn't buy into the stereotype and reminded myself to *"never believe the first truth."*

Exploring Together

Before Karen came to Ireland, her sense of the world didn't stretch much beyond the Pacific Northwest. I tried to explain life abroad over the phone, but nothing matched the daily grind of being there. Once she arrived, we learned faster together, backing each other up whenever something unfamiliar caught us off guard. Ireland was a place where everything felt "*similar but different.*" That phrase became our refrain, and no matter what the surprise, we always said it with a smile.

One afternoon at lunch, Karen asked for an egg salad sandwich. When the plate arrived, something didn't look right. She peeled back the top slice of white bread and found a wilted piece of lettuce covering dry slices of hard-boiled egg. It looked less like a sandwich and more like someone had lost interest halfway through making it. What Americans call egg salad, the Irish call egg mayonnaise. It's "*similar, but different.*"

One evening after work, I offered a woman a ride home. She laughed like I'd said something funny. After asking why, she explained that in Ireland, a man offering a woman a "ride" could be taken as a sexual proposition. I hadn't intended anything like that, but apparently my innocent American offer had nearly caused a scandal. Another *"similar but different"* moment, reminding me that my kind little gestures could carry very unexpected meanings.

As we were learning about the Irish, they were also learning about us. One day, Karen was invited to a buffet lunch with a new friend who had offered to pay. Thinking it worked like the ones back home, she sampled a small amount of several dishes. Her friend stared at the plate, clearly unsettled but not saying a word. Once they sat down, Karen asked if everything was okay. That's when she learned the buffets in Ireland charged per item, not a flat rate for the whole spread. Her carefully chosen variety cost a small fortune. Karen explained the mix-up in the word "buffet" to her friend and offered to pay, but her friend wouldn't let her.

Our cultural knowledge was growing, and it extended beyond just work and daily life. Before she arrived, I'd promised to show Karen the world, and no better place existed than the country we were in. Our first trip explored the immediate surroundings. In Oregon, road signs often advertised the promise of "Food and Lodging." In Ireland, one of the first road signs we saw displayed a martini glass. There's a running joke about the Irish and their drinking habits. They weren't helping themselves.

As we continued on our initial journey, a moss-covered stone ruin appeared on the side of the road. Karen proudly proclaimed it a "thousand-year-old thingy." Since archaeology was not our strength, we remained quite pleased with our newly discovered ancient monument. A guidebook would have set us straight, but we didn't bother to bring one. Upon deciphering the barely legible weathered sign, we learned the truth. The ruin was younger than most American barns.

Undeterred, we kept exploring. Over the next eighteen months, we were immersed in Irish history. Plentiful ruins from different eras dotted the countryside. My favorite ones were the round towers. These tall, slender structures resembled silos, and were used by monks in the ninth and tenth centuries as bell towers. When Viking raiders approached, the monks gathered gold and silver relics from the church, climbed to the top, and pulled the ladder up behind them. The bells rang out to warn of an attack.

The problem with this was that the round towers acted like giant chimneys. By lighting a fire at the base, the monks could be smoked out. Even though these raids had occurred more than a thousand years ago, I decided not to advertise my Danish or Karen's Norwegian roots. We figured it best not to mention we were related to the arsonists.

As our first month passed, each weekend took us farther from home. By Karen's fourth week, we felt brave enough to try an overnight trip. One of the best discoveries we made was the Irish Bed and Breakfast. For less than half the cost of a hotel, we could stay in a private home and wake to a traditional Irish breakfast. No reservations were needed. Licensed B&Bs displayed an official sign with a shamrock, letting travelers know they were approved residences. These weren't the boutique B&Bs we had known back in the States, dressed up with antique wallpaper and inflated prices. The typical Irish B&B was a modest home with a few guest rooms. When we knocked on the door, we were usually greeted with a warm smile and a cup of tea.

The owner served breakfast around the kitchen table, and treated us like family. We quickly learned the anatomy of a traditional Irish fry. It featured dry toast without butter, salty rashers that resembled Canadian bacon, baked beans, a fried egg, a fried tomato, and one slice each of white and black pudding, both sausages. Tea came standard, but orange juice, yogurt, or fruit did not.

Karen never liked the sausage and wouldn't touch it. She didn't want the owner to feel bad, so it became my job to eat it for her. If eating loads of sausage made her feel less guilty and look good, I was all in. My small gesture set a traveling precedent for the next twenty years. No matter what country we were in, one of my roles was to finish whatever she didn't want to eat.

In that first month together in Ireland, I learned more about Karen's likes and dislikes than in the previous eight months. What surprised me was how naturally we fit together. Complementing each other in small ways came with ease. Travel highlighted it. I set budgets and chose the locations. She handled details about lodging, routes, and meals. We played to each other's strengths, and it worked.

With every trip, our horizons were expanding fast, and next up was a weekend to London. We did all the things first-time visitors were supposed to do. We stood in line for the crown jewels, then watched the Beefeater guards pose for pictures with Karen, smiling as if they'd known her for years. At Westminster Abbey, we raised an eyebrow at a coffee cart tucked into a side vestibule. Later, we crossed the Tower Bridge and watched the city stretch out in both directions. A small souvenir stand at the top sold batteries that saved my camera. That night we found our way into the West End to see Cats. Our last-minute tickets put us behind a column, but it didn't matter. We were in London, watching a play on one of the world's great stages. For Karen, the trip was the kind of adventure she had only seen in movies. For me, it was a chance to share a world I hadn't seen since high school.

By the time Karen's fifth week in Ireland ended, she had tasted what life on the road with me would be like. There were still plenty of long, uneventful days in the duplex, but those were becoming the backdrop rather than the story. Traveling around gave color to our lives, and with each shared experience, our bond strengthened.

Blending In

Each week on site, my reputation grew. Meanwhile, The Tasmanian Devil kept stirring up trouble. One of his buildings was constructed a few inches off. Hundreds of connecting pipes no longer aligned and had to be reworked. Tensions ran high as the contractors flooded the trailers with a barrage of change orders and schedule delays. The cleanroom wasn't affected, and managing it with a calm, steady hand, sheltered me. By comparison, the surrounding chaos made me look like the only lad on site who hadn't been raised by sheep.

It helped that my contractors weren't bickering. By treating them like professionals and avoiding micromanagement, I earned their trust. When I needed information, it arrived quickly and accurately. Their responsiveness let me highlight their achievements, and place even the smallest accomplishments in a positive light.

I carried the principle of "craic" from the pub onto the construction site. No matter how high or low a person stood on the work or social ladder, in the area I controlled, everyone merited respect. The locals had little patience for foreigners who looked down on them. Not everyone seemed to understand that.

Doug, my client, certainly didn't. Airtight logic and brute force might have worked in Arizona, but it wasn't a successful strategy in

Ireland. His habit of lecturing rather than listening had already rubbed Mick, his Irish counterpart, the wrong way.

By the time we gathered to discuss why paint had peeled from a cleanroom wall, the tension between them was thick. Doug stormed into the meeting and immediately took charge. He flashed a polished PowerPoint presentation on the wall, complete with graphs, specifications, and recommendations from two paint manufacturers. He spoke with authority, and his delivery had all the precision of a military parade. When finished, Doug looked around the table, waiting for nods of approval. Mick let the silence stretch out before turning his head slowly and mockingly saying,

"That's grand, but what do the real experts say?"

Nobody ever challenged Doug like this. The room went still, waiting to see what would happen. His face turned crimson. He slammed his fist on the table, shouting in an expletive-filled rant about how many more experts Mick needed before he'd be satisfied. Then he threw a stack of papers skyward. Charts and graphs fluttered through the air like startled pigeons. One bounced off Mick's head. Nobody flinched. Mick sat back with a half-smile, letting the chaos settle before speaking. He had no interest in more expert opinions. His only goal was to see how far he could wind Doug up.

Afterward, I pulled Doug aside and explained the game. From then on, he was ready for it. Mick tried again and again, yet never got the same response. Even so, each time they crossed paths, Mick's eyes carried the glint of a man hoping for one more explosion.

Unlike Mick, whose provocations could ignite the room, I chose a quieter approach. Doug's volatile behavior wasn't entirely his fault. Success in his company required an aggressive streak that bordered on antisocial. The meek didn't inherit the earth, they were slaughtered. When he needed information, it usually came as a demand, not a polite request. Minions were expected to get cracking after receiving an order. He was about to experience a very different kind of "craic".

One frosty morning, over a breakfast of greasy chips and baked beans, my cell phone rang. Doug had a presentation due and wanted numbers from the contractor. As usual, the request came with a "drop everything now" urgency. There was no time to finish eating, so off I went, stomach grumbling in protest. Twenty minutes later, after combing the trailers, I returned with the paperwork. Doug glanced at it, then at me, irritation painted across his face. Clearly I hadn't moved fast enough. His lack of gratitude made up my mind. It was time to make a point.

With the delivery complete, I turned my back, blurted out, "Gotta go," then let nature take its course. A long, silent cloud of noxious gas filled the air. I'd barely taken two steps when a groan erupted from his desk, followed by a colorful mix of words featuring my name. He had to finish his presentation and was tethered to his desk. There was no escape. The aroma clung to every surface in his cubicle, a humbling tribute to bad behavior.

From that day forward, every high-priority demand became a potential performance. Doug never figured out when it was coming, and the expletive-filled rants calling out my name were always the same. I still laugh at the thought.

While chemical warfare gave me an advantage in the trailers, I had another secret weapon. Karen had adapted so well that she had been given my car to use during working hours. She became my personal taxi. I was never very good at predicting when the day would end, and this often required some gentle encouragement to leave. Only those with a badge were allowed in the trailers, but Karen became so well known that the guard gave her a warm smile and let her pass. To speed me out the door, she often pitched in and updated my drawings, removing the old, inserting the new, and making sure each landed in the right spot. We made a great team. In a world where the most organized person came out on top, her after-hours help kept me one step ahead of everyone else on the site.

Her real challenge getting me home wasn't in helping me finish work in the trailers. That part was easy. The real challenge was getting me home on Thursday nights. Traditionally, paydays in Ireland occurred on a Thursday, and most of the site went to the pub to celebrate the occasion. Not wanting to miss a strategic opportunity to "network" with the client, the contractors, and my colleagues, I joined in.

There were two obstacles Karen had to overcome when picking me up. The first was in the parking lot. People milled about the front door hoping to get a taxi or a lift home. When she arrived, a wave of bodies swarmed the car like zombies toward the only fresh brain in sight. They banged on her window and tried opening the passenger door, hoping for a lift. Karen hated it, but sobriety had painted a glowing target on her forehead. After beating away the living dead, she would go inside to search for me.

Her entrance triggered a game of pub hide-and-seek. Karen always pre-arranged a time to pick me up, but in the pub, nobody ever looked at their watch. The moment she walked in, a contractor would shuffle me through the thick smoke and crowds of people. A decoy would stroll up and stall her with small talk, a smile, and offers of drinks.

I had already warned her not to trust anyone in a pub. No matter what they tried, their distractions didn't stand a chance. She immediately brushed them aside, and made a beeline for me.

I never encouraged the contractors, and didn't know exactly when the game was afoot. Once she reached my side, I knew better than to offer her a drink. We quickly slipped out the door without saying goodbye as quiet laughter could be heard in our wake. Karen didn't realize it, but chasing her man home from the pub had turned us into a proper Irish couple.

Family and More Travel

Living far from home came with unique challenges. Automatic bill pay and email weren't big yet, so our homes in Oregon had to be managed by a combination of friends, family, the company, and strategic business choices. One of the travel package benefits was that mail could be sent to my company in Portland, who would then FedEx it to Ireland via interoffice mail. Employees who used the benefit too generously quickly earned uncomfortable attention from HR for misusing company resources.

Everyone understood the rules except Karen's cousin, who had her own ideas about how the system worked. She treated the interoffice mail like a snack-and-beverage drop service. Packages arrived containing Kraft Macaroni and Cheese, powdered Irish cream coffee, and other items that weren't asked for and made no sense.

I imagined the clerks' faces as they opened each box. The noodles rattled around, the coffee packets spilled everywhere, and the absurdity of it all made me cringe. What did they think of me? Did they assume I had no taste, no self-control? Each delivery left me sweating. Thankfully, Karen finally convinced her cousin to stop sending packages before HR accused me of running a black-market pantry out of Ireland. I still have no idea what she expected us to do with the powdered Irish cream coffee.

The mail benefit was a one-way service, so anything we wanted to send from Ireland had to go through the Irish Post. Karen quickly became an expert. We frequently mailed packages containing long letters, Irish coins, and small gifts such as an Aran sweater or a local board game. Learning the postal system became a way to share pieces of our life abroad with the people we loved.

My mother had collected postcards when she was young. It became a family tradition to send her one whenever we traveled. Ireland gave me the perfect chance to add to her collection. Years later, whenever Karen and I visited her in Pittsburgh, she would bring out the postcards, letters, and small gifts we had sent. Even as an adult, she still collected every remnant of our lives.

While I sent postcards of ruins and green fields to my mother, the news coming back wasn't always the same. Two of my brothers were struggling, and there was little I could do from afar.

Rick worked a full-time job during the day and chased rockstar dreams late into the night. With three young children at home, his wife didn't appreciate his priorities. To reclaim a sense of independence and get out of the house, she took a part-time job at a local bar. They were both so focused on themselves that they lost sight of being a couple. Hearing about their marriage unraveling from thousands of miles away was heartbreaking.

John wasn't doing much better. My mother would tell me how he drank too much, his wife spent too much, and their six-year-old daughter was often caught in the middle of their arguments. My two closest brothers were headed for a divorce. Their relationships taught me what not to do with Karen, and to be grateful for what I had in her.

As for my nieces and nephews, I realized that beyond gifts and letters, I wouldn't be part of their lives. None of my siblings were sharing the joy they had raising their children. They were too distracted to be bothered responding to their wayward brother. My being so far away meant missing out on special occasions, watching them grow up. Mail and packages are nice, but they could never replace being there.

I couldn't influence much of what was going on back in the U.S., so I instead poured my energy into trying to make things better for Karen in Ireland. Homesickness caught up to her. She loved our weekend trips, but a few hours at the health club each day weren't enough. She missed having friends close by and feeling more productive.

On the occasional Saturday when I had to work, she would come along to use my computer and write emails, but it wasn't enough. One day, I surprised her by coming home early with flowers and a bottle of champagne. She loved the attention, but the demands of work quickly pulled me away again. She was struggling and needed more.

To add some spark to our weekend drives, we bought a deck of cards. Each card showed a different tourist site, and we made a goal of visiting all the obscure places pictured. I hoped the thought of those upcoming trips would give her something to look forward to, but it still wasn't enough. Without a sense of purpose during the week, Karen seemed adrift. As her homesickness grew, neither one of us wanted to face her returning to Oregon.

Looking back, I'd like to think the universe stepped in. It had lent a hand once before when a comet appeared in the sky to bring us together. The time had come for another gentle nudge. This time, instead of a comet appearing, it was a job. Our neighborhood needed an Avon lady. Karen had once sold Avon in the U.S., so she knew how to manage a territory. Customers found her American accent charming, and sales came easily. As a bonus, her hours were flexible, so our weekend adventures weren't interrupted. The homesickness faded. She had found her footing again.

One of those adventures came on a trip to Northern Ireland. Late on a Friday after work, while driving north, we spotted a handwritten sign on the side of the road: "Bag of roosters – 2 pounds." We pictured a burlap sack wriggling with live chickens, their heads poking out in protest. It seemed cruel, but who were we to question Irish customs? As the miles passed, we guessed a rooster was probably some type potato, but we preferred our first interpretation.

Further up the road, the border appeared. I captured our first impressions in a letter:

The border to Northern Ireland is impressive. There's a big guard tower on a hill surrounded by barbed wire. If need be, there's a security checkpoint that all cars could be routed through for inspection. Soldiers with bullet proof vests, helmets, and rifles can be seen patrolling. Since the guard station wasn't manned, we drove right on by. Sad as it may seem, the guard station for the Republic of Ireland in the south is much less impressive. A couple of orange cones and two Garda in warm, fuzzy sweaters gently wave their torch directing cars onward along a small, two-lane road. Karen and I joked about how the Northern Ireland police in their fancy tower probably teased the Republic of Ireland Garda with their little orange cones. Fortunately, the checkpoints are far enough away from each other so this probably never actually happens.

- Letter from Ireland 1997

As our discussion of chickens and checkpoints came to an end, Karen placed one of the CD's we bought at a souvenir shop into the car's player. Irish folk songs filled the air and we sang along as best we could. Silliness and song joined us on almost every trip around the island. Another passage from a different trip captured our spirit.

In fact, at one point we decided to do some hunting. There aren't many people in the Connemara peninsula this time of year, so we stopped the car and quietly snuck up alongside some wild peat. Peat is the earth which burns and is used here for fires much more than wood. Since nobody was looking, and since the peat did not see us approaching, we were able to bag a couple pieces and place them in the boot of the car. Our getaway was clean, and after returning home it was confirmed that the rumors about earth that burns are true. We were also able to solve one other mystery: Is the water in the loughs fresh or salt water? Taste tests revealed the water is unquestionably fresh, and since neither one of us got sick, it is most likely clean, also.

- Letter from Ireland 1997

On the backdrop of our meandering adventures, I had one more surprise for Karen. In the summer, as her birthday approached, I wondered what to get her. She wasn't one for fancy jewelry and we were already seeing amazing things, so I chose something for both of us.

When Karen agreed to come to Ireland, we agreed that all of her bills were my responsibility. That included credit cards. For her birthday, I paid off the balance. She was speechless. Nobody had ever done anything like that for her. If she didn't realize I was serious about her before, she did then. To me it only seemed logical. I didn't mind having credit cards, but keeping a balance on one always bothered me. The interest rates were too high, and the banks didn't deserve the money. Paying off her card freed up money to focus on my dream of becoming a millionaire and continue traveling.

After nine months in Ireland together, we were fully immersed in the culture. At the Waterford Crystal factory, we bought a special edition bowl. It wasn't mine and it wasn't hers. Marriage hadn't entered our minds yet, but buying the crystal bowl hinted at a possible future. Along the ramparts of Blarney Castle, we gripped steel rails as we bent backward to press our lips against a cold stone, all for the mythical gift of gab. Later that evening, torch-lit pathways guided our steps, and vaulted ceilings hosted a medieval banquet. At the Cliffs of Moher, Karen stayed safely back while I cautiously approached the edge to peer down into the sea. There were no guardrails in 1997, not enough tourists had fallen off the cliffs yet. While exploring the island, we drove on endless deserted one-lane roads, spotted ruins, and then trudged across rain-soaked fields with no plaques, fences, or signs. Ireland's remote areas contained a wild, long-forgotten excitement that begged to be explored.

By the time fall rolled around, Karen had heard more Irish music than she ever asked for, and I'd eaten enough sausages off of her plate to gain ten pounds. The charm of a cozy pub had long since worn off, and now the smell of stale beer and cigarette smoke made her growl before we even reached the door. Except for our first visit to London, we hadn't left the island. She was ready to expand her horizons, and I needed to up my game. That was about to happen.

Culture, Cleaning, and the City of Lights

In October, we returned to London with the goal of seeing Phantom of the Opera in the West End. After the play, Karen wanted to go shopping, so we headed over to Harrod's. Designer clothes, sparkling perfumes, and glittering jewelry counters didn't catch her eye. Instead, she zeroed in on the store's limited-edition teddy bear. I couldn't help laughing. Here we were, in one of the shopping capitals of the world, and all she wanted was a stuffed bear. That little bear eventually joined dozens of others scattered through our home.

By this time, I understood that Karen didn't need status symbols to be happy. Experiences mattered more to her than designer clothes or diamonds. I was grateful for that.

As Thanksgiving Day approached, we wanted to do something special. Instead of another quick getaway within Ireland, we planned a trip the way many locals did and booked an all-inclusive package to a small resort in the Canary Islands.

On the plane, the airline sold a limited-edition Travel Barbie complete with suitcases and a garment bag. Karen had always wanted a Barbie as a little girl, and asked if buying it would be strange. I reached for her hand to provide assurance. It wasn't. The Harrod's teddy bear needed a friend.

The Canary Islands are part of Spain, and the island we stayed on had something Ireland did not. It had topless beaches. Fortunately, Karen had chosen the resort, so I couldn't be accused of having ulterior motives. I asked more than once if she wanted to participate in the local culture. She was not persuaded. Instead, we spent our time bobbing in the waves and swimming in the warm water. That was good enough for me.

We both enjoyed the resort and had fun touring the island. On Thanksgiving, we sat down to eat an intimate meal in an ocean-front cafe. I don't remember what Karen ordered, but I ordered the house specialty, garlic squid. Karen scrunched up her nose at my choice. If she hadn't already realized how clueless I was about intimate dinners, the garlic squid confirmed it.

Back in Ireland, on the first day of December the Christmas season officially started. To mark the season, we bought tickets to the Russian ballet's performance of *The Nutcracker* in downtown Dublin. What I really looked forward to was a two-week holiday shutdown of the site. Between our traveling and the pressures from work, I needed a break. The only thing on my mind was some quiet time together, snuggling in front of a warm fire. That's not how it happened.

On Christmas Eve, an unexpected "invitation" arrived, and it was far from welcome. The phone rang and when I answered, the voice on the other end sounded panicked. A sprinkler line had burst over the cleanroom, flooding the area. The fire protection contractor didn't belong to me, but that didn't matter. No one else could be reached. Staying home wasn't an option. I had to return to the jobsite.

The contractors handled the heavy lifting, but leadership mattered too. I spent that night crawling through ceilings, slogging through puddles, and helping oversee the cleanup. My presence gave the client confidence the situation was under control. By the time I returned home, thoughts of cozying up to a fire were replaced with sleep.

Starting in January 1998, Karen and I took several months off from traveling and settled into life at home. Around then, I learned about a government program that recognized the cleanest small town in Ireland. The Tidy Town competition was all about prestige, but our community never placed. On weekend mornings, fast-food wrappers blew down the streets like tumbleweeds in an old west ghost town. I should have guessed the same mess would follow me to the construction site.

The crews in my area showed about as much respect for the cleanroom as the townspeople did for the streets. The work moved quickly, but progress meant nothing if the place didn't look spotless. We could be ahead of schedule and under budget, but if upper management saw a single piece of trash on the floor, they could justify their existence by pointing it out. After hearing me grumble one too many times about cleaning up after contractors, Karen questioned my role. "You're the janitor," she said with a smile. We didn't have janitors. We had laborers and cleanup crews. I got her point.

Whoever said, "Don't sweat the small stuff" never worked in a cleanroom. The cleanup crews were some of the most crucial people on the project, even if they didn't see it that way. If the client was walking through, I rushed ahead to clear booties, facemasks, and gloves from the floor. Staying late earned some playful teasing from Karen, but it paid off. The client came to believe I ran the most disciplined area on the site.

With work well under control, Karen and my thoughts drifted toward more travel. When we first met, she loved that I could speak French. I told her once she learned the language, we would take a trip to Paris. Living in Ireland motivated her to try. After several attempts that left her frustrated, she gave up. It didn't seem fair to let my silly requirement stop us, so I gave her credit for trying and in early February, we planned a three-day visit.

Paris was everything she dreamed of, a city so massive it could never be seen all at once. The subway became our ally, a way to leap across neighborhoods so we could spend more time walking the streets and seeing as much as possible. Our first two days started at 8:00 AM and ended just after midnight. We strolled the length of the Champs Elysees, bought lithograph sketches from a street vendor under the Arc de Triomphe, and watched a fiery sunset behind the Eiffel Tower. At the Louvre, we smiled back at the Mona Lisa, waved at the Venus de Milo, and stood in awe before a hall of paintings that stretched over twenty feet tall.

On the third day, after touring Napoleon's Tomb and strolling past the booksellers on the Seine, we climbed to the top of Notre Dame, where the mist blurred the city and the gargoyles kept their watch. Coming back down, I was already thinking about the next stop, but Karen was done. Her feet ached, her muscles were shot, and she finally put her foot down.

"We need to eat," she said.

"Eat?" I responded. "There will be plenty of time to eat back in Ireland."

The look on Karen's face told me I had gone too far. This was my second time in Paris, and for the past few days the excitement overtook me. Food, sleep, and bathrooms weren't important. These experiences were! At least, that's what I thought until I saw how exhausted she looked.

Karen had been brave up to that point. We had seen more than she ever imagined, but doing it at a pace that rivaled a Formula One race car wasn't what she had in mind. In the interest of reestablishing the peace, we stopped for a crepe, which turned out to be limp, overcooked, and underwhelming. It was hardly worth surrendering sightseeing time for, but it wasn't about me. As we made our way back to the hotel, I knew Paris had only given us a taste. One day, we would be back for more.

Emails about our experiences abroad were getting attention. One of Karen's friends, Donna, had been reading about our adventures and "invited herself" for a two-week vacation. I still had a job to attend to. As long as the entertainment didn't fall on me, I had no objection.

When she arrived in early March, Karen had a packed itinerary ready to go. All I needed to do was get up early, drive them to the bus station, and pick them up at the end of the day looking cheerful.

The first week proceeded exactly as planned. One story of their adventures out even made me smile. Karen told me about a lunch stop at a nearby mall. Her friend had insisted on trying an Irish McDonald's. I didn't think malls and fast food were very high on the tourist list, but thought nothing of it. While standing in line, Donna looked at Karen and said:

"I can't believe how many Irish people are here."

She thought only Americans frequented McDonalds. If I'd been there, keeping silent after hearing her say that would have been hard. Karen had more tact than I, and just made small talk.

During the second week, the intensity at work increased. After a ten-hour day in the cleanroom, the last thing I wanted was to play chauffeur or make small talk at the dinner table. I was hitting my limit. There's a saying about how guests, like fish, start to smell after three days. By the end of day fourteen, I was ready for our home to be ours again. I liked staying in B&Bs, but I wasn't cut out to run one.

Although Donna was the only person to stay in our home, there were many other visitors. Karen and I had developed a reputation for being expert travelers, and we regularly recommended places to stay and sites to see. One weekend, we even saw Mr. Shah, the senior engineer who mentored me long ago. He received a special tour of our favorite castle ruins, and it felt good to give back to someone who had helped me so much early in my career. We even shared a few small pieces of wisdom we'd picked up along the way:

Never confuse an Irishman with an Englishman, or you'll start a fight. "Top of the morning" is only said by leprechauns in Hollywood, not real Irish people.

Don't order Irish nachos, they are just cheese fries. A real Irish coffee is more than just a shot of whiskey in black coffee.

No matter what the signs say, Guinness is not good for you. When Irish eyes are smiling, they're likely in the pub. Never try to outdrink the locals.

Most importantly of all: *Never believe the first truth.*

Wrapping It Up

Doug made sure the reputation of how smoothly our area had been managed spread throughout the client's organization. In late spring, three unfamiliar visitors arrived on site. No one told me who they were or why they had come to Ireland. When I met them in the trailers, the newcomers introduced themselves as Doug's Israeli counterparts. Their project back home had stopped, and they came to learn what they could from the "experts." Left waiting around with little direction, the group welcomed my invitation to tour the cleanroom.

During the walk, I shared what I could about the project, treating each question with great importance. On the way back to the trailers, I noticed them shivering. They explained the cold weather had caught them by surprise. Since they had no plans for the evening, I invited them to join Karen and me for an Irish night out. It felt odd that Americans were showing the Israelis Irish hospitality, but by this time, Karen and I had settled in enough to feel like locals.

When we picked the group up from their hotel, it was clear they weren't dressed for the cold, damp evening. We stopped at our house to grab spare coats, which the visitors accepted without hesitation. During the drive, we visited ruins and discussed local history before ending the night with bowls of Irish stew at a well-known pub. The trio sipped at their pints, but the atmosphere and the hospitality seemed to matter more than the drinks. By the time the band started to play, our guests were ready to call it a night.

The Israelis were incredibly grateful for the attention. Karen and I treated them with the same courtesy we showed everyone else, never thinking the evening was anything special. Still, the effort left a lasting impression that stretched all the way back to their home office.

After my hosting activities completed, one problem remained. The floor tile manufacturer's chronically late deliveries were accompanied by a request for extra costs. Their delays slowed on-site installation contractors and triggered overtime just to stay on schedule. The client wasn't open to paying more. They wanted me to turn the tables and recover as much cost as possible from the floor tile contractor.

It was unusual for someone outside the client's organization to handle negotiations, and I recognized the responsibility. With dozens of carefully organized emails and invoices, I invited the manufacturer to Ireland for a face-to-face discussion. He explained how a cargo ship had accidentally backed into a dock at their factory, causing it to sink. He insisted his company had been heroic for air-freighting tiles to the site at great expense. All I heard were excuses. Nothing changed the fact that their product arrived late, and the project had paid the price.

The client recovered more than they'd hoped for. My section of the project already ran better than planned, and the negotiation simply reinforced the client's trust. I had managed their money as carefully as my own, and it showed.

In late May, Doug called me aside with an unexpected proposition. The Israelis who had visited the site wanted someone to assist with their own project back home. The real surprise was that they hadn't requested anyone from his company. They wanted me. He warned that Israelis were considered hard to deal with, and that neither he nor anyone else in his company was willing to travel there for more than a few weeks.

I thought back to their visit. They had been polite, direct, and extremely curious. Nothing about them struck me as difficult. I got along well with them, and they with me. The past two years had been challenging, but also rewarding. Bringing my experience to a new country sounded like the type work I wanted. I hadn't been home for over eighteen months, so I told Doug I'd need two weeks before shooting off into the world again. It wasn't a problem.

That evening, I told Karen about the possibility of more travel. She'd seen sights beyond her wildest dreams and wanted more, but the isolation from friends and family had taken a toll. My long hours hadn't helped. She needed more than two weeks at home, and neither one of us knew what living in Israel would be like. Israel felt like the next logical step for my career. I didn't like the idea of being apart, but our relationship had grown strong, and I was sure we wouldn't be apart for long. A few days later, Doug had his answer. Send me to Israel.

With our end date near, Karen and I managed one additional trip out of the country, to Stratford-upon-Avon in the UK. I'd studied enough Shakespeare in school to appreciate his influence, and couldn't resist seeing *The Tempest* performed in his hometown. On stage, shipwrecked characters were flung onto the shore of a strange land. I couldn't help but see the parallel. Two years earlier, Ireland had felt like that same unfamiliar distant shore. Now, I no longer played the part of the castaway. Home wasn't tied to any one place. It lived in the life Karen and I were sharing.

The last piece of the project required assembling product information and warranties into a single document. Doug's manager demanded everything be complete before I left, but it wasn't realistic. Some of the warranties hadn't arrived, and waiting around made no sense. There were plenty of Irish administrative assistants onsite that could do the job more efficiently, and at a lower cost than an expensive expatriate.

When he realized I wouldn't personally dot every "i" and cross every "t" he threw a tantrum, yelling and threatening that if I left, he would personally chase me down at the airport. On hearing the tirade, Doug just laughed, congratulated me on being accepted, and told me to get used to it. When my last day arrived, the volatile manager handed me a unique plaque, praising my dedication during the Christmas Eve fire-sprinkler disaster. "I guess you deserve this. Thanks." He muttered before walking away. He didn't hear my sigh of relief.

My original goals when I left engineering and joined the construction group were to make more money, take on greater responsibility and live in a place where I would be noticed. The assignment in Ireland succeeded on all counts. Now, we just had to catch a plane home.

Surviving a long-term overseas assignment came with perks: a cash allowance, two weeks of a hotel, a rental car, and all meals reimbursed. These benefits were meant to ease the awkward transition back into American life. We took full advantage. Shortly after landing in Oregon, Karen and I slipped away on an all-expenses-paid drive down the coast. All we wanted to do was stay in our happy world for as long as possible.

We hated the thought of being apart, but Karen knew that while I was in Israel learning the lay of the land, she would have time to catch up with friends and family. With no thoughts other than being together, we watched the waves crashing upon the log-strewn shores, and then enjoyed the solitude of California's towering redwood forests.

CHAPTER 11

THE FIRST TIME IN ISRAEL

As we had done in Ireland, Karen and I wrote many long letters to our families while in Israel. The letters were always joint efforts, and the excitement of sharing our travels bubbled onto page after page. I did the writing and Karen did the editing. One passage in particular captures those early days, so I'll let my younger self explain how the new assignment began.

With our journeys in Ireland finally complete, it was time to move on to something bigger, better, and more daring. Since China, Iran, and Iraq seemed to be a bit extreme, we chose Israel. Our strategy started out as a simple one. I would go to Israel for the first month and scout out the landscape, making sure all was safe. My biggest challenges at the time included finding good food, letting Karen know what kind of clothing the women were wearing, and making sure I didn't have too much fun while we were apart. I bravely began my portion of the mission on 05 July 1998.

Arriving in Israel, I received a warm welcome from the client's team at the factory. I was invited to places in and around both Jerusalem and Tel Aviv. Aha, I thought, this is the perfect opportunity to begin my mission. The first weekend consisted of a quick trip in and around the old city of Jerusalem, and a brief stop off at the beach in Tel Aviv. I noted the types of clothing being worn, along with places to eat, and reported back to Karen. Unfortunately, I made a critical mistake. My weekend reports sounded like too much fun. In hindsight, it's easy to see why that didn't go over well. Below is a brief excerpt of how I described our conversation.

Karen: *So Dan, how was your weekend?*

Dan: *It was okay, I guess, I spent part of the time hanging out on the beach in Tel Aviv and visiting Planet Hollywood. The temperature is about 85 degrees, and the water is warm. Also, all the women are really thin, and are wearing bikinis.*

Karen: *Huh?*

Dan: *Yup, all the women are extremely thin, and the swimsuits are the smallest I have ever seen.*

Karen: *Huh?*

After two years in Ireland, where women usually wore warm, heavy clothes, the beach in Tel Aviv caught me off guard. My eyes naturally drifted toward the more attractive women. Since Karen, in my eyes, qualified as such, it only makes sense that my description of beach fashion gravitated toward the better-looking women. Despite this logic, she didn't seem to appreciate the pleasure that I was taking in my mission to evaluate Israeli fashion. Karen quickly obtained an earlier plane flight out of the U.S.A.

- Letter from Israel 1998

Arrival

Those initial weeks in Israel left some of the strongest impressions. I spent most of my time with Yoram, the cleanroom manager. Unlike Doug, who leaned on a strict chain of command, Yoram treated me as an equal. He was my age and carried a dry, mischievous sense of humor that I recognized immediately.

Then there was Shira, a young, brilliant, red-haired, free spirit who Yoram couldn't control. He didn't even try. She came and went with the energy of a bouncing rubber ball. On past projects, management would have flagged that lack of discipline immediately. Here in Israel, Yoram just rolled his eyes and chalked it up to youth.

Our offices were in a six-story building with a well-stocked cafeteria. Joining Yoram at lunch became the best way to get his undivided attention. Those meals turned into informal reporting sessions, and more often than not, strategic planning disguised as casual conversation.

Other meetings were more formal, and for those, I had to learn some new rules. To an outsider walking past, it might have sounded like a battleground. As presentations flashed across the front of the room, voices grew loud, and hands gestured wildly. I quickly learned this wasn't anger. It was passion. The Israelis challenged each other freely, especially when they were among equals. No detail was too small to debate. Hierarchy still mattered, though. The tone shifted when an upper manager joined the room. Questions became more cautious.

When meetings began, I often sat quietly while the storm built around me. Loud, impassioned discussions filled the air. Eventually, someone would turn and ask for my opinion. The shift was immediate. They hung on every word as if I were the expert. In those meetings, I was.

If even one person in the room didn't speak Hebrew, a meeting had to be conducted in English. It allowed me to follow the conversation, even if I didn't understand the cultural undercurrents. After a few weeks, if a speaker struggled with English, I asked them to switch to their native language. The looks of gratitude were undeniable, and Yoram always quietly helped interpret for me.

Not being able to understand the language left me at a slight disadvantage. Driving to and from work, I found myself puzzling over the road signs, trying to match the Hebrew letters with the English words beside them. It became a game, and over time I started to recognize words.

At lunch, I would often ask about a phrase I'd read or overheard. The reaction was always surprise, followed by warmth. No one expected an outsider to take an interest, and my self-taught Hebrew from road signs earned respect.

In time, Yoram caught on to one of my tricks. Some words in Hebrew borrowed an English counterpart. I'd pick out a single familiar word and casually ask a question about it. At first, Yoram looked at me with suspicion. Then, a smile appeared. He'd solved the puzzle.

There was one puzzle Yoram and his colleagues couldn't solve on their own. They needed to report construction progress back to colleagues in Arizona. Working closely with Doug in Ireland had taught me how critical clear communication was. Yoram's emails were often full of spelling and grammar errors, which made the Israelis look careless rather than competent. If I saw Yoram drafting a message, I would ask if he wanted me to review the English.

My work expanded from emails to full reports, and soon project status reached Arizona with grammatical precision. Yoram noticed the difference immediately when the U.S. team began responding with more professional respect. He knew that the edits weren't part of any job description. They were my way of ensuring the team's expertise got the credit it deserved.

While efforts at work were being warmly received, Shira helped ease life outside the office. On my first weekend she offered to show me around. When I arrived at her Jerusalem apartment, she had just rolled out of bed. A boyfriend sat hunched over a kitchen table with a cup of coffee in hand. He forced a smile, nodded, then stared back down at his mug. With bleary eyes and frazzled hair, Shira hurried to a back room. Within two minutes, she reappeared looking more than presentable. After waving a quick goodbye to her boyfriend, she bounced out the door, with me scrambling to keep up.

Shira taught me important things, like how to navigate driving through the Old City streets, where to find a trustworthy ATM, and who sold the best falafel. A day later, she and her boyfriend drove me to Tel Aviv to swim in the warm Mediterranean waters. When he started splashing her, she turned away and responded, "Die! Die!"

Wishing death on him for such a minor offense seemed harsh. When I asked about it, her eyes lit up and she laughed. The word *die* in Hebrew means "enough". It quickly became one of my favorite words, and when I told someone, "Die, both in Hebrew and English," they would pause. Then slowly, a smile would appear.

Yoram, Shira, and the rest of the client organization thought of themselves as underdogs. Experts from the U.S. were constantly sent to their factory to point out mistakes. During the short trips, the visitors were always treated with great respect.

Behind the scenes, there was anger over the attitudes of superiority. My first weeks had shown that not all experts were created equal. I didn't tell them what to do. Instead, I explained why, framing it in logic they could follow. That approach connected on a personal level. They also saw I didn't act like I wanted to leave. I was willing to stay as long as they wanted me to. It didn't take long before their acceptance of me took hold, and interactions became livelier.

My eyes were being opened to Israeli culture, and when Karen arrived, the knowledge would be invaluable. Before boarding the plane for Israel, we had long talks. She was nervous about what to expect, and I wanted to put her mind at ease. We mapped out a detailed plan to meet at the airport, complete with backup instructions in case something went wrong.

When her flight landed, I waited patiently at the exit door where passengers trickled out one by one. The arrival hall emptied. The only sound was the light clicking of heels and low rumble of suitcase wheels echoing across the cold floor. We had agreed, if she didn't appear within two hours, I should return to the hotel and wait for her call. Worried, I returned to the car and headed back to my room. Upon arriving, the front desk relayed a message. Karen was on her way.

When she finally arrived, the shared taxi didn't pull up to the front entrance. It dumped her, suitcases and all, in the middle of the dimly lit parking lot. The driver sped off. She stood there, blinking into the dark, unsure which way to go. The hotel windows offered no clues. The lot was quiet. Too quiet.

Then, she saw movement.

A figure stepped out from the shadows. Her breath caught. She gripped the suitcase handle tighter, and thought of running toward the building.

As the figure stepped into the light, her shoulders dropped. Her grip loosened. Fear gave way to recognition, and recognition gave way to relief. I walked toward her, calm and steady, and she let out a breath she hadn't realized she'd been holding. Without saying a word, she wrapped her arms around me and held on tight.

Hotel Living and Long Days

Neve llan is a small, four-story resort located about a twenty-minute drive from Jerusalem, along the road to Tel Aviv. The hotel is equipped with a buffet style restaurant, an outdoor covered swimming pool, a health club center, ping pong tables, and riding stables. The back of the property winds through Kiwi groves, and along the western horizon can be seen the glow of lights from Tel Aviv. At the time we lived there, it was famous for one thing. Weddings.

On a warm August night shortly after Karen's arrival, we climbed a remote hotel stair tower and peered out a window overlooking the pool. A sea of dining tables covered with white tablecloths surrounded a makeshift dance floor. At the far end, decorated with flowers, stood a wedding arch where the bride and groom had recently exchanged vows. Loud cheers and the pounding beat of music reverberated through the air as wedding guests crowded around the happy couple.

I didn't ask questions, or make any suggestions. We simply enjoyed watching the celebration from our lofty perch.

After recovering from jetlag, one of the first places Karen asked to see was the beach in Tel Aviv. She hadn't forgotten my comments about Israeli fashion. I hadn't helped myself by telling her that women in the office often wore tight, low-cut shirts with exposed midriffs. As we strolled along the sand, she pointed out every woman who wasn't thin, or wearing a tiny bathing suit. My prior comments stemmed from surprise at how different things were from Ireland. I might have been slightly clueless, but I got her point. My days critiquing women's fashion were over.

Work often stretched to twelve hours. I liked the Israelis and their energy, but they could wear me out. Most nights I wanted nothing more than to collapse onto the bed and sleep. It didn't seem fair for Karen to go from long days alone, to evenings without company. So, we climbed in the car and went looking for food.

Most of the time, we sat in the nearby mall food court with fast food, or brought a pizza back to the room. On special occasions, we drove to a small restaurant in Abu Gosh. The walls were covered with colorful rugs and the windows contained no glass. They opened directly out into the clear night air. As dusk fell, we snacked on pickled carrots, dipped warm pita into freshly made hummus, and pulled perfectly cooked grilled steak from long metal skewers onto a plate of saffron rice. From loudspeakers on the minaret, the Muslim call to prayer echoed across the hillsides. Its haunting sound drifted over olive groves and crumbling stone walls. However, not every evening had the haunting atmosphere of Abu Gosh.

Exhaustion didn't last long. By the weekend I caught my second wind. In Israel, history wasn't hidden. It surrounded us in every direction. We began with what I already knew, Jerusalem. Shira had taught me how to weave through traffic and into the Old City. The narrow streets reminded me of Pittsburgh. Moving through it felt like returning to an old neighborhood, only this one had towering walls with two-thousand-year-old stones.

On one visit into the Old City, a ten-year old Palestinian attached himself to us as we wandered up the Via Dolorosa. He wanted to be our guide, for a "small" fee. We always negotiated payment with the enterprising little extortionist at the end. His first number was guaranteed to be outrageous. Stopping at the Stations of the Cross and ending at the Church of the Holy Sepulcher brought the story of the crucifixion to life. The attempted shakedowns were part of the show, and they reminded us that even in the holiest of places, someone was always looking for an easy mark.

Down by the Dead Sea, we escaped the hustle of the city and eased into the briny water, our bodies floating as if weightless. The relief didn't last. There was no clean water in sight, and the salt left an itchy crust that clung to our dry skin. From there we climbed to the top of Masada, walking among the remnants of Herod's palace and learning of the desperate stand that ended in tragedy when the Romans closed in.

On another day, at Qumran, the ruins gave way to views of the caves where the Dead Sea Scrolls sat hidden for centuries. An air-conditioned room offered a break and a film explaining the history. The exit, however, funneled us into the biggest tourist shop we had ever seen. Everywhere in Israel, the past rose from the ground, followed closely by someone trying to make a quick buck.

Living for two years in Ireland had accustomed us to cooler weather. There was nothing cool about summer in Jerusalem. After parking along the backside of the Old City walls, we walked over to the Garden of Gethsemane. Young boys hawking olive branches and vendors selling freshly squeezed pomegranate juice filled the sidewalks. On our return, we stopped in the incense filled caves at Mary's Grotto, then started our trek back to the car. By that time, the sun had risen high in the sky, and as we crossed the Kidron Valley an intense heat radiated off of every stone surface. Without any shade in sight, Karen's face turned a bright shade of purple. Although I tolerated the heat with ease, her system wasn't as forgiving. We were already at the car and starting to go back to the hotel. Within a few minutes, she started complaining about not feeling well.

I made a quick detour to a nearby air-conditioned museum, bought a cold bottle of water, and guided her to the ladies' room. Ten minutes later she began to recover, but we both knew we had pushed our luck. I learned to keep a closer eye on her, and on future trips would carefully track "sun points," stopping once Karen had reached her limit.

Israel began to feel less like an assignment and more like home. Unlike a tourist only visiting for a week or two who is shuffled from site to site, we were able to take our time, and see a side of the country rarely appreciated.

Ashkelon may have been where the biblical story of Samson and Delilah took place, but we went for the beach. The wind blew gently through date palms, and Mediterranean waves brushed against a shore crowded with active beachgoers. It looked like a postcard until you noticed the trash and tar balls floating in the water. No one seemed bothered. For us, it was hard to ignore.

The longer we stayed in Israel, the more I noticed that contrast everywhere. Ancient ruins and breathtaking beaches mixed in with the messiness of daily life.

The messiness of life could creep into work. When that happened, my colleagues expected me to sort it out. Communication between an

American contractor and the Israelis had collapsed. Despite never submitting any paperwork, a change order was demanded. Once the Israelis brushed it off, the contractor stopped working.

Both parties were behaving badly. It felt like a Three Stooges routine. I was Moe, knocking Larry and Curly's heads together and telling them to cut it out. A legitimate reason for a change order existed, but it would only be issued after submitting the proper paperwork. The negotiating skills I had learned on my past project were sharpening.

I found other ways to prove my worth. When two visiting American specialists submitted invoices that did not hold up under scrutiny, discrepancy after discrepancy jumped out. Before they could be thrown off site, I showed them how to document their billing so it would stand up to scrutiny.

Yoram appreciated how different I was. Before my arrival, he had seen other Americans demand gas-guzzling pickup trucks while locals rode buses and shared cars. He had watched visitors leave early and brag about vacations in Cyprus, Turkey, and Greece.

In me, Yoram saw someone who didn't brag, stayed late at the office, embraced Israeli culture, and treated his team as equals. I had been warned about how difficult the Israelis could be, yet something in my personality allowed me to act as a bridge between them and the Americans. By the time three months had passed, there was talk of extending my assignment.

Finding a Home and Safety

So far, every negotiation in Israel had been for the client. The time had come to use those skills for Karen and me. When travelers visit a resort, small problems are often overlooked. Karen and I weren't visiting Israel, we were living there.

By the third month, those small problems had piled up. Our sink backed up, the toilet wouldn't flush, and the shower leaked across the bathroom floor. Changing rooms didn't help. Then came ants under the pillows and flea bites across my legs. I had had enough. My company had dragged their feet for weeks about providing better living conditions and was slow in reimbursing expenses, leaving me thousands of dollars in credit card debt. It wasn't only about placing pressure on me. During the day, the people at the hotel's front desk were harassing Karen about unpaid bills.

With my company unresponsive, I needed a new strategy. When Yoram saw my flea-bitten legs, he was appalled. After hearing what we had endured, arrangements were made for Karen and me to move into one of the most expensive hotels in downtown Jerusalem, just steps from the Old City walls. He asked for patience, and while he pressed from his side, I pressed more creatively from mine.

Better living conditions weren't enough. I wanted Karen's flights covered. To communicate in the only language my managers understood, I assembled a PowerPoint presentation titled "What's A Karen." The slides laid out how much value she brought to the company. Doing my laundry allowed me to spend more time working. Being in Israel saved costs that would otherwise have been expensed. Helping me do material take-offs on weekends went uncompensated by the company. Her contributions more than offset the cost of airfare. When Karen first saw it, she couldn't believe her eyes. For the first time, her worth was in writing, projected onto a screen. The presentation gave her more than validation. It made her feel relevant.

After a few days of sleeping on the most luxurious mattress I had ever known, and dining along the pedestrian mall in the New City, the company finally took us apartment hunting. At first, they didn't try very hard. One of the places we were shown was a tool shed, complete with a rusty lawnmower, an oil-stained concrete floor, and the smell of gasoline. The landlord promised to fix it up with an air conditioner, a bed and a light. For a bathroom and kitchen, we could walk into the main house and share with six other tenants. When I told Yoram about the shed, he extended our stay in the luxury hotel for another week.

By the end of the second week, we moved into a real apartment in the town of Ashkelon overlooking the Mediterranean Sea. Shortly after that, expense reimbursements started flowing, and Karen's flights were finally approved. The battles at work were far from over, but once we settled into an apartment, the immediate crisis was behind us, and life felt a little more manageable.

For Karen, that sense of ease didn't always extend beyond the apartment walls. We learned how aggressive Israelis could be. When I wasn't close, she had to stay constantly on guard. Her blond hair drew unwanted attention from men who didn't know the meaning of boundaries.

While visiting a bathroom in the Old City of Jerusalem, a man cleaning the stalls made lewd gestures. Another time, when I stepped away to use a restroom, she was told to stand close to the military police for safety. Even that didn't stop someone from approaching her, though he quickly backed off when the soldiers noticed. At our apartment pool, if I wasn't around and a man wanted her lane, he told her to move with a rudeness that left no room for debate. Karen learned quickly that in Israel, being polite wasn't enough. She had to stay alert and push back, because if not confronted directly, the harassment could escalate fast.

For me, aggressive members of the opposite sex weren't a problem. On a day she visited the office, female coworkers crowded around my desk. Karen gave me a look that said, *Are you seriously not noticing this?* What she still hadn't figured out was that I carried a secret weapon. My focus on work was absolute, and when it came to women, I had the awareness of a brick wall. Someone could have hit me over the head with a frying pan, and I would have assumed it had something to do with the project budget.

Like any place in the world, some areas were safe and others were not. The challenge was knowing which was which. We learned to keep our car out of orthodox Jewish neighborhoods on the Sabbath, since it was considered disrespectful to use machines on holy days. Stories of tourists having their cars pelted with rocks for driving where they shouldn't be were common.

We also knew to stay on main roads and avoid exploring unfamiliar areas. One sign south of Beersheva warned, "Firing Range on Both Sides of Road." We weren't about to test the danger, but we had a habit of pairing seriousness with a smile. Since the insurance didn't cover broken glass, we joked about rolling the windows down in case a stray round passed through.

As much as the places we encountered shaped our view of the world, so did the TV. Evening news reports warned of Iraqi scud missiles, and during my assignment, the United States bombed Iraq. Concerned about our safety, Karen's cousin called with a question that caught her off guard.

"Can you see the bombs falling from your apartment?"

We were nearly six hundred miles away. Karen glanced at the television, then answered with simple honesty:

"Yes, I can see them on CNN, just like you."

Her response wasn't meant as a joke. It reflected how most people back home understood our lives abroad, filtered through news headlines and television images. While we were broadening our horizons, we were also, in small ways, trying to broaden theirs.

Israeli channels broadcast the Clinton impeachment into our living room. The behavior of the U.S. Congress was embarrassing, and my colleagues couldn't grasp why such a scandal warranted these attacks. To us, the President had clearly crossed a line, but the response in Washington felt out of proportion.

For the first time, we saw our country through the eyes of outsiders. The view wasn't flattering. News coverage rarely lived up to its claim of being balanced, and the stories we saw abroad often contradicted the narrative back home. Today, we don't settle for the domestic version of events. We look at how the rest of the world reports on the United States before deciding what to believe.

Traveling Around and the Journey Home

We continued traveling throughout Israel, visiting every National Park and historic site we could. Each location contained out of the way areas far from any other people. Without a formal tour, we were able to take our time exploring each one. Although all of our trips aren't captured here, the shared experiences kept strengthening who we were as a couple.

In the Golan Heights, decommissioned tanks pointed toward Syria, their turrets silent witnesses to recent wars. At Tiberius, we drove up to the Mount of Beatitude and sat on a bench overlooking the Sea of Galilee. Plaques commemorated sayings from the Sermon on the Mount. At Taghba, where the miracle of the loaves and fishes occurred, fishermen cast long, thin poles into the water, hopeful for a catch. Beyond them, jet skis and parasailers raced across the sea, a reminder that these waters were also a place for modern-day recreation.

To the far south, we stayed in a kibbutz before boarding a yellow submarine. Tropical fish lazily swam by as we peered through tiny port holes. The next day, we crossed into Jordan to visit Petra, one of the Seven Wonders of the World. Stone-carved tombs rose before us as we exited the narrow canyon. At the Treasury, the Indiana Jones filming site, we found the interior only thirty feet deep, smelling faintly of too many tourists who had relieved themselves. Even so, the grandeur of the rose-colored rock left us speechless. Karen wasn't feeling well on the way out, so I negotiated for horses to carry us back to the bus.

In central Israel, at Beit Guvrin, we explored an ancient coliseum, our eyes tracing the platform where a governor once judged lives. Walking through cavernous cisterns and beside ancient olive presses, we felt connected to the people who once called these places home.

On another trip, we toured Megiddo, the site of Armageddon. As we traced the outlines of stone buildings, dark clouds gathered. Thunder rolled across the valley, and cool rain soaked us to the bone. Back at the car, lightning struck where we had just stood. Karen's eyes went wide. She looked at me as if the end of the world really was near.

Living overseas meant navigating the local calendar. Unless invited to join in on the celebrations, holidays could be incredibly boring. Everyone was busy organizing their own family gatherings. For us, local holidays were an opportunity to either spend quiet time alone, or explore. In March of 1999, we chose the latter.

Passover commemorates Moses' flight out of Egypt. Karen and I reversed the concept, fled into Egypt for Passover, and designated our trip as Overpass.

I knew the challenges of blending in while in Israel and thought it might be wise to avoid standing out during our trip. Egyptian men dressed casually, like me. Karen was a different story. While browsing in a small shop attached to the gas station where we were meeting our bus, Karen stared at her blond hair in a mirror, aware that in Egypt it would shine like a beacon among the crowds. We weren't looking for attention. We didn't want attention. She looked down at the table in front of her. A blue knit cap, the kind Orthodox women wore on cold mornings, caught her eye. To her, it was the perfect disguise. I saw danger.

One does not enter the markets of Cairo disguised as an Orthodox Jewish woman. One doesn't go dressed as an Orthodox Jewish anything. It wasn't safe. I gently nodded my disapproval as Karen placed the hat back on the table. Instead, she reached for a modest scarf. The bus was preparing to leave. It would have to do.

We rode across poverty-stricken encampments of the Sinai Peninsula and into Cairo, where the tourist industry was still on edge from recent terrorist attacks. Jeeps with mounted machine guns flanked the bus. If the goal was to make us feel more comfortable, it didn't work.

Once there, we let the magic of the place take over. On the Giza plateau, Karen overcame her claustrophobia to crawl through the dim passages of a pyramid. We circled the Great Sphinx, waiting half-seriously for it to come alive. One evening we floated down the Nile on a dinner cruise as belly dancers and whirling dervishes performed on stage.

Before leaving Cairo, we even stopped at a souvenir shop selling custom paintings on papyrus. A colorful picture of a man and woman dressed in ancient Egyptian clothes standing opposite of each other caught our eye. The shop promised to place my name in hieroglyphics beside the man, and Karen's name in hieroglyphs beside the woman. When the picture was presented to us I noticed something was off. The hieroglyphs were arranged so my name was beside the woman, and Karen's name was beside the man.

I asked the shopkeeper about the error. He looked surprised that a customer could read the symbols on his painting, and admitted to the mistake. As a smile slowly came across his face, he told us the painting was an enduring symbol of love. We looked at him suspiciously.

"You see," he said, "the painting is about how your love is intertwined. It shows Karen's name, then a picture of you facing her followed by your name. Her, you, her, you. We loved his creative story so much that we kept the picture. To this day, it sits in a place of honor over our fireplace.

Upon returning to Israel, the awe we had discovered in Egypt ended quickly. We were dropped at a gas station rest area five miles from Ashkelon, only to find our pre-arranged taxi missing. Karen called the driver, who casually admitted he had forgotten us. Her threats to withhold payment didn't faze him. With no other options during the holiday, we hauled our suitcases several miles along the highway until finally reaching a taxi stand.

Our tiring trek back to Ashkelon showed us how hard Israel could be on people. Nowhere was this more apparent than with one of my coworkers, Dorit. When we were first introduced, I noticed heavy circles under her eyes and a constant aura of exhaustion. Karen didn't know Dorit, but she remarked that I often looked the same. About nine months into my assignment, Dorit took a one-month sabbatical. When she returned, the dark circles were gone. People welcomed her back, commenting on how healthy she looked. Her transformation unsettled me. If one month away from work could make such a difference, what was the place doing to me? That question wouldn't be answered for another twenty years.

With one month remaining on my contract, Yoram asked if I wanted to stay. The assignment had lasted just short of one year, and any further extension would have costly tax implications. I knew my work made an impact, but the extra taxes made the cost too high. It took some convincing, but Yoram agreed.

Taxes weren't the only reason. Spending such long days alone in the apartment was starting to wear on Karen. While I fought valiant battles at work, she had her own battles in the apartment. Broken elevators meant climbing eleven stories to get to our front door. Electricity outages meant no air conditioning. Plumbing problems meant strange odors to try to mask.

With a bit of grumbling she could mostly handle all those things, but one item crossed a line. Karen enjoyed doing laundry. Clean clothes brought her a sense of comfort and stability. When another woman in the building aggressively confronted her for no reason, or she found her wet clothes sitting on top of the dryer before the timer ended, it became too much. I needed to get her back to a more civilized environment.

Before we left, the client made sure to recognize my contributions and the sacrifices of the past year. Over the course of three weeks, they honored me with a picnic, a signed coffee table book, and three separate plaques. To top it off, I was given a cash bonus. Client recognitions like these were unheard of, and for me it had happened three times. As the final awards were gathered, I could tell Karen felt overlooked. She had contributed to my success too. We would be heading home soon, and her day was coming. For now, kind words and warm hugs would have to suffice.

For our very last weekend in Israel, Karen and I stayed in a kibbutz at the south end of the Sea of Galilee. By this time, the pressure of work had faded. We spent the day visiting various religious sites and were tired out. The cabin had two chairs outside the front door. On that warm evening, we sat together, watching stars appear while the dark outlines of bats fluttered across the sky. Happy in our travels, I looked over at Karen and asked,

"Is this as good as it gets?"

Neither of us had an answer for that question. I didn't want to forget the moment. In years to come, that simple question became a common phrase. It reminded us to appreciate what we had, and to enjoy the present. The next day we returned to Ashkelon and prepared to say our final goodbyes.

This project assignment had been tough on both Karen and me. Over the past year, we had developed a love-hate relationship with Israel. My frequent negotiations and her long, lonely days were often balanced by professional growth and unforgettable experiences. Evenings could be as peaceful as watching the sun's rays light up the clouds as the setting sun descended into the sea, or as maddening as chasing mosquitoes through our apartment, their bites itching for days.

Of my two international assignments, Israel was the warmest, the most difficult, and the most rewarding. When we left in early July 1999, I was glad to be returning home, but sad to be leaving people I had fought so hard for.

CHAPTER 12

BACK HOME

While still in Israel, management spoke with me about possible next assignments. The day after returning to the United States, anxious for any hint about what the future might hold, I stopped by the downtown office. Thoughts of congratulatory plaques and awards from prior weeks filled my head. As the lobby doors swung open, I pictured trumpets sounding triumphantly as hordes of grateful cubicle dwellers cheered my name. That's not what I got. At the front desk, a receptionist looked at me blankly and said,

"Who are you?"

Who am I? Who am I? I am he who has conquered foreign lands.

Realizing that approach wouldn't work, I humbly explained who I was and asked what floor my department manager's desk was on. She dismissively directed me to the seventh floor and returned her attention to the constant sound of ringing phones. When the department manager saw me, there were no polite greetings, just the question,

"What are you doing here?"

What am I doing here? At least he knew who I was.

Out of sight, out of mind. That saying had never felt more true. Talk about the next assignment had been just that, talk. There was no job waiting. There was no desk. When I asked for two weeks of vacation, he almost seemed relieved. Upon leaving the office, a disturbing realization settled in. I had spent three years working long hours and proving my worth, but I had proven it to a client, not the home office. To them, my name and reputation meant nothing.

From Home to Home

I wasn't going to let the less-than-enthusiastic welcome rattle me. There was much to do besides waiting for work to appear, and it started with getting my personal affairs in order. Ever since she first joined me in Ireland, I'd been covering Karen's bills. We each owned a condominium. It wasn't practical to keep paying two mortgages, especially without the benefit of expense report reimbursements. Our lives had merged, and only one residence was needed. We made a list of pros and cons.

There were strong feelings as to why the other person's place should be sold, but one thing stood out. Karen's condo featured a separate laundry room with a full-sized washer and dryer. Mine offered only a stacked machine in a small closet. Laundry gave Karen comfort. Selling my condo was a small way to acknowledge her many sacrifices.

With that decision made, our attention shifted to family. It had been a long time since I visited Pittsburgh, and except for emails and phone calls, my family didn't know much about the wonderful woman I'd spent the last three years with. We stayed at the house I grew up in, and Karen's love of desserts immediately connected with my mother. She did the typical mom thing, pulling out childhood photos, which felt a little out of place for a thirty-four year old.

At the racetrack, my father was in his element. He turned on the charm and made polite small talk over a meal of steak and crab. When Karen stepped down to the paddock with his fifth wife, it gave us some time alone. Our conversation drifted to the betting. He seemed lost, not quite sure what to say to a son who had clearly become his own man.

The next day, we visited Rick. He politely flipped through photos of our travels while talking about his band and complaining about his ex-wife. His legs sprawled across the couch, leaving me scrunched in a corner. It was his way of reminding me he was my "big brother." The behavior didn't faze me, and I still shake my head at the memory. Back at the house, my brother John told Karen I didn't know how to grill. Since she had watched me master the art of cooking over charcoal in Ireland, his comment made no sense.

We were glad to be meeting everyone, but one thing took us off guard. I'd been away exploring Ireland, England, Israel, Egypt, and Jordan. My professional responsibilities had grown. Yet nobody asked any questions about any of it, and it felt as if they didn't care. Karen smiled through meeting everyone, but I could tell she sensed it, too. My family remained frozen in time. To them, the man who had worked overseas was invisible. Only the memory of a small boy remained.

When we returned to Portland, I made a quick stop at the office. My department's workload still seemed light, and there weren't any projects available. The thought of being laid off felt like a real possibility. I told Karen she may need to get a job. Concerns about having fallen behind with computer skills didn't stop her from pushing forward. When she called her old boss to let him know other companies might call for a reference, he hired her on the spot.

***

The next day was Karen's birthday. We were talking casually in the condo when I asked a simple question.

"How would you like to go to the jewelry store?"

She looked up, surprised but not startled. "Sure," she said.

That was it. Proposal made. Proposal accepted. No candlelight dinner. No mariachi band. Dropping to one knee would have made her eyes roll. How I proposed was plain, maybe even forgettable. For her, it was perfect.

We got in the car, headed to the jewelry store, and bought a ring.

***

The condo sale, the trip to Pittsburgh, and the engagement provided welcome distractions from the comedy of errors at work. At one point, management rushed me across the country to escort contractors on a bid walk. No one showed up. Although the home office supposedly coordinated the visit in advance, I only received a string of apologies. It was a symptom of a bigger issue. Compared to my experiences overseas, my company lacked critical organization and communication skills. My managers focused less on preventing problems and more on reacting to them.

After a few months without any promising project opportunities, a call came in. The company dispatched me to North Phoenix, where a construction manager's recent sudden departure had left a staffing shortage. Responsibilities weren't discussed. They could be figured out upon arrival.

Karen wasn't too thrilled since she had recently started back to work, but she knew the rules of the game. I check out the terrain. She follows. Change and the ability to adapt were the only constants in my career. We'd proven success at managing it in the past, and felt confident we could do it again.

A False Start

Years earlier, a mentor had taught me to ask one question when filling a vacant position. Why did the person before me leave? Colleagues said the prior construction manager left because of the client. No one gave details about what had occurred except to say conditions at the site were intolerable. I knew the person who left. He had a solid reputation, but there was no way to contact him. They also mentioned that a senior manager from the Portland office would arrive with me to investigate project finances.

There wasn't an organist playing ominous music, but there should have been. Within the first few days, alarms were already sounding. The project manager greeted me like a man caught with his hand in the cookie jar. He explained my responsibilities, then guided me to a small office. A whiteboard displaying change order numbers and their status hung on one wall. Our client, Bob, casually leaned back in his chair. He greeted the project manager warmly, then turned his attention to me. He muttered something in a heavy Scottish accent I could not follow. The introduction felt like a reprimand, as if I had done something wrong before the plane even landed.

My job involved shepherding a handful of contractors through a cafeteria retrofit. There were no drawings to review, no contracts to issue, no invoices to negotiate. After settling in, I let out a deep sigh. Sketchy managers, hostile clients, and low levels of responsibility didn't inspire enthusiasm, but the job was only supposed to be for a few months, so I thought, "How bad could it be?"

After one week, I flew back to Oregon to drive Karen, our newly purchased truck, and the motorcycle to Arizona. As the truck pulled into the apartment parking lot, uncertainty filled our heads. The company had started to hint at relocating from Oregon. Neither of us felt comfortable moving, and preferred having the company cover all our living expenses. With my department being slow, this was not the time to make waves. Besides, nothing had been firmly decided yet. Project requirements shifted like desert sands, and I wasn't about to push back on something that might not even be real.

While our future home might have been in question, temporary housing was not. In those days, my company often rented multiple apartments for traveling staff. We settled into a two-bedroom, two-bathroom unit. Our roommate was the senior manager tasked with auditing the project's suspicious finances. He seemed as uncomfortable sharing the living space with us as we felt sharing it with him. Fortunately, he left for work before we woke up and didn't return until after bedtime.

As weeks progressed, the senior manager dug deeper into the financials. Tension on the site was high, and I came to understand why my predecessor had left. The client made life at work miserable by berating my efforts on a daily basis. Karen's steady presence helped, but his unwarranted attacks wore on me. My company's managers ignored the unwarranted tirades against me. They may have been focused on their own problems, but I interpreted their silence as validation of the abuse. It became a lasting lesson in the importance of protecting staff. Karen could see how unhappy I was. We began meeting for lunch to seriously discuss looking for a new job.

I can't say why I stayed. The project environment had rattled me. Maybe it was because the assignment only had one month to go. Maybe I began to doubt if any other company would recognize my international experience. Maybe I simply didn't like giving up, or maybe I found inspiration in an unlikely place.

One day, Karen called from the apartment in a panic. A scorpion dropped onto the floor in front of her. Thinking scorpions were deadly, I asked one of my colleagues for advice. They smiled and said, "Have her put on her shoes and step on it." Apparently, scorpions were not as dangerous as we feared. Surviving this project might require a similar shift in strategy. If Karen could slay her beast, perhaps I could, too.

The next day at work, instead of calmly handling business as usual, I picked up a clipboard, messed up my hair, put on my best worried look, and hurried past the client's office. He briefly looked up, but I kept moving and said, "No time. Emergency!" Once out of view, I returned to my normal self. The next time I saw him, I repeated the worried look. There was no yelling, only a respectful nod of approval. The tactic was absurd, almost comical, but it worked.

A path for surviving the job had been established, even if putting on a show went against everything I believed in. Projects were supposed to be about professionally accomplishing work, not acting. My view of clients and project behavior was changing. I didn't realize the senior manager had noticed the reduced client volatility toward me. He assumed I was doing something right, and there was no reason to give away my secret.

After two months, the job wound down. Both the project manager and the client were fired by their respective organizations. Although I made it to the end, the stress of being someone I wasn't in an unprofessional environment had taken its toll. Whatever glory I'd chased overseas had long since faded. Karen and I flew back to Portland for three weeks off to reset.

Karen knew I needed time to think. Once her old boss found out she had returned, he hired her. He knew her stay depended on my job and wanted her anyway. While she worked, I devoted myself to the noble arts of TV, scratch-its, and beer.

The universe usually doesn't involve itself with trivial matters. In my case, it made an exception. At the end of each day, Karen asked how successful my playing scratch-its was. Every day the answer came back the same. I won.

By the end of three weeks, I had firmly re-established myself as a winner. With luck on my side and a clear head, we flew back to Arizona, unsure of the future. Good news awaited. Relocation discussions had vanished, and a new project in Phoenix needed help.

Lines in the Sand

The new project wasn't exactly new. Design was complete, but construction had not yet started. An invite appeared on my calendar for what looked like a routine hand-off meeting. I entered the conference room, took my seat, and looked around a table filled with unfamiliar faces. It was the beginning of December, my first Christmas season in the United States in three years. As the meeting started, the atmosphere felt more like the Fourth of July than Christmas.

The client lit up the room with expletives, complaining about his company, our company, and everything in between. He bragged about recently clawing his way through an internal power struggle and declared himself in charge. What he didn't realize was what his predecessor had done. To meet the budget, the previous manager had cut interior painting, carpeting, and furniture. For thirty minutes the client berated the engineering team, then leaned forward, eyes blazing, and demanded to know how this disaster had happened. He accused my company of being complicit. The design manager, his face now the color of a stop sign, locked eyes with the client and in a firm voice said,

"I just fucked up."

The words weren't an admission of guilt so much as a way to slam the brakes on the tirade. Silence fell. The design manager stood, gathered his things and walked out as if that settled it. Nobody spoke to a client that way, which only made it funnier. Especially not one wound so tight. The client frantically looked around the room, not knowing what to do. He had fought his way into control, only to inherit a hollow shell with no paint, no carpet, no furniture, and the task of explaining it to his own company.

I had just come from a job with a volatile client, and at first glance, this project looked just as unstable. It wasn't. The other managers in the room ended the show quickly, and after the client left, they explained their plan. The politics belonged to them. My job was to review the drawings, contract the remaining work, and get the construction started. A sense of relief washed over me. This wasn't going to be like the North Phoenix job. On this job, my skills might be useful and have meaning.

The first contract lined up represented one of my more successful negotiations. The contractor's name was Mark, and he was the only bidder. After reviewing his proposal, I returned it, and said it wasn't good enough. He looked slightly dejected, and before he could speak, I continued, "Your rates aren't high enough." I'd managed companies like his before, and thought he had undervalued his work. He could add ten percent to the rates, but I wanted something in return. These projects always had overtime, often amounting to twenty percent extra. I didn't want to see one change order.

Mark usually expected clients to beat his rates down. My offer to increase his billing came as a surprise, and he immediately agreed. During the project, the crew worked at least twenty percent overtime, but it didn't matter. Mark felt I had treated him fairly, so he ensured his team delivered top-notch service.

The main contractor onsite was from New Mexico. I hadn't worked with them before. They were known for quality work, and we got along well. That made my job easier. Only once did they catch me off guard.

While talking with the foreman one afternoon, he casually mentioned a budget his company had set aside for entertaining me. He didn't propose anything specific, yet the implication was clear. I knew the rules. A ballgame or dinner could be acceptable if modest, infrequent, and never tied to a favor. A dedicated budget signaled a breach of ethics. On past projects, I had seen other contractors test boundaries by suggesting trips to the United Kingdom or memberships to private clubs. Some managers accepted, but not me. I refused even the appearance of impropriety and made sure the foreman understood my position.

I wasn't the only one dealing with questionable practices. To help contribute to our expenses, Karen took a temporary job in Arizona. She soon learned that other admins added personal items to requisitions after they had been signed. Senior managers didn't seem to care. When she told me, I knew she shouldn't stay there.

A few weeks later, a plant-wide evacuation forced everyone into the blazing sun. Employees stood in the middle of an asphalt parking lot. Policy barred their return until the senior manager arrived from off-site. The heat reminded Karen of Israel, where her face had turned purple from overexposure. When panic started setting in, she called me, torn between my potential reaction and her desire to quit.

She didn't need my permission. Karen already had my full support. A protective instinct kicked in and I told her to leave. We both agreed she didn't need to stay in a place that treated people that way. Instead of returning to her desk, she confidently went to the car and left.

The temp agency gave her a black mark. We didn't care. Her health and safety mattered more.

Outside of work, Arizona had its lighter moments. My assignment provided an extra benefit, and this one didn't feel sketchy. No longer being confined to a company apartment gave us the freedom to rent our own place. We chose a unit facing a golf course. On cool evenings, I walked the perimeter fence and pocketed dozens of wayward balls. By the time we were preparing to leave, I had hundreds.

Those small diversions filled some downtime, but bigger adventures soon came our way. In January, a surprise visitor appeared whose idea of fun didn't include hunting for golf balls. Yoram arrived from Israel to audit his company's Arizona factory. He asked if Karen and I would join him on a trip to Las Vegas. His company had the same rules about gifts, and he insisted on paying his share. I wouldn't have had it any other way.

Standing at the slot machines, I decided to run a small experiment. Karen, Yoram, and I lined up with cups of quarters. As each pulled the lever, bells and whistles rang. They let their credits ride until the machine drained them to zero. I played the same way with one twist. After every spin, I cashed out. The clinking coins sang their victory song with every payout, no matter how small. Karen and Yoram eyed me suspiciously, wondering how I could be so "lucky." I hadn't actually won. I lost my quarters just like they did. My losing just sounded better.

Las Vegas wasn't our only trip. We hadn't explored the Southwest before and approached it with the same excitement we'd brought to Ireland and Israel. In Tombstone, we strolled down the dusty street and into an old west saloon. Along Route 66, we snapped a selfie while standing on a corner in Winslow, Arizona. After Karen convinced me the Grand Canyon was more than just a big hole in the ground, we took a train, complete with a masked holdup re-enactment. From the rim, we watched passing thunderstorm clouds sweep along the Colorado River far below.

Just like on our prior travels, Karen and I wanted to share our excitement with family and friends. The new adventures prompted more letter writing. Assembling the letters was no small event and could take over a week. I did the writing, then Karen edited. We included handwritten messages so every letter contained a personal touch. Before sealing the envelope, we added coins, petrified rocks, or anything we could think of to share our experience.

Responses to our efforts varied. My mother mostly thanked us during my weekly call to her. Other family members rarely responded. When we received one response, it changed how I viewed writing. A few weeks after sending out tales of our Arizona travels, a letter arrived from my father. He wrote that we should stop sending him "form letters."

Form letters?

Each letter contained personal notes and questions meant to engage the recipient. I didn't appreciate his criticism, and stopped writing to my father. Since we weren't receiving responses from anyone else, other family members wouldn't hear from us as much either. It didn't stop us from documenting our journeys. Future letters were written for the benefit of ourselves, and not for anyone else.

The Road Less Traveled

In May 2000, our lives shifted toward thoughts of marriage. We considered delaying, but a practical reason pushed us forward. The company hinted at sending me overseas. If that happened, I wanted Karen's expenses covered without question. In the past, when I had asked them to pay for her airfare to Israel, they told me to get married. When I explained how my assignments hadn't allowed time for that, they flippantly suggested I get married in Tel Aviv. Not being Jewish made that impossible.

Beside the company constantly keeping me on the move, consideration for our guests was the next most challenging obstacle. Karen's family lived in Oregon, mine were scattered across the country, and nobody lived in Arizona. In our minds, every name came with a reason why they wouldn't attend. My father was broke and struggling setting up a new practice. My mother wouldn't get on a plane, not even to see her own grandchildren. John still drank too much and rarely wandered far from home. Mike's letters carried cutting barbs that neither Karen nor I appreciated. Rick always complained child support left him poor. Kathy had a three-year-old and nothing to spare.

Karen's side didn't fare much better. Our other friends were scattered around the world, and even if they had money, distance made it unlikely they would come. We refused to place the burden of travel on them, and didn't want the embarrassment of empty seats.

I had always imagined a big wedding surrounded by friends and family, but the reality of our situation made that impossible. Karen had already been married before and she wasn't looking for anything extravagant. With my work keeping me on call at a moment's notice, we needed a ceremony that could be arranged quickly and adjusted at a moment's notice to match whatever the company required.

We only sent wedding announcements, not invitations. The lack of response to our upcoming marriage affirmed the decision to have the wedding the way we did. At work, the project manager asked what the minimum amount of time my new bride would accept for a honeymoon. I wasn't foolish enough to ask that question.

As for wedding presents, my mother sent small gifts like bubbles and candy. They felt more suited for a child than for a married couple. My father sent nothing except a card saying, no invite, no gift, and Karen's sister sent a card that said she couldn't congratulate her on remarrying. As of our wedding day, that was it.

The less than spectacular responses didn't shake or surprise us. They made us realize that as a couple, we had become an island. We were okay with that.

Karen and I were married in September by a Justice of the Peace on the Oregon coast. No guests attended. We convinced a passerby strolling the shore to act as an official witness. Since time didn't permit arranging a wedding in Hawaii, Karen ordered leis from Honolulu. They served as a reminder of what our wedding might have been under different circumstances.

That evening we dined at a nearby restaurant, still in our Hawaiian shirts and leis. As we walked in, heads turned, not with smiles but with the kind of side-eye reserved for outsiders. During the meal, we chose to ignore our surroundings, and instead focused on each other.

Traveling so much had stopped making hotels special, so we pitched a tent in an adjacent campground. Toasted marshmallows created the perfect dessert. The evening ended staring up at the stars, just like the first night we met. We were happy, in love, and the day met our definition of perfect.

The next morning, we made coffee over an open fire, and spent the day playing on the sand. After the second night, our backs were sore from the hard, uneven ground, and the early morning air chilled our breath. Neither one of us wanted to spend another night in those conditions. We booked a beachfront spa room near an outlet mall, bought our own wedding gifts, and spent time watching the waves crashing on the shore.

When I returned to work, the contractors greeted me with warm congratulations. They needed my help. The client had been testing their patience by leaving Post-It notes everywhere he spotted a punch list item. Wrapping up the job became my top priority.

Paint in the newly renovated reception area had to match the original wall color, but no matter how many samples the contractor tried, they were told it came out too light or too dark. Apparently, thirty years of dirt and grime is a hard color to match. As a last resort, I directed the contractor to paint the entire room. When the owner returned for his inspection, he beamed. "This paint matches perfectly. I can't tell the difference." The contractor smiled. So, did I. We had our approval.

Everyone considered the job a success, including my company's project manager. Over the past year, his main role had been visiting the site for a few days each month, receiving my updates, fluffing the owner, and submitting monthly invoices. Managing contractor coordination, site safety, schedules, permitting, change orders, quality, warranties, and invoices all fell to me. He had his role, and I had mine. We got along well, and we both knew who really ran the work.

My efforts caught the attention of someone else. The CEO of the company sent a handwritten letter on his personal stationery, thanking me for making the project a success. I couldn't believe it. The person running a multi-billion-dollar company took time out of his day to thank me. I framed the note as a reminder that no matter how high I rise, there is always time to say thank you.

My success also earned recognition from senior managers in Oregon. As a reward, they offered a choice of assignments. One option involved a similar factory in Texas. I didn't really like the opportunity, but the work would be familiar. The other choice led to Taiwan. The company provided little information about the project except that Bill Steadman, the man who opened the door to my construction management career, worked there.

By this time, a pattern had formed. Nobody in my company had wanted Israel, Baltimore, North Phoenix, or even the project I had just finished. Inconvenient locations, difficult clients, and cleaning up messes seemed to be my lot. Texas felt as foreign as Taiwan, but only one of them would move my career forward. My identity in the company was clear. I took the jobs nobody else wanted and found a way to make them work.

Before an answer could be given, I had some final questions. Were there people available who were willing to go to Texas? Yes. More than enough. Were there people willing to go to Taiwan? No. Not a single one. My response?

Send me to Taiwan!

CHAPTER 13

TAIWAN

Arriving in Taiwan left Karen and me completely lost. Since we traveled together, there was no chance to prepare her for what awaited us. We had entered uncharted territory. Even family rarely responded to our mail. That didn't stop me from writing. Looking back, one letter captured our disorientation better than anything I could write now.

A train from Taipei, loaded with young soldiers, winds through a landscape covered with a strange mix of industrial factories and rice fields. Red envelopes rain down from the sky. As the journey ends, Tang Dynasty tri-colored horses prance through the streets in celebration. If you do not understand the beginning of this letter, you have taken your first step toward understanding our adventures in Taiwan. If you actually do understand the beginning of this letter, you are disturbed and should seek medical help. Thus, a very auspicious beginning to a very auspicious letter is complete.

Letter from Taiwan – 2001

Settling In

On the flight from Oregon, some wise, unnamed manager decided that everyone traveling to Asia could fly business class. We were pampered unlike any trip before with wide seats that fully reclined, gourmet meals with real silverware, and a private escort to speed us through the connecting airport in Hong Kong. This high-altitude luxury made it all the more jarring when we touched down in Taiwan and realized that by crossing the International Date Line a full day had been lost.

The Oriental Hotel stood near the center of Tainan in the southern part of the island. We were exhausted after the long journey, and grateful the hotel staff were so polite. They endearingly greeted me by my first name, as Mr. Daniel, and then escorted us to our room. The space was no larger than a walk-in closet, yet it held everything needed to be comfortable.

After a short nap, we stepped outside to explore our new world. The stores on both sides of the street were covered in neon signs with a confusing display of Chinese characters. Hundreds of scooters wove in and out of traffic. Several mounted the sidewalks, cutting in front of us to park or dodge obstacles. Their horns never stopped beeping. Every honk caused me to scan the surroundings for any impending danger. In the air, the smell of exhaust, cigarettes, and rotting seafood added to our discomfort. No other westerners were in sight, and our presence drew stares that reminded us how far from home we really were. After cautiously exploring one block in each direction, we still recognized nothing and retreated to the safety of our room.

Within the city of one million people, there were at least two familiar faces. Bill, the man who had encouraged me to change careers and become a construction manager, was now the office manager in Tainan. My scuba diving friend Lee worked there as well. That night, Bill reached out. The invitation to his apartment seemed polite, though I came to view it as a test. He offered no ride for the one-mile journey and expected us to walk. Not yet able to make sense of the streets or signs, we took a taxi instead.

At his apartment, Bill spent most of the evening smoking on the balcony with Lee, leaving me sidelined. While I tried joining into the conversation, his wife cornered Karen. Nancy immediately demanded her passport to see how old she was, and then made an unusual remark. She said, "You know, when I knew Dan in Massachusetts I could have had him." Karen was stunned. She had already been warned about Nancy's games and refused to take the bait. If a married woman had ever tried something, Karen knew my personality wouldn't have allowed it.

After an hour or so, Bill asked if we wanted a ride back to the hotel. He seemed irritated when we said yes. By the time the evening ended, it became clear the gathering aimed less at welcoming us and more at showing us our places. The message landed differently than they intended.

When the work week started, a different type of welcome provided some relief. Two local employees from the office picked me up at the hotel. They took the assignment of teaching me Taiwanese driving behaviors, showing me how to find the office, and answering any question I could think of. Linda and Shawn both spoke English well, and were invaluable during those early days. There were none of the games I had encountered at Bill's apartment. They treated me like I belonged from day one.

While I navigated the office culture, Karen faced her own challenge at the hotel. She spent her days accompanying an estate agent to find a more permanent place to stay.

Most of that first week blurred together, except for a visit from one of Portland's senior construction managers. On the elevator ride back to my room, he said, "I don't have time for your yearly review. Bottom line is you're low maintenance. You've done great. You are way underpaid." Then he pressed an envelope into my hand. By the time I looked up, the manager had vanished.

In the room, Karen and I opened the envelope together. Inside, we found a double-digit pay increase. For a moment, I just stared. After years of taking the assignments no one else wanted, the payoff finally felt real. That raise tipped the scales on the decision about where to live.

Two main housing choices emerged. One apartment building sat very close to Bill and Nancy. It didn't look as nice, but Karen and I could have made it work. The second choice, a five-story townhome, exceeded our budget. It had polished quartz floors, built-in wood cabinetry, and a private garage. The owner had lived in the U.S. and decorated the townhome accordingly. The estate agent made us promise never to show it to anyone. She knew how angry the other

Americans in my company would be if they found out we had a nicer place than theirs. I had no problem pitching in some of our own money if it meant more comfortable surroundings.

"Comfortable" was a subjective term. We knew the city had pests, and only once did any of them make it into our home. A flying cockroach the size of my hand invaded the bedroom. Memory fails me on how I disposed of the beast, but I picture myself battling it like a lion tamer, clutching a chair in one hand and a whip in the other.

To avoid more unwelcome visitors, learning about trash disposal became a critical life skill. Every day, as a truck slowly moved down the street, small businesses and homeowners rushed outside to heave their bags into the truck. To signal its arrival, the truck played a chiming melody over a loudspeaker that sounded more like an ice cream man than a garbage collector.

Settling in required one final task. Taiwan's heat and humidity are brutally oppressive. Our townhome was a mile away from any store, and I didn't want Karen walking through the heat. With some help from Linda and Shawn, we bought a scooter. Karen had ridden on the back of my motorcycle before, but had never driven a scooter. She mastered the controls quickly, and even found an authentic Barbie scooter on the top shelf of a small shop to pair with the Travel Barbie she had purchased on the way to the Canary Islands years earlier.

The driving habits in Taiwan weren't even close to anything we had experienced while living in other countries. I wrote about what it was like in a letter.

One of the most challenging parts of living in Taiwan is the driving, and the main source of transportation in the cities is a scooter with an engine size between 50cc and 150cc. The scooters weave in and out of traffic in a manner closely resembling bees coming and going around a hive. With sometimes as many as four small children clinging onto their mother, the scooters often travel in the wrong lane and wrong direction, all in a carefree fashion.

Cars and trucks aren't much better, but because of their size, they do not have the ability to move as freely. Red lights are optional and need only be followed if driving in larger cities, in areas using random traffic light cameras, or if there is a policeman around. In the city, narrow streets are lined with cars double-parked in front of stores. Double parking is acceptable as long as your hazard lights are on, and at least one lane of traffic can get by in each direction. Turning in front of other vehicles is also very acceptable, regardless of the color of the traffic light. The rule for cutting off your fellow drivers is that it is okay as long as the actions of your car are continuous and predictable. After having only been in Taiwan for a week, I was given a rental car and told to think of driving in Taiwan like flowing water.

Descriptions of the driving here sound like total chaos, but the system is surprisingly efficient. Unlike driving in the U.S.A, we have not ever heard of road rage, or seen one person swearing behind the wheel of their car. There is a good share of the occasional fender bender, but Taiwan encourages the people to solve these minor accidents privately, and the tangle of insurance companies and lawyers is not prevalent. I actually like the driving system here much better than in the U.S.A. Karen says she will not let me drive much when we return home, because I'll probably end up with numerous tickets, and a few bullets through the car from road raged nut cases.

Letter from Taiwan - 2001

Work and Adjusting

The project site was located forty minutes south of Tainan in the countryside. The office complex consisted of two single-wide trailers stacked on top of each other. The owner occupied the upper trailer, while I shared the downstairs desks with the rest of the managers. Everyone removed their muddy boots inside the door and tucked them into cubbies. As the only American on-site, I moved toward an empty desk while seven blank faces turned and stared.

My colleagues assumed that because the company flew me halfway around the world, I must hold some importance. Among them, one had survived the Hiroshima bombing, another collected stamps and went by the nickname "Weapon", one prepared for marriage, and one possessed a relatable dark sense of humor. Once they realized I wasn't a corporate spy, we became friends.

With papers scattered across the trailer, I quickly faced an early challenge. Contracts, drawings, schedules, and invoices were in a mixture of Chinese and English. Professional translation cost too much, and learning the language took too long. Somehow, I had to find a way to decipher the piles of incomprehensible documents and keep the work moving. Noticing my concern, one of the managers suggested focusing on what I could understand, and not worrying about the rest. The others, who were all bilingual, started to laugh. His words sounded questionable, but they worked.

After orientation, I walked the site. Most of the concrete and steel were already in place. My assignment involved overseeing the cleanroom installation. A superintendent escorted me to my area, and immediately I could see more challenges. Workers used the ladders like stilts to hang wires and install sprinkler piping. During breaks, men in bare feet stretched out to rest on cardboard sheets, while ungodly food smells filled the stairwells. Further along, loosely tied bamboo poles replaced the steel scaffolding I expected. Power cords stretched across the walking paths creating unavoidable tripping hazards. In Oregon, I had previously sat through multiple safety classes. The training proved useful in Ireland and Israel, where American clients followed U.S. safety rules. If there were safety rules in Taiwan, I couldn't see them.

I had received warnings about this. Even though the owner was an American company and wanted to follow American safety standards, Bill told me trying to change the local practices in a day would only cause stress. He directed me to follow the lead of my colleagues. His advice didn't make me comfortable. A project either followed U.S. standards or it did not. The site's choice appeared obvious.

In the afternoon, I attended my first meeting. The contractors all communicated in Mandarin. At one point, the leader noticed me and asked the room to switch to English. The participants mangled the grammar so thoroughly that after ten minutes, I realized they couldn't understand each other any better than I could understand them. I politely told the group to skip the English, assuring them I wouldn't take offense. Once the conversation switched back to Mandarin, I sat quietly and nodded whenever attention turned my way. Discussions requiring my input happened before or after the meeting, rather than during it.

As the weeks passed, my purpose in Taiwan became clearer. Before my arrival, a nearby project had run into legal trouble, causing the Oregon managers to lose faith in both the local staff and the Americans on that job. Consequently, sending me to Taiwan had more to do with safeguarding the company's interests than overseeing the cleanroom. They needed an American with integrity on the ground. It felt good knowing the home office thought of me that way.

My time shifted away from developing professional skills and focused on helping however possible. Occasionally, I covered the site on weekends. Everyone took their turn. I didn't mind the hours, but the knowledge that the contractors spoke no English stayed with me. If something happened, I couldn't help. My colleagues told me not to worry and claimed the workers knew what to do if problems appeared. Sitting in the trailers on those weekends felt like a charade, but if that's what the site needed, they could count on me.

Not being able to develop new professional skills should have bothered me, but it didn't. The work lacked stress. Career aspirations took a backseat to the exciting new experiences. One of those exciting new experiences was business entertainment.

One evening, several managers insisted I join them and a contractor for dinner. They knew I preferred spending evenings with Karen alone, but labeled the event "important for business." Out of respect, I agreed.

After an uneventful dinner, a hostess led us into a private room. Our group consisted of ten men, who all settled onto velvet couches with carafes of whiskey waiting on individual tables. At the front, a karaoke machine gleamed. I was the only westerner in the room and silently hoped they wouldn't ask me to perform *American Pie*, the way the Irish had once done. I didn't realize it yet, but singing would be the least of my worries.

As conversation started and cigars appeared, a beautiful girl in a shimmering gold dress came in and sat next to one of the men. Another in a flowing green gown followed. My mind raced. *Were we allowed to bring our wives? Had I made a mistake?* Then more women arrived. When one sat beside me, it finally clicked. These were not their wives.

The girl beside me poured a whiskey and grabbed my hand. She didn't speak English, and I didn't speak Chinese. Words weren't needed. As her fingers lightly traced outlines in my palm, I finished my glass. Once empty, she filled it again. I remember hearing the karaoke machine start up and thinking, I need to call my wife and let her know about this.

During a break, I stepped out for a brief moment to make the call. Instinct told me there might be more on offer, but I had no interest in exploring it. What my instincts hadn't prepared me for was how Karen would respond. After hearing about my evening, she started to cry. I thought calling would ease her mind, but it only made things worse.

She begged me to leave. I didn't understand the urgency, but complied anyway. Upon returning to the room, many of the men had vanished. I doubted they had gone home. The remaining men were still having a great time. To make sure the host would not lose face, I patiently waited for the right moment, and then politely slipped out.

Back home, Karen started to cry and hugged me hard. I looked at her and asked, "Don't you trust me? I called you. What husband does that?" Tears turned to laughter. Her reaction had nothing to do with suspicion and everything to do with love. Beyond just honesty, she wanted to be together. Clueless as I could be, the feeling was mutual.

There were other places my lack of awareness showed up. Several months after our arrival to Taiwan, my hair started looking scruffy. Asking where to get a trim seemed innocent enough, and the other managers were quick to offer advice. Their advice came with a warning. Men's haircuts, they explained, could come with extras. Attractive young women might give you a massage. Sometimes it went further, finishing with what they politely called a "happy ending." Every man in the trailer smiled at the description, which told me plenty.

That evening I told Karen the story over dinner, as I always did. Her eyes went wide. She had already heard a few local customs from the women she lunched with, and this one did not sit well. I shrugged it off as another oddity of life overseas and finished my meal.

After dinner, Karen came out with a pair of scissors and announced she would be giving me my first haircut. I never did see the inside of a Taiwan barber shop, and I still can't confirm whether the stories were true. What I did know is that Karen wasn't going to take any chances. Twenty-five years later, she is still cutting my hair. What began as protection became a ritual of love. I never missed the barber, because as long as I had Karen, I already had my happy ending.

Beyond the domestic adjustments, there were other cultural practices we had to learn. Every fifteen days, businesses and homes followed the lunar calendar with customs we learned to respect. On store sidewalks and in front of the construction trailer where I worked, people arranged tables with offerings of fruit, tea, chickens, and sometimes even beer or Pringles potato chips. Next to the tables, metal containers held stacks of fake paper money that were set on fire. At first, I heard the burning sent wealth to ancestors in the spirit world. Later I learned some believed it kept wandering ghosts content or brought prosperity to businesses.

Our own townhouse contained a barrel in the garage for money-burning. The estate agent told us about a foreigner who once mistook the ritual for a trash incinerator and tossed his garbage inside. The neighbors nearly killed him for the insult. We doubted the story, but it made us laugh, and it drove home an important lesson. Gestures made in innocence could easily be mistaken as disrespect.

With these traditions so visible and openly practiced, I became more aware of how people looked at me, too. There were times in my life where I struggled to be seen. Taiwan wasn't like that. At one point at work, when the other managers were away from the trailer, I noticed one of my company's project assistants giving me a strange look. I casually asked what she was looking at. At first, she appeared embarrassed. It was my arm. She said the men she knew did not have hair on their arms and asked if it was ok to touch me. It surprised me, but I didn't mind, even if it felt a bit like I was a zoo animal.

Being different extended beyond the construction site. It occurred any time we walked out our front door. To capture what that felt like, I'll let my younger self once again speak through a letter written in 2001.

The one part that we will probably never get used to is being constantly stared at by strangers. In Tainan, there are not many Westerners, and we are definitely a minority. We do not ever feel discriminated against. The people of Taiwan are extremely friendly, but it still feels strange to have small children point and say may-gwo-ren (American). They don't mean to be rude. It makes us feel like movie stars. Frequently high school aged students will gather enough courage to practice their English on us by saying "Hello, how are you?" On the upside of being a may-gwo-ren, I recently learned the literal translation of the word. May-gwo-ren means beautiful-country-person.

Letter from Taiwan – 2001

For all of the ways we were different, there was one way that I was the same as everyone around me. At 5'-6" tall, off the rack clothes fit me perfectly. If any tailoring was required, it came with the suit, no extra charge. My entire formal outfits were upgraded at costs much more reasonable than in America. Despite the adjustments, something about Taiwan felt easier than we expected.

Food

Anywhere we traveled, life became easier once the basics were figured out, and finding food ranked high in importance. Taiwan offered constant culinary adventures. Some welcome, others not so much. My writing included passages about food, and the following captures some of our experiences ranging from the exotic to the routine.

The safest places to eat are usually the most familiar, so after getting settled, we looked for American fast-food restaurants. McDonalds appeared first. The menu is pretty standard fare, so don't even think about McRice, McMuGuGaiPan, or McFortune Cookies. The second fast food place we found was Kentucky Fried Chicken, and once again, the menu was identical to the U.S.A.

We continued to explore the city, and the third place we came across was a Pizza Hut. Everything looked normal at first glance, so we took a seat by the buffet table. Our first bite into pizza number one dashed our hopes for normal pizza. It was a Cuttlefish and cheese pizza. Pizza type number two had shrimp and coconut, pizza type number three was smothered in hotdogs. Five-spice chicken, soybean pods, and bitter gourd accompanied the salad bar. We have not been back to Pizza Hut since.

At this point you may be wondering why we didn't just eat at the local restaurants? A typical restaurant in Taiwan is a small shop with seven or eight tables stretching from inside the store out onto the sidewalk in front. The smells of car and scooter exhaust, sewer, and rotting seafood perfume the air. Menus are not in English and most of the food is unrecognizable. Guessing at a menu item is not advisable since it could result in marinated duck tongue, baked chicken feet, squid on a stick, sea cucumber, goat nose, or one of a million other mysterious items. Some of the restaurants are very good, and have a much better environment than what is described above, but we are typically very cautious of eating at local restaurants, and try to avoid playing Russian Roulette with our stomachs.

Letter from Taiwan – 2001

There were times we did take chances with our stomachs and when we went out with friends, figuring out what food arrived at the table became a game. If something looked unusual, we would ask what it was. Our host usually waved us off, saying not to worry and to try it anyway. Often, we were told the item on our plate was good for men or good for women. Other times we were told there was no word in English for what we were about to eat. That made me suspicious. I would then ask if it was animal, vegetable, or mineral, which always drew a puzzled look. Dining out was definitely an adventure.

Just like our days in Ireland, if Karen didn't like the food on her plate, my duty was to bravely finish whatever it was. Whether at a restaurant or with a friend, not eating made the host lose face. Eating her food had to be done with stealth. Garlic beetles, fish balls, stinky tofu, and all other kinds of colorful fare made it into my stomach. I always survived.

On one occasion while out with eight other Americans at a sushi restaurant, Karen and I took our seats around a table on the sidewalk. The gutter below our feet carried away fish scraps, and the smell couldn't be ignored. Karen leaned in and whispered that the food should more appropriately be called "sewershi."

One of our dinner companions had grown up in Japan. He taught us about sushi. After his lesson, Karen let everyone know she preferred her sushi cooked, which drew a round of smiles. As dishes were served and beer flowed, scooters zipped past, sending black exhaust over the table. At the end of the evening, about the time Karen started turning a mild shade of green, the Japanese man explained that sushi was as much about the atmosphere as the food. He rated the restaurant. Food: 10. Atmosphere: 0.

To avoid the adventurous hazards of dining out, most of our meals were eaten at home. Enough time in the country had passed that we felt ready to host a dinner for the two people who had been so helpful upon our arrival in Tainan. Shawn and Linda appeared at the front door carrying what looked like a green football with sharp spikes. Linda, whose family was from Malaysia, wanted to share her love of durian. The fruit more closely resembled some medieval weapon than a tasty treat. All I knew about durians was its nickname: "stinky fruit." We had experienced enough adventures with food by then, and I wasn't eager to taste anything with that name.

After dinner, Shawn cracked it open revealing a mushy, yellow flesh. Linda spooned it into bowls, smiling as if she were presenting a dessert fit for royalty. I took a tentative bite and immediately regretted it. She noticed my hesitation and said durian tasted better cold, more like ice cream. Relief surged as my bowl whisked its way back to the kitchen. The relief didn't last.

A short time later, Linda checked again. She asked if it was cold enough. I said no. Karen took a bite and disagreed. She confidently declared that it seemed cold enough to her. I shot her a look meant to convey *never cold enough*. She didn't get it. Then it hit me. Karen and I hadn't yet perfected that unwritten communication couples are supposed to have. Fifteen minutes later, the routine repeated. Another check. Another pleading look toward Karen. Another reluctant spoonful. By the third round, I realized I was trapped in a durian Groundhog Day. Not wanting to extend the evening any longer, Karen took over Linda's role of asking if it was cold enough, except she wasn't really asking. I was trapped. After surviving the ordeal, I realized any food with the word "stinky" in it should be avoided.

Inviting people to our home for a meal did not become common practice. Trying so many different foods in Taiwan meant that we ate extremely well. Unfortunately, that came with gaining weight. Well into the assignment both Karen and I realized we were rounder than we should be. Karen started first by dropping ten pounds. Once I saw she was serious about losing weight, I joined in. My routine included running up and down the townhouse stairs two at a time. Thirty minutes of climbing from the first floor to the fifth and back was followed by sit-ups, push-ups, and lifting ten-pound dumbbells. After two months, Karen dropped thirty pounds, and I lost twenty. Our lifestyle in Taiwan made us healthier.

A Real Honeymoon and Outside Forces

After getting married in Oregon, the company hadn't afforded us much time off. When visiting Thailand for ten days, we didn't plan for it to be a honeymoon, but it was. Being there felt as luxurious as the trips my father took me on when I was in high school. The following description from my younger self captured our adventure.

Phuket(pronounced poo-ket) is a small island at the southern tip of Thailand, located in the Andaman Sea. We stayed at Le Meridien resort in a suite that more closely resembled an apartment than a hotel room. It had eleven restaurants, a private beach, several pools, a massage spa, squash courts, dive facilities, private gardens, a scuba center, and a golf driving range.

Our trip had two main highlights. The first highlight was an elephant tour. A minibus picked us up at our hotel at 8:00AM, and drove past rubber plantations and banana trees for two hours. We arrived at a protected section of Thailand's rainforest in Phang Nga National Park. The driver handed out pineapples so we could feed and make friends with our elephants. At first, the elephant eyed us suspiciously, but then took the fruit in her trunk, and rolled them into her mouth.

As we hopped on board a two-person wooden chair strapped onto the elephant's back, our driver hopped onto the elephant's head. After about 45 minutes of lolling along the jungle paths, a small, isolated pool at the base of a waterfall appeared. Small pieces of natural tin, remnants of the area's early tin mining days, glistened in the pool like small pieces of gold. Our group enjoyed diving from the surrounding rocks, and leisurely swimming in the water below.

After about an hour, we were served a lunch of fried shrimp, cashew chicken, and fresh fruit in a make-shift tent. On the way back, our guide encouraged me to sit on the elephant's head and act as the driver for a while. The trip was unforgettable.

Our second highlight was Karen's birthday. She started the day with room service on our hotel room balcony. The waves gently lapped the shore, and as we finished the last bites of our meal, a rainbow appeared over the Andaman Sea.

After breakfast, she took a snorkeling lesson in the hotel pool. Out of the pool and into the ocean for some late morning wave jumping topped off a busy morning. A facial appointment and massage at the resort's spa filled the afternoon.

In the evening, we rented the resort's private yacht for a sunset cruise and had the full attention of our Captain. He even allowed Karen to command the wheel. After an hour's ride along the coast, and endless wine and hors-d'oeuvres, we arrived at the island's most famous sunset point. Just as a rainbow greeted the start of Karen's birthday, a rainbow appeared in the sky to bid the day farewell. As the sun descended, rays of light created a golden fan stretching from the bottom layer of clouds into the ocean.

The trip was one of the best vacations we've ever had, and upon leaving through customs, we practiced our Thai language one last time. Pressing our hands together (like a person praying), I said "kahp koon kahp," the traditional Thai words for a man to say thank you. Karen said "kahp koon kah," the traditional Thai words for a woman to say thank you. Without any questions, the customs agent smiled, responded politely in Thai, and waved us through. We already want to return.

Letter from Taiwan – 2001

Although my writing described many of the exotic experiences, it never told the whole story. One untold detail was what happened after the honeymoon. My assignment allowed for periodic home leave. As long as a trip cost less than flying back to Oregon, it was supposed to be covered. When we returned from Thailand, the company rejected my expense report.

The dispute turned into a classic teacher versus student match-up. Bill had first introduced me to construction negotiation back in Massachusetts. Oregon, Ireland, Israel, and Arizona had all battle tested me.

He claimed I hadn't followed the intent of my travel letter. I replied that contracts are based on words, not vague intent. He passed me off to Human Resources in the home office. After several back-and-forth exchanges, they set aside logic and leaned into accusing me of trying to "game the system." It wasn't true.

Frustrated with the false accusation, I approached Bill and played my final card. Paying for the trip wouldn't be a problem, but I reminded him the company still owed me a home leave. The trip to Thailand had been much less expensive, and going home would cost the company fifty percent more. In addition, with travel time and jetlag considered, it would take me away from billable work for seven to ten days.

Bill shook his head, and stared across the desk. I stared back, and in a deadpan voice said, "It's not my fault. You taught me everything I know about contracts." It wasn't true, but it made him smile. He knew the negotiations were over. The company paid for the entire trip.

The company's antics weren't the only thing that attempted to dampen our happy life. One family member tried as well, and he tested my patience. Except for an occasional email, Karen hadn't met my brother Mike. When sending messages, his humor came at my expense, and he thought he could convince her to join in. The messages weren't playful. They were sharp and meant to divide. I didn't like it, and neither did Karen. He didn't realize there was no space between us.

Even his casual comments felt like interference. After living in Tainan for over a year, we had already successfully navigated the culture and fully adapted. Despite never living in Taiwan himself, Mike decided to impart some unsolicited guidance. He suggested foods to try, phrases to avoid, ways to "blend in." The advice could have been harmless, but with him, it rarely was. Every suggestion came with sarcastic barbs, cutting remarks, and a condescending tone.

Karen knew how he had treated me in the past and prepared to come to my defense. It wasn't needed. I knew his emails and comments couldn't touch what we had built. Making him disappear was as easy as hitting "Delete."

There were other outside voices that were hard to ignore. Every day we received The China Post, an English language newspaper. The paper was typically one day behind in news because of the time difference, but it had cartoons, sports, finance, international, and local stories. Articles were often taken from U.S. sources such as Reuters or AP, and were to the point. Murder, drownings, rapes, molestations, drugs, and sex scandals weren't splashed across every front page. After comparing newspapers from Israel, Ireland and Taiwan to the U.S., we understood why many foreigners were afraid to visit America. Karen and I liked the news in Taiwan, and wanted to remain in our happy bubble for as long as possible. The bubble burst on the night of September 11th, 2001.

When the twin towers in New York came down, it was around 9:00PM in Taiwan. I noticed the stock markets were not open, wondered why, and asked Karen to turn on the TV. We watched as the second plane hit, not believing what was unfolding before our eyes. That night, we went to bed shocked at what we had seen, not sure what the next day would bring. Our Taiwan news bubble was shielding us from the sensationalism in the U.S.

At work, my Taiwan colleagues continued as if nothing had happened. They were curious about my reaction and how I felt, but nothing changed throughout the day. Airports weren't closed. Meetings went on as usual. Reports had to be written.

When I arrived home that evening, Karen gave me an update. She had scrubbed the internet looking for news from across the world. We knew we weren't in the storm of emotion sweeping the U.S., and felt like being in Taiwan permitted us to view the events with a more objective lens. When we sent emails to family back home, Karen's sister dismissed what she wrote because we weren't living in Oregon. She said we didn't understand what it was to be an American.

The response was insulting, but it wasn't anything new. Karen's sister often chose dismissal instead of understanding. What struck us most weren't just the words, but how quickly she brushed aside Karen's perspective. It was a reminder that we were living in a different world, separated not only by oceans but by how we saw and processed events.

By early 2002, the construction started to wrap up. The project hadn't really taught me new skills, but it had broadened my horizons. In general, I knew the construction industry could be hard on everyone involved, but in Taiwan some behaviors were worse. Upper managers thought they owned those working under them. There were mornings when my contractor could be found head slumped over, asleep at his desk. He often worked through the night to produce whatever his home office managers demanded. I didn't make unreasonable requests and recognized his limitations. He respected that I treated him like a professional.

Not everybody on the jobsite behaved similarly. The owner's U.S. representative asked me to make demands of my contractor that I viewed as unethical. When it became known that I wouldn't be following his request and why, he threw a tantrum.

I had run across enough bullying in my life, and wasn't about to back down, even if not following the demand meant removal from the job. The onsite project manager from my company smoothed things out, and convinced the client there had just been a misunderstanding. I suspect someone went behind my back in Chinese and directed the contractor to do as the owner said, but that is something I will never know. What I did know was that my values could not be compromised.

There was another time I refused to adapt to the local culture. A metal floor manufacturer offered a tour of his factory. He hoped my company would use his products instead of importing from a foreign competitor. After the tour, we sat in his office where he offered a small cup of oolong tea. He explained how to avoid patent issues by taking the other manufacturer's product, making a few minor changes, and then producing it in Taiwan. I thanked him for his time, and returned to the office to share the experience. My colleagues told me the manufacturer's behavior was normal business in Taiwan. It would never be normal business for me.

As my contractor completed the final punch lists, a Taiwanese manager replaced the owner's U.S. representative. The new manager didn't like Westerners. He tried to treat me as disrespectfully as he treated other locals, but his limited English failed him. He couldn't convince me of anything other than his own madness. It was almost comical. Past assignments had already taught me how to navigate difficult clients. With the contractor by my side, I listened intently to words I didn't understand, nodded respectfully, and left with all the seriousness the situation demanded. My contractor interpreted for me afterward. As far as I could tell, the work finished without issue.

When my last day on the job arrived, my contractor presented me with a small gift: a frosted glass dragon wrapped around an eight-inch crystal ball. I hadn't expected anything. It came to represent the respect we had for each other. In years to come, the glass dragon would break, freeing the crystal ball from its clutches. If staff members or clients questioned my advice, I would simply point to the crystal ball and tell them I could see all. It was a bit of office theater, but it carried the hard-won perspective of a project where I had learned to see exactly what I needed to, even when I couldn't understand a word.

Business Development

The end of the project didn't mean my time in Taiwan ended. Bill knew work was slow across the company. Instead of sending me back to Portland and into a wave of upcoming layoffs, he suggested I take a few weeks off. I had a four-week sabbatical saved up, and getting paid while traveling felt like a bonus.

Karen and I used the time to travel throughout Taiwan. We had already explored different parts of the island, and decided to spend some of our break at the southern tip in Kenting National Park. We enjoyed two days at a private resort by a beach located along the Taiwan Strait, where we drove through tea fields, climbed the deserted ruins of a neighboring town, and strolled along forest paths. From the beach, we watched the sun slowly descend into sparkling blue waters that reminded us of the Red Sea. In the distance, we could see a damaged Greek oil tanker being salvaged. The story made world news, and we enjoyed having a front row seat.

On our way out of town, we found one last surprise. A nuclear power plant sat inside Kenting National Park, less than half a mile from our resort. It felt like seeing a reactor in the middle of the Grand Canyon, and we smiled at the uniqueness of Taiwan.

Another trip took us to Taroko Gorge, a breathtaking marble-walled canyon. We stayed at the gorge's only hotel, in a Japanese-style room. The "bed" was a thin roll-out tatami mat tucked in a closet, and in one corner, a table sat a foot off the ground with legless chairs.

Karen's first words were, "Where's the bed, and who vandalized this furniture?"

After an uncomfortable night's sleep, we hiked a nearby path up through banyan trees filled with chattering monkeys. On another trail, a spider large enough to eat small birds for lunch stared down on us from his web. We never found out if it was poisonous, but decided spider-free resorts with Western amenities were more our style.

The sabbatical had been a clean break from the prior project. Walking back into the office, something felt off before I even reached my desk. Bill had been telling the staff not to worry about the lack of projects. There was more work than anybody knew what to do with on the horizon. Words didn't mean much to me. When asked to assist with some business development proposals, something didn't feel right.

Between long uncomfortable meetings strategizing how to win more projects were uncomfortable lunches. At noon, three or four people would rush out the door for a thirty-minute break with me in tow. They entered one of the small, garage-sized restaurants nearby, and as fast as everyone sat down bowls filled with dumplings were placed in front of each person.

I tried to keep up with the pace of eating, but never could. Others at the table gulped down dumplings in one bite, reminding me of seals swallowing fish. With each dumpling disappearing down their throats, I half expected to hear them bark. One colleague, Clement, noticed I ate more slowly. To save me from losing face, he matched my pace until we both finished together. Although we always ended lunch in thirty minutes, I was never a match for the trained seals at my table.

While I struggled through performances at lunch, performances with our clients didn't go much better. On one of our trips to Taipei, we attempted a presentation. Afterwards, the client looked across his desk and said, "Your competitor has twice the number of people. Can you explain why?" I had to think quickly, and responded that our crew was more experienced. We didn't just throw warm bodies at a project. If he were at a doctor, would he rather have one really good physician, or five people who had never practiced medicine before?" I wasn't convincing enough. We didn't win the proposal.

Winning a project in Taiwan was always going to be a difficult battle. U.S. labor cost four times more than the local staff, and that was before travel and taxes were included. We needed to either have a technological advantage, or to be selling something the locals couldn't offer. We had neither.

Trying to win work with the deck stacked so heavily against us was deflating. After hearing feedback from one client about how bad the proposal was, Clement stopped by my desk to congratulate me. I was confused. We lost. He explained, "In Taiwan, there is bad, really bad, and downright terrible. You were only bad. That is a huge success." I knew there was some truth to what he was saying, but I also knew that he was trying to boost my spirits.

Shortly after my first proposal attempts, a U.S. manager, nicknamed The Hatchet Man, flew in from abroad to conduct layoffs. I watched as colleagues from my prior project were ushered into a conference room. About an hour later, they came out trying to hold back tears. It was heartbreaking to see people I knew in such pain.

The Hatchet Man hadn't only come to the Tainan office to cut staff, he wanted me to accompany him on a proposal in mainland China. The first stop was Hong Kong, where I needed to obtain an entry visa. While there, I watched as my companion walked narrow alleys to pick up a tailored suit, and then stopped at a restaurant to make sure his private cigar locker was stocked. I had heard rumors he was corrupt, and watching him move through Hong Kong like an international spy only reinforced the belief.

Next, we flew to Shanghai, where within twenty-four hours business cards with my name and title were produced. The office appeared incredibly efficient. One afternoon, I stopped by the Hard Rock Café to pick up a few guitar pins. After the meal, it struck me. In Shanghai, from office staff to restaurant workers, the tone was cold, more reserved than in Taiwan, where almost every interaction carried warmth. When colleagues back in Tainan later heard my description, I could feel their smiles.

After Shanghai, we headed to Tianjin. At the construction site, a manager asked how to improve his project. I didn't have enough information to give a real answer. Everything he described to me sounded like a textbook example of a well-run project, and I let him know. It would take more time to properly evaluate his site. We didn't have more time.

The Hatchet Man wasn't thrilled I hadn't put on a better show, but I was about analysis and careful thought, not off-the-cuff answers. As we returned to Tainan, my prospects for chasing new projects seemed to be fading. It didn't bother me, though. I preferred working in a world of actions and results, not words and empty promises.

Over the next several months, there were more layoffs and more unsuccessful proposal attempts. The Hatchet Man disappeared to chase work in Russia. It wouldn't be long before the company fired him for shady practices.

As September 2002 approached, Bill could no longer extend my assignment in Taiwan. My last few days in the office went better than the business pursuits. At work, one person gave me a small picture of two golden carp circling a lotus flower. It was a beautiful symbol of Karen and my journey together. Clement gave me a door hanging of a Chinese lion with a sword in its mouth, a guardian for our future home. The owners of our townhome treated us to dinner and small gifts of colorful Koji pottery and a homemade kit to make boba tea. Boba hadn't caught on in the U.S. yet. A small pouch still sits in our pantry, its scent carrying me back. In return, we told them their home had excellent feng shui and were sure a much-desired child would follow. Nine months later, they had a son.

One of our last stops was a large souvenir shop in Taipei, where we purchased a replica of a fifteen-inch-high, tri-colored Tang Dynasty horse. Many of the warm gifts received are still displayed throughout our home today. The horse holds the central position.

CHAPTER 14

RETURNS

When my mother found out I was going to live in Ireland, she told me to be careful. The IRA was setting off bombs in Northern Ireland, and she didn't want her baby boy getting killed.

When my mother found out I was going to Israel, she told me to be careful. The Israelis and Palestinians were fighting like cats and dogs. Being in the wrong place at the wrong time would mean certain death, and she didn't want her baby boy getting killed.

When my mother found out I was going to live in Taiwan, she told me to be careful. War could break out at any moment. The mainland Chinese have weapons pointed at the island, and she didn't want her baby boy getting killed.

When my mother found out I was coming back to the U.S., she finally relaxed. Home meant safety.

When we returned home, safety wasn't my biggest concern. The first thing the company asked me to do was update my resume. I didn't know what that meant for my future, but it sounded like the most dangerous thing I had faced in years.

Adjustments

In September 2002, when we first walked in the front door of our condominium, it finally hit us that our time abroad was truly over. Karen and I had spent the past two years outside of the United States living in a modern townhome and experiencing things we had only dreamed of. Everything in the condo now looked tired and dated. Our place didn't have modern polished quartz floors and beautiful inbuilt wood cabinetry like what we had been living in. To top it off, the hot water heater didn't work. Exhausted from the journey, Karen sat in the front hall and cried while I tried, unsuccessfully, to comfort her.

I reminded myself there were things we could control and things we couldn't. Upgrading our home was something we could do, and the various projects would help us re-adjust to life back in the United States. We sat down and created a plan that would give us the best "bang for the buck." I could refurbish cabinets, paint, tile floors and countertops, refinish the fireplace, and stain the deck. Contractor help would be needed for vinyl flooring, a new pantry, upgrading interior doors, and anything electrical or water related. It was a big list, but it gave us something productive to focus on.

Planning and getting started on the projects also helped us adjust to sensory overload that we hadn't expected. In Taiwan, the product choices in our small grocery store were limited. Now, we had entire aisles full of different laundry detergents. We stared down the aisle for several minutes, feeling the need to run away. There were powders, pods, liquids, scents like mountain breeze and lavender sunrise. The products didn't just sit on shelves. They shouted at us, demanding to be chosen.

For the past two years we had tuned out all of the surrounding conversations. My knowledge of Chinese could get me by if needed, but those were one way conversations. I could speak basic sentences, but struggled to understand what other people said. Now, every voice cut through. Complaints, gossip, family plans for the weekend. Our brains hadn't built the filters yet. They were used to simplicity, and the comfort of not knowing. The sensory overload overwhelmed us.

In Taiwan, we never had to deal with unwanted phone calls. Back in the U.S., our phone didn't stop ringing. To discourage the intrusions, I recorded our answering machine message in Chinese. For a while, it worked. Then one evening, two calls came back-to-back.

The first sounded hesitant. "Uh… is this… Chinese? Yeah, never mind." *Click*. Success! My Chinese had fooled someone. The second message, though, came in fluent Chinese. I froze. That wasn't supposed to happen. I hit replay and hunched over the machine. Tone by tone, I pieced the words together. The caller wasn't a telemarketer. It wasn't even a wrong number. It was the Social Security office. The U.S. government had breached my "unbreakable wall."

While adjusting to life at home, another change appeared quickly. Within days, the company asked me to take my resume and interview with a client. Carrying a resume into an interview made me question why I still belonged to a company that had so little work of its own.

At the interview, a woman sat across the table and asked about my past projects. She wanted to understand my knowledge about a specific scheduling software. Any decent construction manager could build a schedule. They were nothing more than puzzles. Unfortunately, I had never used the program. From her questions, I assumed the interview was over before it began.

As I prepared to leave, she smiled and told me I'd be perfect for the position. My reputation from Ireland and Israel hadn't disappeared, and she couldn't believe her luck that I was available. I sat there wondering if we had just been in the same conversation. I had admitted I didn't know the software, hadn't I? She explained that the current scheduler was Israeli and could teach me whatever I needed to know. Work began the next day.

By asking me to be her scheduler, she had done the one thing that motivated me most. She trusted me. If someone trusted me, I was going to work twice as hard to make sure it was deserved.

When I arrived at the trailer complex, the scheduler patiently walked me through the software and the logic behind each activity. His assignment ended in two weeks, so my education had to happen quickly. By the time he left, I was navigating the software with ease.

Schedules were exactly the sort of challenge I needed. The original work was slowly taken apart, then put back together in a way I could clearly understand and explain. To increase the chance for success, I visited each contractor and asked how they thought the work should be done. They were delighted to have someone ask that question. As long as their approach made sense, I incorporated it. Piece by piece, the schedule took shape. With each step, my confidence grew.

The schedule wasn't my only challenge. Another building on site had finished construction just before I arrived. My client didn't want to pay the general contractor to stick around and complete the punch list. Whether the subcontractors felt they were owed extra costs didn't matter. The client wanted the work done for free.

Convincing the remaining companies to finish whatever the client wanted became my secondary focus. I wasn't just the scheduler anymore, I was the guy sent to ask for favors without any authority to give something in return. The subcontractors saw the task assigned to me and had sympathy. They understood that with this billion-dollar semiconductor client, the cost of doing business included some free work. The experience taught me a lesson about business. This client typically gets what they want, whether they are right or not.

Unrealistic expectations extended beyond the client and into my personal life as well. Two months after landing in Oregon, Karen and I had a surprise visitor. My father wanted to see how we were doing. His timing couldn't have been worse. Our home improvement projects were in full swing, and the toilet sat in the middle of the bedroom, disconnected and out of place.

We still had a few weeks left in the company's temporary housing. Despite our pleas to reschedule the trip, or at least stay in the company apartment, he insisted on doing the trip his way. His visit wasn't eventful. We took him to the Oregon Coast where we'd been married, and shared photographs of our travels. Then, as he was leaving, he looked around, gave me a serious look and said, "You can do better, son." I didn't respond.

Our home wasn't in a poor part of town. The grounds were clean. The interior was in disarray, but for good reason. If my company sent me halfway around the globe, the condo let me walk away without worrying about maintenance. His assessment relied on material values that completely failed to grasp my strategic lifestyle. I shouldn't have let his comment bother me, but it did.

As 2002 closed, another adjustment hit us. Ever since the return from Taiwan, Karen's hair had been falling out. By Christmas, it was almost completely gone. It hurt to witness such emotional pain. Despite regular exercise and excellent health, the loss chipped away at her confidence.

I didn't love Karen for her hair. I needed to show that this change didn't change what we had between us. Music offered a way to say it.

In the old Randy Travis song, *Forever and Ever, Amen*, he sings about loving someone even if their hair falls out. That was exactly how I felt.

A doctor's diagnosis confirmed Alopecia. After we found a wig that matched her old style and she adjusted to wearing it, I encouraged a trip to the mall. We sat on a bench and watched the crowd. It was astonishing how many women had thinning patches, crooked cuts, or hair that looked like they'd just rolled out of bed. With every sighting, Karen's confidence ticked upward.

When her emotional strength seemed to return, I gave another gentle nudge. A return to work would prove the world accepted this new version of her. She nervously agreed and phoned the company that always seemed to have a job waiting. Before the call ended, she had her old job back. If her old boss noticed the change, he never said a word.

Seeing Karen return to her old self was a relief. Through it all, I had stood steady, loved without hesitation, and served as a reminder that she was more than a reflection in the mirror. She offered thanks, but none were needed. Loving her through the crisis was never a choice. It simply was who I was.

Into the Unknown

In the summer of 2003, the scheduling project wrapped up without issue. Back in the office, management looked surprised to see me. I had become accustomed to their welcome of silence followed by a vague suggestion to take vacation. It felt like the corporate version of "Don't call us, we'll call you." I had once again assumed it was their job to assign work. Maybe I misunderstood.

With no pressing assignment ahead, Karen and I decided to take a vacation. We had explored other parts of the world with energy and excitement. It felt like the right time to do the same in the U.S. Our backyard didn't include bears or moose, so I suggested Alaska.

We went white water rafting and rode horses through forested trails. A hydrofoil took us to watch eerie blue glaciers calving while sea otters played in the water below. One part of the trip even included a dog sled ride. The other activities were fun. I wanted to see bears.

We boarded a float plane to a remote lake, expecting a rugged wilderness experience. At the lodge, shallow bowls of a watery stew were slapped down on a table with wooden benches. When someone asked when the main course would be arriving, they were told this was it. Our excursion wasn't about the food, so we focused on the excitement of the main event. A boat took us across the lake and anchored fifty feet from a well-known watering hole. Off to the side, a twenty-foot observation post stood above the water, staffed by researchers. To our surprise, a dozen fishing boats sat between us and the shore. For the same price, their tour came with deli sandwiches, salmon, and front row seats to the bears. Ours came with gruel and a view of their sandwiches.

The float plane excursion had been both underwhelming and misleading. The brochure showed bears in Katmai National Park fishing for salmon. After returning from Alaska, Karen managed to get half our money refunded. Apparently, I wasn't the only one with negotiating skills.

In September 2003, there still weren't any new projects on the horizon, so we planned our next trip. I hadn't been back to see family in Pittsburgh for almost three years. Once there, it felt natural sitting around the kitchen table talking as my mother wandered about the kitchen.

Being in Pennsylvania gave me the opportunity to show Karen where I went to college. It had been sixteen years since my graduation. The drive to State College reminded me of the rides with my father when he drove me to and from the university.

Walking around the Penn State campus stirred memories, but something felt off. Backpack-laden students were still rushing from class to class along the mall. Others could be seen sleeping in the lounges. Watching them, I felt more like a visitor than a former student. As we left, I realized it wasn't the campus that had changed. I had moved on.

A few days after our visit to Pittsburgh, the company called. A job in Idaho Falls needed immediate help. Construction was well underway. They lacked coverage for the night shift on a task that would run twenty-four hours a day for three weeks. I hadn't worked nights since my college days. During slow times, saying no to work offered a fast path to unemployment, so I packed the car, kissed Karen goodbye, and started the twelve-hour drive east.

When I arrived in Idaho Falls, a manager laid out the details. I would work fourteen-hour days for the next two weeks without a break. Despite company policy, they wouldn't pay overtime. When Karen heard the conditions, she was angry. Her past work in Portland taught her the labor laws. I understood the frustration but told her this wasn't the time to make waves.

A safety representative greeted me during my first night. When he suggested we could save the company money by bringing bag lunches instead of grabbing something at the local Wendy's, I pictured him falling into one of the concrete pours. Sadly, he never did.

The construction crew lived as nomads, drifting from one major project to the next. They worked just long enough to collect a paycheck, then vanished until their money ran out. In the early hours of the morning, when break time rolled around, they made street tacos using propane stoves located on the scaffolding, a hundred feet off the ground. At the end of two weeks, the site manager asked if I would stay on the night shift. I agreed. It wasn't really a choice.

Three months of fourteen-hour shifts, seven days a week, left me exhausted. My life shrank to a cycle of hotel breakfasts, frantic sleep, and rushing back to the site. Laundry became a luxury that robbed me of valuable sleep. Finally, a manager in Portland noticed. He knew my capabilities and couldn't believe I was still pulling the graveyard shift. "What are you doing working nights?" he asked. "Our team is getting killed during the day." Within twenty-four hours, the company moved me to the day shift. I didn't argue.

Relieved to finally escape the nights, I barely had time to enjoy it before the other managers played a trick. Once they saw me on days, all five decided to take in-house vacations. They dropped seven of the site's ten active contracts in my lap. My time onsite climbed to twelve-hour days. It was better than the fourteen hour night shifts, but not by much. I'm sure they found the stunt funny, but I didn't see the joke. When a contractor needed help, someone had to respond quickly to keep the job moving. They expected me to fail because they didn't know me. I had a secret weapon.

Karen arrived in Idaho and immediately hunted for an apartment. While my world narrowed to work, hers expanded to utilities, mail, groceries, and car maintenance. She handled everything to ease my mind. Later in life, I'd shrug and say I didn't know how the world outside of work functioned. In reality, she built the foundation my work depended on. Without her, the version of me that showed up to work every day wouldn't have existed.

My contractors were a gritty bunch. The foremen included a retired rodeo clown, a gravel-voiced Kansan named Rusty who collected antique tractors, a Native American who told stories about his past, and a journeyman whose crew worked in complete silence. As an outsider who sounded like management, I wasn't one of them.

To me, they weren't any different from other construction workers I had come across. They tried pushing their luck with change orders, but didn't know the rule about whoever is most organized, wins. My observation notes were thorough and backed by photos. I rejected inflated claims with airtight logic and paid fair costs without question. It was all part of the game.

I told them if they planned to fool me, they had better do it well so I could live a happy life. If I caught them, no one would be happy. After a few months of testing my limits, trust set in. When the retired rodeo clown invited Karen and me to a family barbecue and showed us the mountains where he once rounded up cattle, I knew we'd been accepted.

Just as the contractors started to come together, my brother's life began to unravel. In January 2004, my mother called with news. Rick had attempted suicide. He was in the hospital, but she insisted I stay away. The news left me unsteady, grasping for a way to respond.

He wouldn't take visitors or talk with anyone. We had just seen Rick a few months earlier in Pittsburgh, and although he appeared a bit jumpy, that wasn't unusual for him. My mother asked if money could be provided to help. I didn't like making family loans, but this wasn't a loan. I would have given anything she asked for.

The isolation felt the toughest. In the coming weeks, I couldn't reach Rick except through my mother. She even discouraged me from sending a package. I wanted to respect his space, but I felt helpless. Sporadic updates arrived, and over time, it was as if the whole event never happened.

Years later, I saw a document that was never intended for my eyes. Rick described unbearable back pain, and an addiction to oxycodone. When the doctor cut him off, the withdrawal broke him. He recovered, but for several years, a distance I never understood remained between us.

Rick's troubles were extremely serious, and I needed something to keep my mind from dwelling on his collapse. Work unknowingly helped. My colleagues weren't exactly friendly. Their management styles caused more trouble than results. One raised suspicion by using his contractor's trucks in ways that looked like special favors. It won him support from that crew, but not from anyone else.

Another manager agreed to cover for me while Karen and I took a long weekend in Yellowstone National Park. We had barely driven an hour down the road when my phone rang. He had confiscated a contractor's bulldozer keys because he didn't like the parking spot. The contractor was furious. After a few brief calls, I calmed the situation and ensured the keys were returned. Karen breathed a sigh of relief, grateful we didn't have to turn the car around.

Yellowstone offered a welcome distraction, one of many escapes Karen and I managed. As work settled down, we threw ourselves into the countryside with real enthusiasm. In Idaho, we picked our way across the lava fields at Craters of the Moon, then stood in the deep wagon ruts of the Oregon Trail, imagining the thousands who had passed before us. The bears in Alaska had been a letdown, but at Bear World, they strolled right up to the car.

In Salt Lake City, I asked the temple guide so many questions he thought he had a convert on his hands. Karen politely took a pamphlet and moved me along. At Bryce Canyon, we stayed in a cabin on the rim and watched the sunset paint the orange and white rock formations. Against the fading sky, they looked like giant Dreamsicles rising above the horizon.

In Zion, beside the Virgin River we paid tribute to Ireland by breaking into our own version of *Riverdance*, laughing at how ridiculous we must have looked. In Arches, we hiked the entire Dark Angel Trail, ducking under massive stone spans and trekking across narrow ridges marked by small piles of carefully arranged rocks.

Our souvenirs became predictable. We collected postcards, magnets, mugs, and T-shirts at every stop. Combined with hundreds of photographs, they were the only evidence we had that we'd actually made it that far.

In September 2004, as the project came to a close, I picked up a different kind of souvenir. The facility produced malt, which is nothing more than toasted baby barley sprouts. When one of the first trucks spilled some grain onto the ground, I scooped up a handful and placed it in an empty beer bottle with the client's label. It later sat on my desk in Oregon as a reminder of Idaho. It also reminded me of a promise to myself. I would not expect uncompensated overtime again, and I would never assign anyone to fourteen-hour shifts, seven days a week, for months on end.

Choir Practice

The company owed me two weeks of temporary housing after the Idaho job. With a four-week sabbatical also waiting in the wings, Karen and I decided to have some fun. Staying put was never our style. We booked a riverfront hotel in Portland and spent the first few days strolling downtown and eating our way through local restaurants.

We started in San Francisco, where the Golden Gate Bridge appeared clear one minute and vanished into the fog the next. Farther south, we lay on the ground in Big Sur and stared up at the Milky Way's white bands. In Disneyland, Karen braved a roller coaster that flipped her world upside down. She made me promise to never put her on one again.

Watching a live sitcom taping in Hollywood revealed behind-the-scenes magic. Producers encouraged us to laugh by throwing candy and gifts into the audience. The journey north took us through Yosemite just as a flash snowstorm hit. The valley transformed. For a few hours, the roads were impassable and we were trapped inside a snow globe. We safely escaped, but fighting to put chains on the tires proved harder than anything I dealt with at work.

By the time we returned to Portland, I felt well-rested. The semiconductor client I'd served so many times before soon had me in their sights again. Over the years, I took on whatever role they needed and made it work. I designed foundations, managed installations, negotiated contracts, and built schedules. Whether in Oregon, Ireland, or Israel, I delivered. Those projects helped the client's managers advance their careers. Whenever they needed help, they called for me. A sudden vacancy gave them the excuse to bring me back.

My company sent me to a nearby site to oversee mid-level managers. Unfortunately, the site had its own politics. Because I hadn't come through their chain of command, the local leadership saw me as an outsider. They weren't eager to see me in a senior role and assigned me menial tasks.

Years earlier, a colleague warned me that if I wasn't in a real management role by forty, it might be time to move on. Forty had come and gone while I was still waiting. For the next five months, Karen's diary helped explain why I stayed. Many days contained the same line: "Dan came home again today saying he doesn't know why they have him there."

Other entries didn't read like a crisis. Instead, they described long lunches, weekends at the coast, and shopping trips with no particular purpose. After the grueling pace of Idaho, the lack of responsibility in Portland became a comfortable trap. I stayed because it was easy to let the days slip by when no one cared if I bothered showing up for work or not.

That peace was temporarily broken in February 2005 when I received an unusual email. My father wanted a substantial loan. At seventy-four, he was chasing financing for a new animal hospital. The banks had already turned him down. He spelled out the terms and explained it was all to give his fifth wife long-term security and help cover her daughter's college costs. I stared at the screen.

Did he forget who he was writing to?

There were plenty of reasons to say no. He had walked away from his family responsibilities when I was three. What would stop him from doing it again? His first wife, my mother, had no security. In high school, he manipulated me into convincing her to assume the mortgage he was supposed to pay off. When I bought a motorcycle before my senior year of college, he stopped paying for tuition. My wife was older than his.

It wasn't that Karen and I couldn't afford it. Like the bank, I considered him a bad investment. If we gave him the money, I knew we'd never see any of it. I wrote a short email explaining that I had my own wife to look after, then wished him well. He didn't reply.

By April 2005, friends in the client's organization heard I was wasting away in Oregon and decided to fix it. With only two days' notice, my company told me to head to Arizona for a one-year assignment. The client wanted me to oversee the civil and structural engineers from my own company on their behalf. I smiled. My own company wasn't promoting me, but the client was. It sounded like a conflict of interest, but if everyone was comfortable with the arrangement, I would live up to the trust.

During my orientation into the client's organization, a recruiter noticed how often I had worked for them over the years. She asked why her company hadn't just hired me directly. I didn't have an answer. I simply said, "I don't know. You tell me." Nothing came of it then, but the idea of joining a company that appreciated my effort stayed with me.

On the project, I walked a fine line with the design team. At one point, the Civil Engineer asked me to stop finding so many mistakes because it made him look bad. I explained that returning drawings without comments would make the client wonder why they had hired me. He grumbled and walked away. Behind the scenes, the client remained satisfied with him. To me, that balance looked like success.

The fine line didn't end at work. My manager in the client's organization wanted everyone on the team to be singing from the same page. Every Wednesday, he gathered the engineers and contractors at a nearby golf club for "choir practice." Spouses weren't invited. There might not have been songs, but there were plenty of appetizers and beer. Coming home often meant facing Karen's less-than-pleased looks. I survived them, but never imagined something as wholesome as choir practice could be so hazardous.

Karen and I had lived in Arizona before and visited many of the National Parks and Monuments, but we had more to see. To take the sting out of choir practice, we explored the Southwest with gusto. In Saguaro, the cacti stood like guards, and I half-expected Wile E. Coyote to pop out with an ACME anvil. Monument Valley gave us a sunset that turned the rocks fire-red before fading to muted tones. At Four Corners, we knelt to touch four states at once. I called my mother in Pittsburgh and told her it counted as four separate calls. She didn't buy the logic.

We looked for the traces of those who came before us. In Chaco Canyon, we wandered ruins built with impossible precision. A ranger let us peek through a telescope at black sunspots. Wupatki reminded us that foreign countries didn't have a monopoly on ancient history. A picture of the orange stone structures against the blue sky still serves as my computer's screen saver.

On one weekend, we broke away for a short trip to Pittsburgh, then came back and continued exploration of the southwest. Launch buttons were pressed in a decommissioned missile silo near Tucson. In Roswell, New Mexico, the streetlights wore alien heads, the gift shops acted far too seriously for what they sold, and the McDonald's hid a UFO inside. We stopped at a pistachio farm, sampled a few, and kept driving. When we reached White Sands, Karen swore the insect chasing our car was a top-secret government drone attempting to retrieve our allegedly stolen nuts. I pulled down my hat and stepped on the gas.

Near the end of our stay, we saw Johnny Mathis in concert. His voice pulled me back to the small boy waiting for his crew cut as a transistor radio filled the air. With every location we visited, we collected a magnet. Today, those magnets hang on a whiteboard in our home. They are a simple record of the miles we put behind us while the company figured out where to send me next.

Another Open Door

As April 2006 came to a close, it was time to return to Oregon. A few weeks later, my company asked if I'd assemble a proposal for a project in Boise, Idaho that would be designed out of Portland. I was officially a construction manager, but with work drying up, they wanted me to move back to the engineering group. The irony of the request wasn't lost on me. For the past year I'd already been acting as a design manager, only within a client's organization.

Management basics were the same whether they applied to a contractor or an engineer. Both worked to schedules, stuck to budgets, and stayed within scope. The difference was in what drove them. Contractors were focused on tangible results. They were high-energy, goal-oriented, and willing to do just about anything if the money was right. Engineers were different. They were eager to please, loyal to their clients, and motivated more by intellectual collaboration and problem-solving than money. My view was simplistic, but experience had proven it true.

Switching career paths for the second time wasn't a hard decision. I needed to be where the work was, and Engineering Management provided more opportunities.

The company still didn't understand my capabilities. They made me second-in-command to a senior design manager who had no time for Boise. Since other work already filled his schedule, the plan was for him to be the face of the project. He managed the client and invoices while the structure and execution were mine to control. I led the proposal, arranged travel, coordinated meetings, tracked budgets, and submitted change orders.

The architects and engineers weren't sure what to make of me at first. I came from the construction group, and stories had circulated about how tough I had been on the engineers in Arizona. Slowly, their trust grew. It started when the team was reminded that my structural engineering license was still active. I was one of them. It also helped when I stood up for a senior architect who had left a DUI off his background check. The client wanted him removed, but I convinced them to let him stay. Over the next seven months, the project went extremely well.

Two significant things came from that job. First, the senior project manager didn't take all the credit. He made sure the company knew about my performance. Second, the assignment allowed Karen and me to stay at our home in Oregon for most of the project. Between work and short trips across the state, we spent our weekends on long, relaxing motorcycle rides through the nearby vineyards and orchards. With the wind in our faces and the engine revving through each curve, all seemed right with the world.

By February 2007, my work on the Idaho had decreased so much that the company started looking for another project for me to take on. When an old client in Arizona asked about my availability, the company had me transfer my existing project to a junior manager and pack my bags. I didn't mind returning to the southwest, but after proving myself as an engineering manager, they asked me to serve as a client representative monitoring construction. I had gone from leading to observing. It was a career step back.

I couldn't fully blame the company. My own success was coming back to haunt me. Ten years earlier in Ireland, I helped Doug succeed. He wanted to create a team of trustworthy people, and when his company wanted something, my company delivered. That "something" was me. As Karen and I traveled back to Arizona, I made a mental note to try harder to cause problems.

My role was to watch over a contractor's work that was already well underway, and report back on their progress. Doug viewed it as proper oversight. The contractor viewed me as a spy. I viewed it as busywork.

Early on, trouble appeared. A foreman made false claims about my directing his crews. Instead of backing me up, Doug said, "I don't know who to believe. I wasn't there." His reply shocked me. Over the years he hadn't just been a client, he'd been a friend. If he wasn't going to trust my reports, what was I doing there? The site seemed tense enough. Confronting the issue directly would come across as too aggressive, so I decided on a different strategy.

To improve communication and strengthen trust, a sacrifice had to be made. Each day, Doug and I headed out for lunch together. He chose the spot. Weekly, I valiantly chowed down on burritos the size of a fire extinguisher, and even survived the spicy chicken wings of death. By the end of the project, the tension had cleared and all was well.

Karen, however, had a knack for creating her own adventure. One evening, while taking a walk, she tripped on an uneven sidewalk and fell. When she became too dizzy to stand, I called for paramedics. By the time they arrived, she was looking better, but the wheels were already in motion. Two guys and a woman bounded out like television stars. Muscles bulged, ponytails bounced, and million-dollar smiles flashed. Fortunately, a trip to the hospital wasn't needed. The paramedics didn't do much, but their arrival seemed to help. I knew better than to compete.

It wasn't all stressful. Just like we had done in Oregon, Karen and I continued treating the southwest like our playground. We made it back to the Grand Canyon and stayed in the historic El Tovar hotel. Our reservations were last minute, and the only room available looked like a converted broom closet in the basement. We didn't care. We weren't there for a luxury room. It was about spending a night on the rim, or as we liked to say, "Living on the Edge." One weekend, we even visited California to dine beside the tank at SeaWorld's Killer Whale Experience. We loved the vacation opportunities so much that Karen once joked about asking if I could convince my company to send us to her next vacation spot. I knew she was teasing and told her that wasn't how my company worked.

For my career, Arizona was only supposed to be a small detour. My company had other thoughts. As the project ended, a new request came in. Past successes were haunting me again. One of Doug's colleagues had reached out and decided where I could best help their company. It was the same manager I had interviewed with years ago for the scheduling job in Oregon. She was working in Israel, but she wasn't the one who needed help. I was being sent to support one of the Israelis Karen and I had loaned our coats to in Ireland back in 1998.

The assignment made my head spin. Why was the client choosing my next projects? Wasn't that my company's responsibility? This was another two-month construction management role, not engineering management. I no longer knew where my career was headed. Still, overseas work paid well. I had some leverage, so I made one firm request. If they wanted me, Karen's travel had to be included. They agreed. That softened the sting of a path that felt increasingly unclear. I didn't realize it then, but something bigger was already in motion.

In July 2007, when I arrived in Israel, everything on the project was already in crisis. Trust with the general contractor had fully broken down. I sat through client-run sessions about construction progress and upcoming work. They called the meetings task forces and held them in war rooms.

The biggest problem was that key people were missing from the room. The managers overseeing the work weren't there. The client kept making commitments to themselves, and promising deliverables no one had agreed to do. If the contractors didn't meet expectations, the client huffed and puffed, and paraded out more meaningless presentations. I'd never witnessed this type of charade.

The games didn't only happen in the war room. When I asked why progress had stalled, the contractor claimed they were searching for missing parts, but the lie quickly became clear. The parts weren't missing. They were damaged, and the replacements wouldn't arrive for another month. Still, they kept telling the client they were searching the warehouse.

Each morning, my Israeli counterpart talked about missions. My mission rarely had a clear goal. It was subject to unpredictable change and often made no sense. I valued structure and discipline, not chaos and reaction. To make things worse, I never knew when the assignment would end. It kept getting extended two weeks at a time.

When the last day of the last week arrived, the client promised another extension. I knew adapting to change was part of the job, but this was ridiculous.

Having Karen with me helped. She didn't like not knowing when we were leaving, and she definitely didn't like seeing the stress I was under. To pass the weekends, we revisited the Israeli national parks and tourist sites from eight years earlier, snapping then-and-now pictures. It was fun revisiting the places and trying to recreate the poses.

At one point, we snuck away from the madness for a long weekend in Istanbul. The elevator in our hotel was the size of a phone booth, with two gates guarding a dark wood paneled door. It reminded me of something from an old movie. The towering spires of the Hagia Sophia and Blue Mosque drew us in, and we listened to stories of sultans and harems in Topkapi Palace. On Princes' Island, where no cars are allowed, we toured flower-lined streets in a horse-drawn carriage. It was a throwback to a quieter era. The trip was a welcome escape from where we had come.

After four months of shifting missions and a client who seemed over-caffeinated, my company reached out with a lifeline. The new president of my division had once practiced structural engineering, just like me. He knew my work, and thanked me for my patience. He didn't want the client making an end run around his plans and told me that the next time they asked for an extension, no matter how hard they begged, I should say no.

Finally, someone in my own company was looking after my career again. I was no longer adrift. The client tried to beg. I said no. Those bigger things already set in motion were waiting, and they were in new places and with new people I had yet to meet.

CHAPTER 15

SHUFFLING THE DECK

Within my company, each technical discipline had its own professional focus. Architects were driven by aesthetic vision, which sometimes meant rapid changes in direction. Structural engineers kept their heads down and carried the load. Chemical engineers often viewed their process knowledge as the undisputed command center of the project, expecting deference from other disciplines and resisting any challenge to their technical authority. The list went on.

In the home office, people often worked with the same group for years. They learned each other's strengths and weaknesses. My projects weren't like that. The teams changed with each new job. I never considered managing people one of my strengths.

To survive the upcoming role, I needed to up my game.

Scotland

After arriving home from Israel, the company provided details of my new assignment. A client in Sicily had stopped the design and construction of a factory years earlier. A partially constructed building shell sat in Catania, Italy, waiting for completion.

My company proposed a split strategy. First, finish the design remotely in Scotland, where the original engineering team lived. When complete, the team would relocate to Sicily and support the construction. Before beginning, the client needed to approve me. In November 2007, I stayed home just long enough to enjoy Thanksgiving with Karen, and then boarded a plane to Italy.

My hotel room in Catania offered only the basics. A single bed sat in the middle of a room with bare walls and poor lighting. In one corner, a shower enclosure lacked enough space for me to turn around. After the long flight, washing off the film that always clung to me seemed like a good idea. Exhausted from the trip, I fell asleep on my feet. Bumping into the narrow walls kept me upright just long enough to wake up and drag myself across the cold tile floor into bed.

The next morning at breakfast, I met Peter, the Scottish office manager who had assembled the proposal. We hit it off immediately. His dry humor and steady manner resonated with me. At the client's office, I entered a structure known as the Banana Building because of its curved shape. The contrast between the playful name and the overly serious nature of the semiconductor industry struck me. I liked it.

My company's Italian construction manager met in the lobby. Sandro had a hangdog demeanor. Every word he spoke made me think doom awaited. He had arranged for the hotel, and when Peter asked about the modest accommodations, a mischievous smile appeared. He explained how the Phase One engineers had lived extravagantly, and wanted to ensure the team projected a humble appearance to the client. Peter and I exchanged a look. Although small, the hotel met professional standards. Ownership of the budget belonged to me. I smiled back and nodded with approval.

We entered a large office with floor to ceiling windows. The client, Mario, sat behind a large wooden desk. He swiveled slowly in his black leather chair, as if he were sizing us up. Everyone briefly shook hands as Peter made small talk. With formalities complete, we were motioned to sit down. Then I just listened.

Mario explained how the project in Italy won a competition. His company recently purchased a factory in Israel, and only enough money remained to retrofit one location. My experience with the Israeli site, where I managed construction years ago, made me lean forward in my seat.

The two factory managers met at his company's corporate headquarters to make their case. The Israeli manager spoke first. He said the factory should not be built in Italy. Catania lies in the shadow of Mount Etna. The volcano could erupt at any moment and destroy everything. The factory must be built in Israel.

The Italian manager followed. He said the factory should not be built in Israel. Rockets from Gaza or Iran could rain down at any moment and destroy everything. The factory must be built in Italy.

Mario kept turning slowly in his chair, never saying how Italy won, but smiling at the result. When we left, Peter and Sandro said Mario had Mafia ties. If he shared that story, it meant he liked me. I was in.

That evening at dinner, Sandro and I had a chance to get to know each other better. He told me about his love of food and how he farmed ancient varieties of wheat. I told him how much I loved my mother's baked spaghetti growing up.

A pained expression flashed across his face and his nose wrinkled. To him, spaghetti was pure and simple. Tomato sauce placed over pasta. Baking it was a crime against the culinary arts. We weren't even twenty-four hours into the project, and I had already offended his religion.

On the next trip to Catania, I met my design team. It was a mixed group. Two of the Americans started bickering on the first day. The Scottish contingent consisted of a fast-talking electrical engineer who reminded me of a used car salesman, and a mechanical engineer with the grumpiest attitude I'd ever seen. My architect was Italian. Her mother lived in Catania, and she would have done anything to make sure the project moved forward. Despite feeling an unhealthy tension within the team, weaving this group together would be critical to our success.

We gathered at an abandoned office trailer complex. The lights didn't work, the heat was out, and worst of all, the coffee machine was broken. As we sat around the table, each person summarized their scope and explained what help they needed. When it came time for the grumpy mechanical engineer to speak, he said, "It can't be done." I calmly asked for clarification. He responded, "The design doesn't work." When I asked if the client should be told of our failure, he said, "Yes, and we should all go home." The room went silent. Everyone looked at me for guidance.

I knew the technical problem could be overcome. With engineers, there is always a solution. It's just a matter of time and money. I told the team to finish their planned tasks, and we would regroup back in Glasgow. That afternoon I called Peter. He already understood the behavior I was dealing with, and told me not to worry. Another solution existed. A new engineer with a better attitude was starting in a few days, and he would replace the troublemaker. The project moved forward, and my leadership of the team had passed its first test.

Karen and I spent Christmas of 2007 together in Oregon. My work visa came through quickly. Karen's would take six more weeks. While I settled into Scotland, she had to keep everything running smoothly at home. We didn't like being apart, but passport control doesn't care about personal preferences.

When I arrived in Glasgow, the engineer who had caused problems in Italy had left the company. His replacement was young, ambitious, and believed she could make anything work. Changing one person transformed the group, and the underlying tension I had felt in Catania vanished. The job settled quickly into a steady pattern of uneventful days and monthly trips to Catania for client meetings.

Karen arrived in early February. With our apartment next door to the office, we were able to have lunch together every day. As a bonus, work finished at a reasonable hour. I loved the stress-free life of not driving in crowded traffic, and she loved the extra time we had with each other. Since we had no car, it also helped that the train station was just five minutes away. Karen had fond memories of train trips as a child, and couldn't wait to explore the countryside. With no drama in the office, I happily obliged.

It always felt respectful to explore the country we were living in first, so we started our adventures within Scotland. On the outskirts of Stirling, the sword used by William Wallace stood taller than me. His statue looked strangely like Mel Gibson from the movie *Braveheart.* Inverness and Loch Ness greeted us with tales of Nessie and a boat ride across the dark waters to Urquhart Castle. During one adventure, our train crossed the Harry Potter viaduct on the way to Oban, where we sipped whiskey that stayed on my tongue for two days. Every stop offered a generous serving of local food, and we sampled dishes like haggis and cullen skink.

Over time, our trips expanded beyond Scotland. In Liverpool we did a Beatles tour, visiting famous spots like Penny Lane, Strawberry Fields, and the Cavern Club. When the opportunity arose to travel to Norway, we didn't hesitate. The *Norway in a Nutshell* self-guided tour stretched from Oslo to Bergen, and gave Karen a chance to see where her ancestors came from. Traveling past towering waterfalls and through deep fjords reminded us of Glacier National Park.

In early July 2008, Mario notified me there were funding problems. He asked the engineering team to wrap up whatever they were working on.

No design is perfect, and there's a standard of care that accounts for that. Most owners don't understand. During construction, contractors always find flaws in the drawings, and every question carries urgency. When the engineers respond too slowly, the pressure does not land on them. It lands on the project manager. I knew how technically difficult the project had been. Stepping away from that pressure came as a relief.

Closing the project had its own challenges. One designer demanded perfection and could not bring himself to abandon an incomplete masterpiece. When he asked for a few more days, I used my best crowd-control voice and told him, "Stop. Pencils down. Step away from the drawings." He didn't use pencils and could hear the playfulness in my voice, but he also knew I meant it. He wrapped up his work as best he could.

Another designer tried to submit a questionable expense report. The project had a clear written policy that I reviewed with him before his one-month assignment. I was sympathetic to travelers and always gave them the benefit of the doubt, but he ignored the policy and tried to implement his own financial system. It took several firm exchanges before he complied with the requirements necessary to pass a company audit.

After hand delivering a copy of the final drawings, I decided this was the most perfect design in the history of engineering. No errors. No revisions. Only one conclusion could be drawn. My management had been amazing.

Footprints and Forks

Returning to Portland followed a familiar pattern. Schedule a few weeks off to catch up with family, remind my management when I will be in the office, show up in the office at the scheduled time, receive puzzled looks from management wondering what I was doing there. It shouldn't have bothered me, but it did.

At my desk, a colleague handed me an invitation and asked me to sign a card. A senior engineer I'd met years earlier was retiring, and had planned a reception for that evening. Spending time with people who barely noticed whether I came or went didn't sound like fun. Karen was always glad to see me. I chose her.

The next morning, someone stopped by and said I'd been missed at the reception. When they called my name, no one knew where I was.

My name had been called?

I hadn't seen the engineer in years, yet he had mentioned me in his farewell speech. We once played racquetball in Pittsburgh, and I made him work for every point, no matter the score. At the retirement party, he thanked me for teaching him the value of always giving your best.

Once alone, I sat with the thought. Something I'd dismissed as insignificant had left a lasting mark. Over the years, thank-you notes had arrived from people I'd written a reference for or mentored, but those never seemed like much either. My footprint was larger than I had realized.

A few weeks later, a new assignment came through. We packed the car and started on the long drive to Albuquerque. My role was to support the project manager. I knew him from past projects, and respected his approach. The long hours were wearing on him. Except for moral support, I wasn't really needed.

One event stayed with me. Large semiconductor clients could be highly demanding, often asking for free design services. To promote goodwill, project managers often agree to handle a few small extras. When this client didn't get their freebies fast enough, they threatened to withhold payment. I saw the stress building on my colleague's face.

The team was already taking care of the extra requests, and couldn't move any faster. The threat accomplished nothing but damaged trust.

The issues were solved quickly, but the attempted bullying stayed with me.

Since I was just in town to provide support, there was no stress on me. Karen and I were able to enjoy Albuquerque and loved its southwest flair. From our hotel, we could see balloons from the area's famous festival rising into the air. Taking a tram to the top of Sandia Peak gave us a sweeping view of the valley floor, and on one weekend we even snuck away to Las Vegas to see The Blue Man Group.

The food was the most amazing of all. We loved the hint of chile peppers that seemed to flavor every dish. Even McDonald's asked if we wanted green or red chile with our Big Macs, and no meal felt complete without a fluffy sopapilla drizzled with honey. As a souvenir, we bought a ristra made of red peppers that later doubled as a Christmas wreath.

When we returned to Portland in January 2009, we tried to carry a little of New Mexico with us by creating our own dish. We started with a basic white sauce, then folded in tender chicken thighs, stirred in mild green chile for attitude, and added a generous sprinkling of coarse black pepper for a tiny kick. Ladling the sauce over a bed of fettucine completed our masterpiece. It wasn't authentic Southwest or Italian, but something that belonged only to us.

Coming home wasn't prompted by the job ending. A new opportunity had surfaced. The architectural department manager was eager to land a large software company from Washington state on his resume. He assigned me the role of proposal manager.

From the first meeting, something felt off. The team was the most entitled, arrogant group I had encountered. All senior engineers. All highly opinionated.

Before moving forward, I did some research. As project manager, I had indirect visibility into salaries and quickly realized mine lagged behind most of the other managers. It wasn't the first time I'd noticed that pattern.

This group was guaranteed to be high maintenance, and it didn't sit right that the person responsible for them earned the least. My negotiation instincts kicked in. Whether the company felt persuaded or simply desperate to get me started, I couldn't say. When the raise appeared in my paycheck, the reason no longer mattered.

Managing the group proved as difficult as expected. One team member refused to follow my instructions. He disagreed with my interpretation of the contract's complex incentive clause. When directed to focus on his assigned areas and not on mine, he balked.

My first instinct urged me to remove him from the project, but I didn't have the authority to do that. After taking a deep breath, I asked the architectural department manager for support. That's when the shock came. Instead of backing me, he acted as an arbitrator. He removed the financial component from my responsibility and handed it to the belligerent employee.

I had given everything to pull the proposal together, and now, an arbitrary decision threatened to throw it off course. I felt angry, but couldn't let it show. In this world, emotion signaled a person out of control. That wasn't me. After composing myself, I pulled him aside and questioned why he had undermined my authority. When he asked what I wanted him to do, I said, "You wanted me as the project manager. The next time support is requested, give it. Don't act like a referee." He stood speechless as I shook my head and returned to my desk.

The challenges didn't just come from the team; they came from the client, too. At a dinner, he approached me and made what sounded like a threat. I'd been warned about his behavior and about the expectation of kickbacks. Nothing he said could be directly challenged, so this wasn't the moment for confrontation. Still, I kept my guard up.

Weeks later, after the team presented the proposal, the architectural department manager approached me. He expressed surprise that the client told him the financial incentive section had been presented incorrectly. His earlier decision still grated on me. I reminded him that my original interpretation had been correct. He stared at me blankly.

In the company hierarchy, he held a higher position than I did. That moment probably should have told me that politics weren't one of my strengths, but it didn't. All I knew was that telling him felt good.

The client's decision on the proposal didn't come quickly. To find relief from the pressure of work, I took long motorcycle rides with Karen through the countryside. Focusing on the road ahead while the engine roared beneath me always cleared my mind. Within minutes, the stress faded and the beauty of Oregon's rolling hills, mountain peaks, vineyards, and orchards took over. With Karen holding on tight, every curve came with a reminder of what mattered most.

After a few weeks, a new opportunity appeared. One of my old clients wanted to start a new project in Israel, and I was the only person in my division with management experience there. That made me the expert. Two programs were on the table. One had a corrupt client and an unsupportive management structure. The other offered freedom, respect, friends, and a return to international work. I chose the latter.

When the architectural department manager heard of my decision to accept the new project, he was not pleased. He thought I owed him because he had been instrumental in my pay raise. I didn't see it that way. The company should have already paid me more to make up for all the previous years. I couldn't say it out loud, but sure wanted to.

In the weeks that followed, the manager's frustration cooled. He later told me that although my presentation in the Washington meeting had been successful, the client canceled the project and changed direction. If I had stayed, I would have been left drifting once again. Instead, my choice opened a door to the largest and most complex assignment of my career.

Paving the Way

The new assignment didn't constitute an actual project yet. It was merely a proposal request for the first of four phases. With help from a business development contact and a team of senior engineers, I owned the response.

Clients loved making vague requests, so ensuring clarity was critical. Anything left open to interpretation invited conflict. I combed through every line, documenting questions and coordinating a reply.

As the proposal hinted at big changes in my professional life, something more personal brewed in the background. I was looking to buy a house. The condo had been a good home base, but it was time to move up. Karen insisted we use her cousin as our real estate agent. After mild resistance about mixing family with business, I gave in.

We'd done our research and had a general sense of the market. Staying within budget, having air conditioning, and finding a place with a view were my minimum requirements. When her cousin scoffed the requests, I knew we were headed for trouble.

She provided several listings, but none of them came close to meeting our needs. They were either ridiculously over budget, or they had a "view" of a dumpster. Instead of playing her games, we took matters into our own hands by finding a property with a beautiful city view of the surrounding hillsides in an upscale neighborhood that was only three miles from our condo. When her cousin saw the house, she said we couldn't afford it, and didn't want to be blamed for our disappointment. She was wrong. She knew the budget we had told her, not the budget we could afford.

During negotiations, her cousin represented the homeowners more than she represented us. They were real estate agents who had fallen on hard times. She identified with and felt sorry for them. I wanted to fire her cousin, but knew that would not help family relations. We really did like the house, and her cousin's unprofessional behavior didn't stop us from buying it.

Years earlier, when my father visited Oregon, he wasn't impressed with the condo. We had been upgrading it, and hadn't wanted him to visit until the work was complete. Before leaving, he'd said, "You can do better, son." After buying our new home, I had done better. We sent him a picture. He never commented.

While Karen handled our move, I prepared for a different kind of adventure. My proposal for the first phase won approval, and I needed to begin. This three-month stage of the project was one of the most enjoyable. Using an experienced staff, it focused on studying the client's concept to uncover anything that could significantly delay the schedule, such as utility or permitting constraints.

A team assembled, and to my surprise, my friend Lee was one of the engineers. He'd served as a mentor when I first joined the company and a colleague during our time in Ireland. Now he was part of my team. He wasn't used to seeing me as the top dog, but he respected my position, and his seal of approval gave me instant credibility.

The senior engineers and architects didn't need much management. This group had left their egos behind years earlier. Once they were briefed on the project structure and requirements, they knew what to do. For me to be effective, I had to know when to step in and when to step back. For this phase, my role focused on staying out of their way and gently guiding the process.

In June 2009, the team scheduled a four-week trip to Israel. To prepare them, my meetings in Oregon ended with lessons from my time living there. Common phrases, driving habits, areas to avoid, and local cuisine all became part of the discussion. I also explained that in Israel, yelling in meetings usually didn't signal anger. It signaled passion. By the time they boarded the plane, the team was ready.

Even though the company didn't pay for her flight, Karen came with me. We always worked better together, and arriving a few days early let us pave the way for the entire group. During those first days, we bought cell phones for everyone and programmed key numbers into them. If an emergency arose, they could reach our client, a colleague, or me.

Once the team arrived, Karen and I took steps to ease any concerns they had about their new surroundings. One weekend, we guided the group through the streets of Jerusalem. On another, they experienced sites around the Sea of Galilee. Each trip came with a small dose of my humor. While everyone was reminded to be respectful at the tourist sites, once out of earshot I told them how the Apostle Paul had been a plumber who installed a rubber sprinkler system in the Garden of Gethsemane. They could see the hoses, and since I was the project manager, it must have been true. I said it in jest, but the ones who nodded in agreement let me know who the yes-men were.

I wanted the engineers to love Israel the way I did. Happy employees are productive employees. There was another reason for making sure everyone enjoyed themselves. If the project moved forward, more staff would be needed for later phases, and some would be asked to relocate to Israel for up to a year. I viewed each person as an ambassador who could help attract future talent.

Showing the team my passion for where we were was only part of my plan. The client needed to feel included too. After our first presentation in Israel, when the engineers said thank you and spoke a few simple phrases in Hebrew, the client sat stunned. It didn't take long before they were teaching everyone about Israeli holidays. They prepared presentations, answered questions, and were energized by the engineers' curiosity about their culture.

Before the first phase completed, I started working on the next proposal. Three more months were needed to refine the scope, and find ways to cut costs. Since the client had confidence the project would be constructed, the next phase also included a one-year work visa for both Karen and me.

Most of my company's management acted in a reactionary manner. They preferred to wait until the last minute to make a decision. I knew that approach would fail in Israel. Everything moved slower in the international arena. Old lessons had taught me that organization leads to success, so I planned at least three months ahead. My visa process dragged. Documents arrived in pieces, and I had many questions. By the time the process completed, I understood every step. Clearly documenting the process and having the team gather their records in advance saved the team two weeks. It was a small thing no one noticed, but leadership wasn't always about speeches, authority, or even recognition. Sometimes, it was just about seeing what needed to be done, and doing it.

The second phase started well. The team trusted my cultural guidance, but they weren't yet convinced of my ability to lead technical presentations. I had a specific way I wanted their work shown, and they weren't used to doing things differently from their other projects. Three weeks before the final presentation, one of the engineers stopped by my desk. He said he had finished his studies and hadn't found any issues. His presentation pages were blank.

I stared back and slowly shook my head. The client had paid millions of dollars for a presentation summarizing our work. I asked if he had just spent a few million dollars, would he accept a presentation that looked like a crumpled twenty-dollar bill? He hung his head and responded no. When the team next gathered, I told everyone the same thing.

It took extra coaching and steady encouragement to help the senior staff embrace my format. By the time the final presentation completed, everyone's work looked like a million bucks, and the client let them know it. They said it was one of the best presentations they had ever seen. Afterward, the engineers couldn't stop congratulating themselves on the success. I didn't say a word. My reputation was growing.

At the end of every project, the company held a Lessons Learned session to review what went wrong, what went right, and why. I wasn't allowed to run the meeting. Management thought a project manager's strong personality could influence the feedback.

A colleague conducted the session while I silently watched. Before long, a pattern emerged. Every problem fell on the project manager. No matter how small the issue, it was never their fault. If someone had an uncomfortable airplane seat, somehow that became the fault of the project manager too. I knew it was lonely at the top, but this was ridiculous. Some of the engineers seemed to enjoy themselves more than they should have. After that, I managed the Lessons Learned sessions, and never let another one of those meetings happen on my project again.

CHAPTER 16

MAKING A NAME

Early in my career, I learned that responsibility and influence rarely went to those who waited in the background. I wanted to be noticed. While I embraced a hardworking and ethical approach, I could not accept a quiet professional life.

On previous projects, I had managed to stand out. Clients noticed my work, the CEO sent me letters of commendation, and awards filled my wall. Yet, every time I gained momentum, someone seemed to knock me back down. I never truly vaulted up a corporate ladder. Instead, I fought a constant cycle of progress and setbacks.

In Israel, the spark of opportunity lit again. This time, I didn't focus on a title or a ladder. I focused on cementing my reputation and securing my position. It was up to me to ensure the fire didn’t go out.

A Steady Hand

Karen and I returned to Portland for Christmas. Although the second phase of the project completed successfully, no time remained for rest. The Israelis understood the holiday, but that didn't mean they expected work to stop for it, and the next stage represented the most intense work yet. I had to prepare for the overall project's detailed design.

Before the third phase could begin, I had contractors to negotiate with, team travel memos to write, and a thousand small details screaming for attention. In addition, sixteen people were relocating to Israel. I felt the weight of each one.

In January 2010, two weeks before departing back to Israel, I stopped by the office. While passing a conference room, I saw a whiteboard filled with notes about how to manage my project. The approach failed to grasp the complexity of working internationally, and worse, it ignored the contract entirely. At first, I assumed it was just an exercise.

Being curious, I found the two people who had drawn it up and asked about their intent. One of the managers immediately became defensive and started ranting. She wasn't interested in listening, only in talking. With the pressure of organizing the upcoming work, I only had so much patience for her behavior. After being aggressively brushed aside and interrupted several times, I finally told her to "calm down," and to "take a Valium." The room went silent.

In hindsight, I could have chosen more professional words, but my reaction wasn't just about fixing a flawed strategy; it was about understanding why they hadn't included me on a plan that I would ultimately have to execute. Their approach posed a real threat to the project's success, and I sincerely wanted to know what they were doing. The two managers departed in a huff. I never found out.

With two days to go before departure, the team's work visas still hadn't arrived. I'd been working with an expeditor, and wasn't ready to cancel any travel plans. As hours ticked by and pressure built, the schedule remained unforgiving. It didn't care about excuses for being late. Team members nervously called multiple times looking for updates. It was like being in a car with children in the backseat constantly asking, "Are we there yet?" With each call, I calmly told the team to have faith, and that everything was under control. The final documents arrived just hours before departure. The team didn't see me breathing a sigh of relief, but I did.

Beyond the relief of that moment, something had changed in me. I always took my work seriously, but never felt the level of ownership like this before. The past six months had brought some intense moments, and took all of my energy. I was about to weave together over a hundred fifty engineers and consultants from the United States, Ireland, Scotland, Qatar, and Israel. All of them depended on me.

It felt as if the project was an octopus that had wrapped its tentacles around my brain. I nurtured it, guided it, and protected it. The project became a part of me, and while that may have been good for the company, it wasn't necessarily good for me.

In Ben Gurion airport, Karen and I waited to confirm everyone made it through security. When two people started wandering aimlessly in the wrong direction, I took off after them. Karen stayed with the bags. She was startled I'd left so quickly. Eager taxi drivers swarmed around her asking if she wanted a lift as other arriving passengers jostled her about. After rounding up my lost sheep and returning to her side, she glared at me. I barely noticed. On the way to the hotel, she let me know her displeasure. I was starting to lose sight of what really mattered, and it wasn't work.

Adding to the stress was that Karen and I still led groups on excursions around Israel. The trips had become famous, and at times, as many as fourteen people joined. Managing the project late into the evenings proved challenging enough. Herding cats around ancient aqueducts was even tougher.

At the end of a long work day, the engineers would often see Karen sitting alone in the lobby, reading a book. When they asked about my whereabouts and she said I was still at the jobsite, they looked embarrassed and shuffled quickly to their rooms.

By the time February rolled around, we needed some quiet time for ourselves. Instead of having breakfast in the hotel with everyone else, we broke away to sit at our own table. Some still stopped by to discuss work, but most understood. They knew how much I had devoted to them, and the project.

In April, during the Passover holiday, we had a weekend to ourselves and took a trip to Shivta National Park, home to the ruins of an ancient Nabataean city. They were nomadic traders who crossed the desert selling frankincense and myrrh. The man who invented the Colt pistol helped excavate the site, and his home had been converted into a crude Bed and Breakfast. Pistols decorated the walls, and stray cats perched on the rustic, wood dining tables.

That night, Karen and I sat under the stars. In one direction, we could peer into a darkness filled with crumbling walls and ancient history. A mile away in the other direction, the glow of a military tank post lit the sky like a misplaced stadium.

We tried turning our back on the lights the same way we tried to turn our backs on the project, but work didn't always cooperate.

My cell phone rang, its sound piercing the night air. A manager in Portland, not associated with the job, couldn't stop himself from interfering. He told an architect in the United States to immediately board a plane and fly to Israel. A low-level client manager was unhappy with the local architect and had complained. I had already solved the issue the prior week, but that didn't stop the overly reactive manager from panicking.

I didn't tell the architect not to come. I just pushed back his departure date. If he came when directed, my Israeli counterpart would have been upset. During the Passover holiday, the architect would have nothing to do. Wasting money like that would upset the client every time, even if they weren't paying for the trip. I knew once back in the office, I'd have to smooth over the unnecessary chaos. Unless the architect's manager intended to foot the bill and handle the security, he had no authority to send anyone.

It wasn't the first time Oregon had reached into my work. I was coming to understand that this geographically remote management often behaved with a disproportionate sense of authority, frequently overriding established protocols. My actual manager, Peter, was in Scotland. We worked together before and got along fine. If the client was unhappy with how I ran the project, that was the proper chain of command.

After Karen and I returned to Ashkelon, others continued to test their limits on my project. One senior manager in Portland tried changing a travel policy that I knew would hurt morale. Every country was different. Travel policy wasn't something to turn upside down in the middle of a project. Another supervisor accused me of failing to follow proper procedures for client change orders, even though I always did.

My survival depended on organization and persistence, but one factor mattered even more. A senior manager from Scotland advocated for me from behind the scenes. He shielded me from the company politics. I could often see the attacks, but with his support, they never gained enough momentum to knock me off balance.

As external managers kept me on my toes, so did my own team. Every day brought a new reminder that I was managing people, not just projects. The drawing coordinator stayed up all night to meet a deadline. When I saw him sleeping at his desk in the morning, I gave him a gentle kick in the pants. Working in Idaho Falls on the night shift had taught me about working to exhaustion. I told the team they could never work more than twelve hours in a day, sixty hours in a week, and must always have at least one day off per seven.

On one occasion, the two managers underneath me were bickering. I pulled them into a conference room and reminded them that while managers can fight behind closed doors, they must never do so in front of the team.

While celebrating a project milestone, one of the engineers had too much to drink and acted rudely to the client. I drove him home, and as I turned the car into the entrance to the town, he opened his door and threw up. A police car sat nearby, facing our direction. I was grateful the policeman didn't see him, and that it wasn't my car.

Another engineer ignored my security warning and walked aimlessly across the rooftops of Jerusalem. When he got lost, he tried exiting through an open door. It happened to be someone's home. The Old City could be a powder keg. I told him he should be glad he wasn't shot.

A Bucket of Cold Water

By July 2010, I was running on fumes. Karen and I took a quick home leave. We needed a break from the constant demands of my job. Rules for working hours applied to the team, but I never followed them myself. I typically worked six days per week, twelve hours per day. The constant phone calls and tapping of my computer late into the night grated on Karen. When the time came for me to return to the jobsite, she chose to stay home.

I knew how hard the trip had been on her. She couldn't work like she had done in Ireland or Phoenix. We were living in a small hotel room, not the beautiful townhouse like we had done in Taiwan.

The hotel sat on a cliff overlooking the Mediterranean Sea. We could hear the waves gently lapping on the shore, enjoy clouds lighting up the sky at sunset, and even watch the palm trees swaying gently in the cool evening breeze. Those things were great when I was convincing people to come to Israel for a short period, but living in a hotel for months presented its own challenges.

Karen saw what was behind the curtain. Cockroaches scurried across the dining room floor, children ran screaming up and down the hallways, and she had no privacy from hotel staff or others on my team.

When I returned to Israel and stepped into the hotel room, the loneliness hit me. I paused for a moment and looked at the four small walls. All thoughts of work slipped away. As the reality of what she was enduring sank in, a deep sadness overcame me. For once, I didn't try to hold it together. I sat on the bed, put my head in my hands, and closed my eyes. We had tried carving out some personal time just for us, but it wasn't enough. She was due to return in four weeks, and I knew when she did, things had to change.

When Karen returned, my focus started changing. We needed more time for ourselves. Travel had always acted as a constant in our lives. It became a refuge to look forward to in challenging times. One benefit of living in hotels and flying around the world is points. To take the sting out of the cost, we could get free hotels and free airfare. It had been a year since we'd taken any real vacation, and Europe sat on our doorstep. Bucharest came first.

For one week, we camped out in a luxury hotel and branched out into our surroundings. One private tour took us to Transylvania to see the beautiful wood carvings and decorated rooms of Peleş Castle. We felt embarrassed as our driver announced the crowd needed to make way for the VIPs and ushered us to the front of the line. Other tourists stared as if we were movie stars. That evening, we entered the town of Sighişoara. By the time we arrived, the restaurants had closed. The best our guide could find was a small establishment that offered a cheese sandwich paired with a shot of a red liquid called Dracula's Blood.

During the long drive back to Bucharest, our driver claimed he knew a great place for authentic Romanian food. Our previous stops had disappointed us, so we looked forward to the experience. When he pulled into a roadside gas station, Karen and I looked at each other with apprehension. Inside, we were served a plate of pork and beans that looked as if they had come straight from a can.

We were glad we hadn't come to Romania for the food. The sights more than held our interest. Private limousines shared country roads with horse-drawn carts full of hay. Long rows of tall, nondescript apartment buildings stretched down isolated roads in remote towns. The driver said the out-of-place buildings were remnants of communism. Except for the meals, we loved every moment of our adventure. It reminded us that even in the middle of constant work, the world was still waiting.

In October 2010, we visited Pittsburgh to celebrate my mother's eightieth birthday. At the airport, Israeli security started asking their standard questions. When they wanted to know the purpose of our trip, I told them it was for my mother's birthday, and added that I hadn't seen her in three years. The security agent's eyes grew wide. Then the unexpected happened. The agent scolded me. "You are a bad son. Go! Visit your mother. No more questions." As we passed, I hung my head and then smiled. I was being treated like a local.

December brought even more travel. After spending Christmas in Oregon, we returned to Israel recharged. Taking a trip every three months breathed life back into Karen, and gave her something to look forward to. It didn't make the days in the hotel any easier, but that was about to change.

By January 2011, we moved out of the hotel and into our own apartment. We were finally able to cook familiar foods. Our favorite store became the Russian grocery. They sold the taboo product from pigs known as ham, or as my Israeli friend Shira called them, small cows.

Something else happened in January. Construction was underway and Phase Four had received full approval. The engineers were fully funded to assist the owner and contractors through completion of the building shell. Many of the original engineers finished their one-year commitment and returned home. Others, drawn to the excitement of international living, stayed on. I worked with each person to ensure a smooth transition.

The two project managers who helped set up the work both decided to return to the United States. The project would not have succeeded without their efforts. One discussed leaving and then changed her mind a month later, but her change of plans came too late. A replacement was already on the way.

The second manager never told me he wanted to leave. I heard it from the Portland office instead. That hurt. I thought we had become friends. Among the entire team, he was the only person who felt uncomfortable telling me his decision. I didn't let him know of my disappointment. Like everyone else who had sacrificed a year away from loved ones, I gave him a sincere thank you and honored his contribution before he left.

The new staff arriving in Israel fit right in and benefited from the knowledge the old-timers shared. The site maintained a one hundred percent success rate for personnel completing their original assignments, but that streak was about to end.

My responsibilities covered Phase Four, but there was also a Phase Five involving semiconductor equipment installation. I knew the work from my construction days. The company won the contract, and because the work was so specialized, a new team with a new territorial manager arrived onsite. Unlike my set-up, he skipped the cultural lessons, and ignored people management. I didn't agree with his approach, but could only offer to help. It wasn't my project.

One of his team members hadn't disclosed the need for medication to stabilize her mental health. She stopped taking the prescribed pills, and became increasingly afraid of her surroundings. The manager washed his hands of the situation, assuming Human Resources would handle it. He stayed focused on getting his new project off the ground.

Human Resources was half a world away. They were completely incapable of helping. Both the company's and the manager's lack of support bothered me. I couldn't let someone unravel while others looked away, so I stepped in.

She trusted me after our first conversation. I can't explain why, but my being nearby helped her stay grounded. A day later, she checked herself into the local hospital. Since she didn't have any in-country support, I stayed with her until 1:30 AM. Karen understood, and even joined me in the waiting room.

After checking out of the hospital, more challenges arose. In the mornings, she bought a ticket to go home. As the afternoon approached, fear took hold and she refused to board the plane. My days were consumed by fielding frantic calls, and visiting the hotel to keep her from spiraling.

I couldn't keep spending so much time away from my other responsibilities, but felt it was my duty to do so. By the end of the week, I coordinated a new strategy. The company paid for her sister to fly to Israel. The day she arrived provided a huge sense of relief.

Others noticed how much I cared for team members, even if they weren't mine. Being there for the employee was about more than one person helping another. I worked hard to make sure the team felt a sense of community. Friends and family who could support them in the United States weren't in Israel. There was a phone number to call for a medical emergency, but it didn't cover daily issues.

One person lost their car keys in the Dead Sea, another didn't feel well and needed a ride to the doctor. These weren't emergencies, but having someone nearby to lend a hand provided peace of mind. I told everyone they could call me for anything, anytime. If uncomfortable calling me, they needed to find someone on the team they were comfortable with.

When two young engineers asked if they could relocate to Tel Aviv, I hesitated. In Ashkelon, if they got in trouble, I could find them in minutes. Tel Aviv was a maze. They said they had experienced all Ashkelon had to offer, had met all the women, and wanted more. That didn't sound like a great reason. I approved their request under one condition. They needed to live close enough to each other so if one needed help, the other would be there. Without even looking at each other, they enthusiastically nodded their heads in agreement.

Paris in the Springtime

By April 2011, the project was running smoothly. The team stayed busy responding to client change orders and contractor questions. The one person who replaced my two supporting managers worked out well. We shared the same birthday which made an immediate connection. He fully embraced the local culture and how I ran the job.

Back in Portland, a senior manager noticed the progress and asked if I could write down my secrets to success. I wasn't sure how to respond. Most of it already existed in a Project Execution Plan, but few people bothered to read it. The best way to connect with a team was in person, not through a dry procedural manual. Guidelines were necessary, but this wasn't about following a cookbook. A project is a living, breathing thing that evolves.

I never did respond to the request. Success came from how I applied my values to rapidly changing situations. It was just me being me, and capturing that would have meant writing a book.

It wasn't always like that. Sometimes, being me meant being "we". With the job running smoothly, Karen and I decided to take an extended vacation. We had only been to Paris once, and there was still so much to be seen in and around the city. We planned the trip as carefully as I had planned the project. Our adventure alternated between Paris and the French countryside.

We spent the first day gathering our standard souvenirs like Hard Rock Café pins and a Starbucks mug. At night, after the tourist crowds thinned, we made our way to the top of the Arc de Triomphe. From our lofty vantage point, we watched the Eiffel Tower light up as its beacon spun around in the darkness. Karen took a picture she still uses as a screen saver on her computer to remember how special that moment felt.

Looking at Monet paintings in the Orsay and Orangerie museums was interspersed with train rides to the royal Palaces of Vincennes and Fontainebleau. I had visited Versailles in high school, and loved taking Karen through the Hall of Mirrors. The palace provided new experiences as well, and we strolled through the expansive gardens to Marie Antoinette's private guest house, the Petit Trianon. Since Versailles wasn't part of a guided tour, we walked through the palace a second time, just to cement the memory.

For the castles of the Loire Valley, we switched gears and took a bus tour. Being herded like sheep took away from the beauty. At a brief lunch stop, the waiter chased after us with our dessert in a box as we hurried back to rejoin the group. It wasn't necessary. The bus ended up being late. By the time the tour completed, Karen felt she missed the magic of what we had just seen. I told her the memories would have to live in the hundreds of photos I had taken. It didn't help her disappointment.

Other trips into the countryside were conducted on our own. We took a fast train to see the picturesque fortress of Mont-Saint-Michel. Crossing the causeway and climbing narrow streets to the monastery at the top rewarded us with commanding views of the surrounding sea. Nearby in the walled city of Saint-Malo, we saw the grave of Chateaubriand. During dinner, I proved my language skills were still strong enough to avoid ordering deep-fried pigeon.

By the time we returned to Israel, France had provided us a lifetime of memories. Knowing the pressures of work weren't going away anytime soon, Karen and I still took short trips back to Portland. From our Oregon home balcony, we watched Fourth of July fireworks light up the distant hillsides. On another four-day trip, we enjoyed scrambling to make Thanksgiving in our own kitchen. The long days and project challenges kept coming, but the travel made our time in Israel feel less stressful.

That year, we stayed in Israel for the Christmas season and scheduled a tour to Bethlehem on December 24th. While waiting for the visit to begin, a man tried to convince us that our guide wasn't coming. He had died, the man insisted, and his own gracious offer couldn't be refused. We already knew the predatory tricks played on unsuspecting tourists and politely declined.

In Bethlehem, we toured Shepherds' Field, visited a plastic baby Jesus in the Church of the Nativity, and listened to a marching band playing Christmas carols in Manger Square. Karen held on tight, making sure crowds filling the streets didn't separate us. For an encore, on New Year's Day we took a tour underneath Jerusalem's Western Wall. A Santa Claus selling bagels at one of the Old City gates waved us goodbye as we returned to our car.

In early 2012, the president of my company's division called. The project's reputation was well known. I had been chosen for a Health and Safety Service Award because of how I looked after my team. The CEO presented the award, which had never been given to anyone in our group before. Being in Israel, I found it impractical to fly halfway across the world for a pat on the back. The president still wanted me to hear the speech he would give.

One part stuck out. He said, "Dan doesn't need to be told to do the right thing. He just does it." Small words of recognition like that were more powerful than any company award. He promised to send a copy of his speech. He never did, but it didn't really matter. I still heard the words.

Fire and Reign

Life in Israel came with risks. In March 2012, two hundred rockets rained down from the Gaza Strip. We were only ten miles from the border, and the Iron Dome defense system lit up the sky overhead.

To me, the rockets weren't scary. The only time we heard of injuries was when people ignored Israel's Home Front Command's advice to take cover. We understood why people got hurt. The draw of watching interceptors turn in the sky and track down incoming threats was mesmerizing.

To help my team put the danger into perspective, I asked if anyone in my group ever played golf in a thunderstorm and held their metal club high in the air. They all knew how unsafe that was, and the importance of ending the round and heading inside. I explained that the rocket attacks were similar. The moment they heard the sirens, they needed to stop what they were doing and follow the appropriate guidelines.

When the time came, my team knew what to do during a rocket attack, and once the danger passed, they all checked in to confirm everyone was okay. One week after the first sirens sounded, a ceasefire was brokered.

There were other risks besides rocket attacks. My friend Lee loved swimming off the coast of Ashkelon. One evening at dinner, he described battling the big waves of the Mediterranean Sea. Fishermen on the rocks shouted for him to get to shore. Lee had served in the Polish Navy and wasn't intimidated by rough seas. With energy in his voice and a smile on his face, he looked across the table and said, "Swimming today was great. I almost died. You should come with me next time." Karen gently kicked me under the table as I replied, "Um, no thanks."

Oregon must have been concerned about harm coming to their award-winning manager because in late March, I received a call. They thought my job had become too easy and wanted me to return home. Well, that's how I remembered it. They also mentioned something about needing my help on another project.

Over the past two years, I'd heard about trouble on a project in Oregon. It was for the same client I'd been working for. The engineers described the management there as being like the Keystone Cops. Staying in Israel wasn't an option. I notified my client counterpart, and prepared to leave. As everyone offered an obligatory thank-you, one stood out.

An Israeli drawing coordinator who didn't believe in her own abilities had been amazing. I knew she had children, and after repeatedly doubting herself I explained the tale of *The Little Engine That Could.* The story made her eyes light up.

Upon returning from one of my trips back to Oregon, I presented her with the book. She greatly appreciated my point, and the chance to share the story with her children. When it was my time to go, she gave me a personalized mug listing the traits of a good manager. The misspelled words only made the gift more precious.

After receiving everyone's thanks and words of praise, it was time to make a small update to my title. Over the years, I had become one of the most successful and experienced project managers in my division. In emails and on business cards, my title changed to *Senior* Project Manager. My mother always warned me about getting a big head, but this was earned. The quickly graying hair confirmed it.

All the kind words weren't just for me. I knew others made it possible to maintain focus on my job. When Karen saw the attention I was getting, she gave me a gentle nudge and asked, "What about me?" The company didn't give awards to spouses. She would just have to settle for my love and attention.

While living far from home, there were friends back in Oregon who made our lives easier. They also never received any special speeches or awards. At the beginning of our assignment, Karen and I were concerned about who would care for the house we had just bought. Fortunately, some good friends agreed to look after the home, giving us one less thing to worry about. Their kindness provided a peace of mind that kept Karen steady so she could focus on me, and I could focus on my job. They kept our cars in running condition, scanned mail, and monitored contractors who had to repair a major water leak.

Our friends knew that years earlier, Karen and I barely had time to move in, let alone furnish or paint. After hearing my thoughts about colors for the home office, they offered to help and jumped into action. Unbeknownst to us, their enthusiasm leaked into another room.

Once back in Portland, we walked through the house to make sure everything was in order. As we opened the door to our upstairs spare bedroom, an eerie glow lit the entire space. The walls were painted bright orange. With matching curtains and white furniture, it felt like sunglasses were needed to stare into the brightness. Karen and I stood in silence.

Our friends had converted the bedroom into a craft room for Karen. She didn't need a craft room. They didn't realize that the office was her space. As the intention behind it all sunk in, we smiled. A couple who cared about us had created the room, and as much as any corporate award or praise, our friends' gesture was exactly the type of thing that helped us succeed. As we settled back home, the room became my space. Entering it always reignited a smile, and it became a reminder of friends who care.

CHAPTER 17

DESCENTS

The Portland office had a reputation for being the premier location for any manager in my division. Amazing people worked in other offices, but the division's executive team sat in Portland. It was one of the reasons I had originally relocated there.

After returning from Israel, I expected to be placed in charge of what was considered the flagship project. That did not happen. A younger manager received the top role, and the company asked me to mentor him. He had never managed a job of the size and complexity this project had, and got the position because he had worked alongside one of the local senior managers who supported him.

I could see from the start he was struggling. Even with my help, I wasn't sure if it would be enough. Missing out on the lead role disappointed me, but I had my marching orders. Sitting passively beside the young manager in meetings felt awkward, as if the company had put me out to pasture. I wasn't ready for that yet.

Transitions

The president of our division once told me that the hardest thing he ever had to do was let people make mistakes, not the kind that couldn't be reversed or would damage confidence, but the kind that promoted learning. I knew that was what I had to do with the young manager.

Within a few weeks, he started to miss meetings. His newborn son had medical issues, and the timing could not have been worse. Early planning is when a project finds its footing. My managers saw the risk and asked me to take the lead.

There was never any doubt about my answer. The only question I had was for Scott, who had placed the young manager in that role. On the last project in Oregon, the client asked that Scott be removed. For reasons that did not make sense to me, he received a promotion and was on a trajectory to become the next division president.

Before stepping into leadership, I requested a few minutes of his time. I asked what had gone wrong on his previous project. Scott had a good reputation and said everything had gone without incident. I knew the client in Portland treated project managers like clay targets at a skeet shoot, yet his version didn't match what the engineers told me.

There wasn't time to dwell on the discrepancies. My focus had to be on getting the new project off the ground. It started with a team meeting that included the client and all levels of management.

With this group, a firm hand and strict discipline were the only way. I looked across the conference room filled with more than twenty battle-tested managers and laid down the law. We reviewed the rules of engagement for handling disputes, and I challenged them to not hide from the tough problems, giving examples of the ones that needed attention. One by one, they nodded in agreement. These weren't my rules or even my company's. They were the client's rules. The only real question was whether everyone would follow them.

That first meeting went well. The tone of the project had been set. Now I had to line up my supporting managers. The first one came from Ireland. In Israel, he acted like royalty. He had tried pushing me aside so his incoming group's work could take precedence. It didn't go over well at the time, and having him designated as my second in command concerned me. I made those above me aware. Whatever his manager said to him before he arrived must have worked, because from day one he was fully supportive.

Another proposed manager had worked with Scott on the previous project and was still cleaning up loose ends. He said he preferred staying in his current, much easier role. I wasn't used to people turning away work. What hit me even harder was that two years later, he received a promotion. By then I had noticed a discouraging pattern. People could work on unsuccessful projects and still be promoted if they had the right connections.

I still needed more management support, and the company gave me two strong-willed people. Both were highly competent, fiercely independent, and respected my position. This was the A-team. I knew they would be successful as long as I didn't try to "manage" them too much.

Another part of the project that looked promising was my client counterpart. He was the same person who had worked closely with me on the successful project in Israel. His company wanted to capture the same magic we'd found before by placing us together again.

All the pieces were in place. There were plenty of normal ups and downs, but my leadership team remained steady. The company also viewed it that way, and placed me in a program reserved for the best of the best.

In November 2012, with the project fully under control, Karen and I planned a one-week vacation. We'd seen the Elvis Café in Israel and joked about Las Vegas weddings. Then inspiration hit. We'd been married quickly along the Oregon coast just before our assignment to Taiwan. Renewing our vows in Las Vegas at an Elvis Chapel sounded like a lot of fun.

For the ceremony, I wore a tuxedo and Karen wore a long gown. We snapped a few pictures outside by a pink Cadillac and then headed inside. Except for Elvis, we were the only people in the chapel. We were offered a choice of songs, and there was one that struck me as being just right. "I Can't Help Falling in Love." As the ceremony progressed, Elvis gently scolded me for kissing Karen too soon. She cried through the whole thing. After all the nights she patiently waited for me to come home from work, I hoped they were tears of joy.

After the ceremony, every activity followed the wedding theme. For the honeymoon, a helicopter flew us to the bottom of the Grand Canyon where we toasted champagne. The play *Nunsense* added a touch of religion. We enjoyed dinner while watching heroic knights joust at the *Tournament of Kings. The Jersey Boys* musical acted as our band, and for a wedding gift, we visited the shop featured in the television show *Pawn Stars.*

Our renewal didn't start out as something serious, but when we looked back on the ceremony, it was. More importantly, in years to come, our time in Las Vegas let me remind Karen that I married her, twice.

By March 2013, Karen and I fell into an old pattern. I worked long and demanding days, while she planned our next trip. Before we met, I had an assignment in Massachusetts, and when a ten-day vacation window opened up, it felt like the perfect opportunity to show her someplace new. We started in Salem with a tour through the House of the Seven Gables. I'd never read Hawthorne's novel, and made sure to buy a copy in the souvenir shop. At lunch, we shared a bowl of New England clam chowder at a restaurant guarded by a wooden witch.

The coast pulled us north to Bangor, Maine, where we cracked fresh lobster and took a single-engine plane tour over Acadia National Park. After seeing the park from above, we had to see it from the ground. Along the shore, we soaked our feet in the cold Atlantic water. On the way back south, we managed a few photos beside a snow-covered moose before a blizzard whited out the roads.

Cape Cod offered long stretches of beach, where we sat on the sand and had a picnic lunch. At Plymouth Plantation, costumed Pilgrims reenacted history with practiced cheer. Karen tugged my sleeve when I asked too many questions. We paused at Plymouth Rock, unconvinced it was the real landing site from 1620.

Boston was our final stop. We ate lobster rolls in Faneuil Hall, walked the Freedom Trail, tossed a fake bale of tea from the deck of the Boston Tea Party ship, and soaked up the history as if it were new.

Both Las Vegas and New England were amazing, and work wasn't causing any problems. For the first time in years, life felt balanced, even celebratory. It wouldn't last.

The Betrayal

By late summer, several changes occurred in my company. The division president who had always supported me, and another senior manager I had gotten along well with, both moved on. These people possessed high integrity and knew my history with the company better than anyone. They didn't both leave at the same time, but in the days before their departures, they appeared stressed. Although rumors suggested they were being pushed out, no one ever explained why.

There were also changes on the job. My client counterpart, with whom I got along so well, left the project and returned to Israel. His company thought he needed to be tougher on costs. As a large project progressed, this client became unreasonable about change orders. My counterpart never acted like that. Our cost negotiations were consistently tough but fair. Sometimes my company made money, and sometimes they didn't. I suspected the real reason for his removal was that the locals wanted to exert more control.

The replacement manager had once worked for my company as an engineer. She thought I had a hidden slush fund. That may have been the way she managed, but it wasn't mine. I was always transparent on costs and felt hiding money was dishonest. She didn't believe me.

Project negotiations became more challenging because of her continuous requests for freebies. I told her any change order had to follow a strict process. She didn't like that and saw the process as an obstacle to overcome. This wasn't what her company insisted upon when the project first started. I had worried about the client following their own rules back at the start, and now my concerns were coming to life.

While she played games with costs, the team worked at an efficiency level higher than I had ever seen. All the meetings remained amicable, and on the surface, everything looked alright. My problems weren't about what could be seen.

When the phone rang on my twenty-third anniversary with the company, I thought someone was calling to thank me for all my hard work. That wasn't what happened. All I remember is being told the client had requested my removal. My head spun. It didn't make sense. I'd followed the rules the client set out. The project was progressing at high efficiency. The problems weren't any bigger or smaller than any other project.

I remembered prior conversations about when Scott had been removed. Was it possible the client thought removing a project manager was a normal part of business? No one had ever requested that I leave before. My clients asked me to stay.

Back in the office, the message was even more mixed. One group said I had done an amazing job and promoted me from Senior Project Manager to Program Manager. Another group claimed they needed to repair client relations and asked me to reflect upon what went wrong. The only words that came through were: "Bad dog. You know what you did wrong." Except I wasn't a dog, and I didn't know what I had done.

After reflecting and asking internal questions, there were no clear answers. My manager told me that because of the project, my bonus and raise would be affected. I'd been given an elevated title and punished, all at the same time.

My client counterpart took me to lunch to say goodbye, which felt like a nice gesture. I asked why her company had requested my removal. She expressed surprise, then mumbled something about how she hadn't meant for it to happen. When I asked her what I possibly could have done to merit removal, she just stared.

Her silence landed like a slap. The confusion and dejection I felt turned into disbelief. The mumbled words and embarrassing silence revealed complicity. Lunch ended uneventfully, and upon leaving, I didn't say a word.

It took years before the truth came out. I hadn't been the problem. It was someone who wasn't even in my orbit. Shortly before my removal, the company hired a new senior manager named Todd from the client's organization. He wanted to make a name for himself and decided a high-profile project manager would make a good target. He played politics with those around me and convinced them I was a problem.

In time, my department manager apologized and admitted he had been manipulated. He told me he didn't remember the part about reducing my raise and bonus. I couldn't forget it.

Years later, the client had another major project. They wanted me to lead it. When I hesitated and explained to my management why I didn't want the job, they looked confused and said the client never asked for my removal. The words were not credible.

As for Todd, upper management realized his attitude didn't belong in a professional engineering company. He left the firm after less than one year.

Confirming what happened in the years to come would be comforting, but in the aftermath of my removal I felt betrayed. Years of my life had been dedicated to the company's success. Instead of letting my actions speak for me, they let themselves be manipulated and readily believed the worst about me.

I had always naively thought an unspoken contract with my employer existed. If I put in the hours and competently produced results, the company would reward the effort. I had kept my part of the agreement. They had broken theirs. The trust would never be fully repaired. The company never tried.

I wasn't alone in my feelings of betrayal. Karen had accompanied me on past assignments, often helping in the background. In her diary, she wrote that my departure from the project felt like a funeral. During those first few days, we took long motorcycle rides, ate at our favorite restaurants, and just tried to re-center ourselves.

In August 2013, feeling disillusioned, I headed to Denver for a previously planned executive training seminar. There were lectures, speeches, and charts. It was a condensed version of the slick management books that crowd the bestseller lists. Each presentation came with a list of seven things to do, or twelve successful habits. I was struggling, and my head wasn't in the right space. I couldn't invest myself further into the company after what had just happened. It all came across as meaningless drivel that some consultant who never managed real work dreamed up.

The worst part was the personality test. I prided myself on being able to adapt and adjust to rapidly changing situations, and here the company was trying to define who I was through probing questions about my social life and friendships. I didn't like being labeled in high school, and liked it even less here.

By the end of the week, I started doubting who I was as a manager. It wouldn't last, but being made to question myself didn't sit right. My position required high levels of confidence. Uncertainty was viewed as weakness, and the weak didn't survive.

Emerging from the Fog

Once the corporate double-talk ended, Karen and I had a five-week sabbatical scheduled. We'd driven from Portland to Denver for the seminar, and the time off started with a slow, wandering trip back home.

My sister lived about an hour outside of Denver and was on the way, so our trip started with some catching up. It had been a long time since we'd seen each other, and it felt good to be around family again. Recent events at work weren't brought up. They were my burden to carry, not hers.

After visiting Kathy, Mount Rushmore was our first stop. It took about six hours to drive from Denver. Our first peek at the presidents on Mount Rushmore occurred at night. The mountain's white glow made it even more striking. For me, the carved figures represented what people can accomplish in hard times.

We had arrived late, and after dinner we noticed a jewelry store still open. Karen saw a sunflower pendant made of black gold that she liked. I'd never been to the Black Hills of South Dakota and it was the first time I'd seen this type of jewelry. The sunflower is a symbol of renewal. Karen had been feeling the stress caused by my work situation. Restless nights and pained expressions affected her as much as they did me. We both thought "renewal" was the perfect theme for our journey.

On the way to Wind Cave the next day, I enjoyed watching the prairie dogs popping their heads in and out of the ground. They could retreat to safety when danger arose. I envied them.

When we continued on our slow journey home, we saw Wyoming's Devil's Tower from miles away, and hiked through the trees and around its base. Custer's Battlefield in Montana stood as a testament to Native Americans beating the odds. The Oregon Trail Interpretive Center in eastern Oregon paid homage to those who made the treacherous journey to an unknown world. I could see reflections of work in every place we visited, and although I enjoyed the sights, my fog hadn't lifted. I was glad when we finally arrived home.

Since departing Oregon, we had traveled over 3,800 miles in eleven days and crossed eight states. Most couples would have stopped there. Karen and I didn't operate that way.

We hadn't seen my parents for two years. The second part of our sabbatical took us back to Pittsburgh. It was as much a responsibility as it was a vacation. After a few days of fulfilling our obligation, we headed to Niagara Falls. The hotel gave us a commanding view of both the American and Canadian falls. During the day, we packed onto the Maid of the Mist and approached the roaring waters. Karen didn't enjoy crowds, but went along with it for me.

To get more personal with the water, we descended into the rock behind the falls and peered through the deafening curtain of water. When Karen's make-up dripped into her eyes, she became uncomfortable, and was allowed a special trip up on the elevator. Niagara Falls might not have been her favorite trip, but it was a memorable one. For me, like her mascara, thoughts of work were starting to wash away.

Back in Pittsburgh, we switched gears and visited Fallingwater, a home designed by Frank Lloyd Wright. Nearby, we stepped back into history by visiting George Washington's Fort Necessity, the outline of the old wooden fort a reminder of our country's past rise to glory.

After returning to Oregon, we still had ten days of remaining time off. The first part of the sabbatical had been anchored to work. The second part had a family theme mixed in. The third part was going to be different. I had never been to Hawaii. This trip wasn't going to be about anything but fun.

We flew into Honolulu and settled into a hotel near Waikiki Beach where we took a ride in a submarine. As the sub descended into clear green water, sea turtles glided among the ruins of sunken ships.

On land, we traveled to the Big Island of Hawaii and stayed at Volcano House hotel, nestled within a National Park. At night, the orange-red glow of lava rose in the distance, and above us the Milky Way stretched across the sky. The sheet of stars across the sky might not have seemed memorable for someone living away from city lights, but it was something we rarely saw.

The volcano took center stage again when we boarded an open-door helicopter. As it hovered over fields of flowing lava, we could feel the heat rising up from the ground below. On our way back to Hilo, we stopped at the Mauna Loa macadamia nut factory. The free chocolate-covered samples were a perfect way to end the day.

No trip to Hawaii would be complete without a visit to Pearl Harbor. Walking the memorial and learning about those who sacrificed themselves felt like a requirement for every American.

On our final day, we thought about spending time on Waikiki Beach, but the sand was too hot, so we made other plans. Iolani Palace sounded interesting. We didn't know anything about it. Touring the rooms deepened our appreciation of Hawaii's history and its people.

When we finally arrived home and posted the pictures from our five-week adventure, friends asked if I had retired. They couldn't believe how much we had done. We would have kept going, but the calendar dictated otherwise. The fog remained, and the thought of returning to the office only brought dread. Yet, even with that weight, picturing another career seemed impossible. Finding a way forward was the only option. Exactly what that looked like remained a mystery, but I would soon find out.

Into the Fire

Returning to the office after five weeks away only confirmed what I already suspected. No one in the office knew what to do with me. I walked the halls feeling like a condemned man no one wanted to talk to. When an opportunity finally appeared, I had to put together a resume for an interview in Idaho. That wasn't comforting.

Karen and I made the twelve-hour drive across Oregon, where I met with a hospital director. The position sounded more like public relations and had little to do with my technical experience. One of the other candidates was a more experienced manager from Arizona. I had worked closely with him on past projects and respected him greatly. Neither of us were chosen. The director decided on an engineer with no project management experience who had grown up in the area. I wasn't surprised.

A short time later, rumors circulated about relocating me to Saudi Arabia. That was even less comforting. Israeli work visas already filled my passport. When Karen researched what expat life would be like there for Americans, the restrictions on women were extreme. I pictured holding her hand in public like we always did and getting thrown in jail.

Three months passed with questions swirling, and by Christmas 2013, everything was steeped in uncertainty. The company seemed determined to send me to Saudi Arabia. I spent thousands on a new wardrobe, including several suits. A second passport with blank pages arrived via expedited mail. When Karen looked at the photo, she barely recognized me. She said my eyes were dead, as if the fire in my soul had been extinguished.

A few weeks before departure, a different option appeared. A familiar client in Israel was preparing a new project and questions started trickling in. Management didn't know how to respond and looked to my past experience in the region. After providing initial responses, I told management that once I got on the plane, I wouldn't be able to help them. Communicating with Israel from Saudi Arabia would not have been in my best interests, and I made it clear that they would be on their own. With only a few days left before leaving, I was told to cancel my plans and catch the next plane to Tel Aviv.

Arriving in Tel Aviv didn't mean returning to the same environment I had known. While I had been away, the landscape had changed. When I saw the Israeli manager that had worked so closely with me in Israel just three years earlier, and again in Oregon, he told me his company had shuffled him into the background just as mine had done to me. The camaraderie we shared on our previous two projects had vanished, replaced by a cold aloofness. I understood what his company had done to him, but I never understood why that changed the friendship we had built over the years.

There were other bigger changes. Management consultants often have a strange view of business. They constantly promote new methods, regardless of prior success. I understood why. If clients were told they were already doing everything right, the consultants would be out of work. My prior 2009-2012 project in Israel had been successful. It met cost, schedule, and scope requirements. That didn't stop the consultants from convincing the client that major changes were needed.

Just over two years had passed since I left Israel, and my reputation for success remained well known, but the client no longer hired engineering companies directly. Consultants convinced them that projects would go better if they kept all parties under one roof and let a construction company subcontract the engineers. It was a bad model.

Neither the chosen general contractor nor their selected engineering firm had ever worked in Israel. Even worse, they lacked experience on a major semiconductor facility. The solution involved bringing in another experienced engineering company to calm nerves. My company sold my reputation and experience as the glue that would hold everything together. The problem was that no one asked my opinion about the arrangement.

I had no authority to influence the general contractor or the new engineering firm. They both saw me as an outsider. I knew trouble was brewing during the contract negotiations. The general contractor didn't understand engineering firms and cut the design fee so low that I knew it wouldn't meet the client's needs. My opinion didn't matter. Only the cost did.

One month in, the client began asking for everything they had traditionally received. I was happy to restore services to the desired level, but that came with a price. They didn't like that answer.

At the time, everyone else from my company was still waiting for work visas and couldn't come to Israel. The general contractor sent daily requests to revise proposals, prepare presentations, and chase down pointless tasks. My workweek stretched from Sunday through Friday, starting at seven in the morning and ending just past midnight. None of this was normal. Even as exhaustion crept into every part of my day, I pushed harder, convinced I could prove my worth again.

The initial project organization started coming together well. My company's engineering team made excellent progress remotely in Arizona. The local subcontractors were on board, reviewing the drawings and preparing permits. In a few more weeks, the installation of the computer network would be complete, everyone could join me onsite, and I could finally exhale.

Before that could happen, I received an invitation to attend an offsite team-building meeting with the site management. Memories of how powerful establishing a sense of community could be encouraged my mood.

The meeting took place at a nearby hot springs resort. When I arrived, folding metal chairs lined the perimeter of an empty conference room. A facilitator guided the discussion as each person shared project concerns and thoughts on increasing productivity. Since the room contained a large number of the general contractor's people, the discussion focused mostly on their concerns. When my turn came, I spoke from the heart and asked:

"Does anyone in this room understand that the engineers are entering their busiest time? We need your support."

That was how projects worked. Early on, the engineers were a flurry of activity as they developed the documents. The construction team supported them by reviewing drawings and offering preferences. A solid design formed the foundation the contractor stood upon. Undermining that foundation undermined the entire project. As a job moved forward, the roles reversed. When construction reached its peak, the engineers supported them by approving alternate products and answering questions quickly.

Everyone's eyes turned to me. The energy in the room shifted from an amicable discussion to an unspoken accusation of "What are you complaining about?" Except, I hadn't complained.

The meeting devolved into an ambush. Accusations about not getting along with the client and not responding quickly enough to the general contractor's needs took me off guard. I had met every deadline and thought I had a strong relationship with my counterpart.

They suggested I spend some time alone with the client and smooth things out. *Smooth things out?* It made no sense. The conversation hadn't been about relationships. It had been about everyone's concerns and how to efficiently get the job done.

When I spoke with the client, nothing new emerged. They wanted a large number of costly services for free, and I wasn't willing to give them away. If that was a problem, they had the wrong manager.

I casually stated that it wouldn't have hurt my feelings if they wanted to replace me. The client's eyes got momentarily larger. Apparently, that wasn't an option. I didn't leave the meeting feeling closer to the team. I left feeling isolated.

One major distraction remained. Rockets from Gaza were being fired into Israel, and daily sirens sent Karen and me to shelters. We had experienced this before, only this time the intensity was much greater. Karen could feel the hotel windows rattling and limited her time outside. We weren't afraid, but we weren't comfortable either.

The attacks didn't let up. In the office, we left our desks several times a day and walked to a protected shelter. After work, while driving home, I saw a rocket trail arching toward the road ahead. As I considered stopping the car, it began to curve in midair and I realized it was an interceptor. I was safe.

Another time, the sirens sounded while Karen and I drove through Ashkelon. We pulled to the side and looked for cover. A woman grabbed Karen's arm and pulled her toward a bench while I crouched beside a wall. When I looked up, white interceptor trails lined the sky. No one around us showed fear. Rockets had become part of our life.

The general contractor was terrified. Every time a siren went off in Tel Aviv, their phones screeched out alerts that were more disconcerting than the sirens. I knew they'd brought their wives, but when I learned they'd relocated small children and pets, I couldn't believe it. As Israeli tanks lined the Gaza border, the general contractor ordered an evacuation to Rome.

Wars don't last forever, and when a ceasefire came, I planned on having the engineers hit the ground running. To remain on schedule, I still needed one more week to finish setting up the computer network, but the engineering needs didn't matter. Staying in Israel while my construction counterparts fled made them look bad. That wasn't acceptable.

When I told Karen we had to evacuate, she wasn't disappointed. She'd never been to Italy, and a few days in Rome sounded like fun. Private flights were arranged, and although I felt guilty leaving my Israeli friends behind, we left with our group.

In Rome, the general contractor continued acting like the design team didn't exist. Meetings revolved around their preparations and never discussed impacts to the engineers, who were still entering their busiest time of the project. As fun as Rome was, we couldn't stay there forever waiting out the conflict. I still hadn't given up on the thought of creating a unified team and suggested we all regroup in my company's Phoenix office. Curious looks stared in my direction, and I pictured little lightbulbs appearing over their heads. The contractor was also based in Phoenix. They enthusiastically agreed, then let our client back in Israel know and congratulated themselves on the plan.

As the meeting ended and I emerged from the conference room, Karen rushed across the lobby and grabbed my arm. Earlier, I had faced an ambush in Israel. Now she described an ambush in the hotel.

The general contractor wives had cornered her. They bragged about designer bags, trips to spas, and the joy of being away from their husbands. Karen didn't care about status or belittling a partner. These women operated in a world Karen didn't recognize, and didn't want to. Once she spotted me, she excused herself from their clutches and escaped to my side.

The next day we got some distance by walking the streets of Rome and collecting the standard magnets, mugs, Hard Rock Café pins, and t-shirts. We stood in St. Peter's Square in Vatican City, staring at the domed Basilica rising before us. There wasn't time to take a tour, but we vowed that one day we would. Our lunch overlooked Rome's Colosseum and the waiter openly flirted with Karen. I knew it was harmless, and it was hard to compete with the towering ice cream sundae he made just for her.

Walking among the ancient ruins only whetted our appetites for what was to come. That night, we had dinner at the restaurant that created the dish Fettucine Alfredo. The chef tossed the pasta and cheese at a makeshift table beside the diners. We would have loved to spend more time exploring the city, but duty called, and a project awaited.

If the ancient Romans could hold their empire together by absorbing other cultures, perhaps there was hope I could weave a general contractor from Texas into the Israeli world. We said our farewells and headed to Arizona

The Burning Man

By August 2014, the fighting had eased enough for us to return to Israel. Phoenix had given me a brief sense of renewal. It didn't last.

My team was still waiting on visas, so for the first week it was just me and one computer specialist from Dublin. The smaller engineering firm ignored the visa rules and already had their team on site. No one cared that my company followed the law. All they saw was that the other group was there and we weren't.

When my team arrived, it felt like a breath of fresh air. Working alone in Israel was stressful but manageable. The real pressure came from the growing list of problems. The general contractor was over a month late providing information we needed to start. Schedules were already tight, and the client made asking for more time or money off limits. It felt like being told to make bricks without straw.

As we worked to catch up, new problems surfaced. The contractor met with the client and presented their own version of the design without informing the engineers. When the client saw unapproved changes, they were furious. Everyone knew the situation wasn't under my control, but because I was part of the contractor's organization, some of that anger landed on me.

My Israeli client counterpart understood and quietly advocated for the engineers. We tried coming up with ways to help the general contractor understand the design process, but they refused to listen, and their behavior rattled the entire client organization. After one of our futile brainstorming sessions, he looked across the table at me. In a monotone voice that sounded like Eeyore from *Winnie the Pooh*, he said:

> *We have a plan.*
> *It's a bad plan.*
> *We don't like the plan.*
> *But we have a plan.*

After the meeting, those words started repeating in my head. He wasn't trying to be funny, but I couldn't help smiling at the thought. It served as a small light in the surrounding darkness.

Problems came from more than just the general contractor. My company was experimenting with creating designs in 3-D. I was used to paper drawings I could highlight and walk around with, but the industry was changing. To survive, we had to stay on the cutting edge. Despite offers of extra training, both the contractor and client struggled to understand the new format. The confusion strained the budget and schedule, which meant even more pressure on me.

The last time I had managed a project in Israel, creating a community was vital to our success. My company's travel policy had changed, and I had less influence over the team. The tight-knit feeling from before no longer existed.

On top of that, one person who had been with me in Israel on a prior project worried me the most. He flaunted his disregard for rules and constantly reminded everyone how indispensable he was. I knew better. His subconsultant could manage independently, and while she acknowledged his help with the client, she bristled at any suggestion she couldn't handle the work herself. I didn't extend his assignment.

At the end of 2014, as my fiftieth birthday drew near, I noticed my hair turning snow white. The stress was taking a toll. Pictures of my older brothers showed they had some gray, but nothing like mine. It wasn't just me feeling the pressure. Behind the scenes, the client had also reached a breaking point.

Construction costs and schedules were not on track. When the client requested detailed reports, the general contractor promised they would be provided in two weeks. Two weeks later, the reports hadn't arrived. After excuses were given, the reports were once again promised in two weeks. It was like watching Lucy promise Charlie Brown she wouldn't pull the football away. After several months, the client wasn't having it anymore.

I wasn't part of the top management meetings, but heard the general contractor and client both agreed that the tone of the project had to change. Communication on the project just wasn't working. Each side received permission to remove one person from the other company. The general contractor went first and chose the head of the client's organization. It was the right choice. The manager was absolutely toxic, and his style filtered through everything.

The client chose next. The right choice would have been to remove a lower-level person who worked for the general contractor. That individual caused chaos in the client's world and mine. That isn't what happened. The client couldn't have their top person removed and respond by removing someone in a lower position. That would be like trading a king for a pawn. Instead, they chose the top person in the general contractor's organization. It was a terrible choice. The client removed a highly competent and experienced manager who wasn't at the heart of the problem, all because of kindergarten politics. I didn't know whether to laugh or cry.

As the first months of 2015 went by, I noticed a change. The client didn't seem too upset about losing their manager, and pressure from that side of my world eased. The general contractor was too busy with its own power struggles to pay much attention to the engineers. We remained an afterthought.

That didn't mean the contractor stopped making trouble. One day, one of their managers stormed over to my desk and began yelling. The Israelis treated me as one of their own, and the engineers were protective of me, so the scene drew immediate attention.

I grabbed my computer and asked the manager to continue the conversation in a conference room. In corporate speak, I said we needed to take his comments "off-line." Once inside, I let him vent and then walked him through each complaint, showing him that I had already addressed every issue. After a few moments of silence, he apologized. I told him that treating me that way in front of the others hurt his standing with both the engineers and the locals.

When we stepped out, he loudly proclaimed that he'd been wrong and was very sorry. Heads popped out of cubicles like prairie dogs. No one ever yelled across the office, much less twice in one day. I had kept my calm, but underneath, I could feel myself burning.

CHAPTER 18

RESTORATIONS

The management changes helped ease the temperature onsite, but the previous year had worn me down. Although I maintained a calm exterior, anger consumed me from within. The construction group continually dismissed my advice and demanded more free engineering services than any of my past clients. Even after a full year in Israel, the general contractor still didn't understand the local culture. Instead of accepting Israeli practices and turning them into strengths, they fought against them. Through early morning meetings, I sat through their struggles like someone watching a performance, not a project.

I believed in organization, logic, and direct communication. Scope, schedule, and strategy could change. What could not be changed was who I was.

I had become a shell of my former self. Old-time crooners kept me company on the drive to work. Johnny Mathis sang about someone used and worn out who just wanted to go home. The song fit the way I felt.

I needed a break.

Long Weekends

When discussing places to visit, I asked Karen to avoid flights that would require us to wake up at 3:00 AM, or flights that had multiple connections. The only other thing I wanted to avoid was anything associated with World War Two. We needed something upbeat.

A guided tour of Munich and its surrounding area met all of those requirements. Also, after dealing with an undisciplined general contractor, Germany promised a sense of order and efficiency. As an added bonus, letting someone else plan the details took pressure off of Karen, who when she planned trips, worried so much about what could go wrong that she sometimes forgot to enjoy herself. I notified Adrian, my second-in-command, that I'd be gone for a long weekend, then headed out the door without looking back.

The tour started at Neuschwanstein Castle, the place where Walt Disney found inspiration for the Cinderella Castle. Without a bus to shuttle the group up the hill, everyone hurried along the steep incline to the castle gates. After visiting the massive 19th-century furnished rooms, we quickened our pace toward the back of the property. I wanted an iconic picture from a distant bridge. Unfortunately, there wasn't time to traverse the fifteen-minute walk and get back down the hill to the bus. Our pictures ended up being of the postcard variety.

The highlight of our trip was a day trip to Austria. The guide began in Salzburg by showing us film locations from *The Sound of Music.* We stopped at a treed garden where the Von Trapp children played in their homemade clothes. After crossing the river, we walked through the cemetery and gated fences where the family hid from their Nazi pursuers. As the tour continued, a boat carried the group across an Austrian mountain lake to see nearby towns. My favorite part occurred on the return trip when the boat speakers played Julie Andrews singing "The Hills Are Alive," and I found myself getting lost in the music and surroundings.

The other big draw in Salzburg was Mozart. Costumed actors and life-sized cardboard cutouts welcomed us into stores selling Mozartkugeln, round chocolates filled with pistachio, marzipan, and nougat, then coated in dark chocolate. They were delicious. During lunch, we tried a Salzburger Nockerl, Mozart's favorite dessert of three meringue peaks drizzled in raspberry syrup.

Our final day ended taking a bus ride along the Romantic Road to the town of Rothenburg ob der Tauber. The shop windows were filled with pyramids of stacked snowball-sized pastries covered in powdered sugar, and we had to try one. They looked better than they tasted. Karen told me about Germany's famous Christmas markets, and although it wasn't the holiday season, we made time to visit a Christmas shop where we bought an ornament for our future tree.

After arriving back in the office, Adrian asked where I'd been. My long weekend had lasted five days. Leaving him in the dark might not have been fair, but I wanted to see how he would manage. There weren't any problems requiring my attention, and except for him, the site hadn't noticed my absence. That told me more than I needed to know.

Although Germany had improved my outlook, I still needed a break. Two weeks later I notified Adrian of my plan for another long weekend. The conversation included much praise about how well he had managed the site during my prior trip. That made him suspicious. Before the conversation ended, he raised an eyebrow and asked, "Can you define the word weekend for me?" I just smiled.

My family always thought our grandmother immigrated from Hungary. She never talked about it and no one really knew. Germany and Austria had only reminded me of how much joy I found in traveling. I was about to find it again, only this time, it would be in Budapest.

Our room at the Intercontinental Hotel didn't seem remarkable at first. A curtain covered one entire wall, and when we drew it back, the panoramic view made us gasp. Across the Danube, illuminated government buildings crowned a majestic hill. I pressed my camera against the window to keep it steady, and started snapping pictures.

The next day we explored the city by touring Parliament, and then taking a bus ride to Heroes' Square. At one stop we entered a large basilica. In the back were the bones of St. Stephen's hand and wrist. For the cost of a few coins, a dim light brought the relic out of shadow. It struck us as morbid, so we focused on the decorative stained glass windows instead.

On the last day, a boat drifted along the Danube to towns whose names I could never remember without looking them up. There were more churches, statues, and shops packed with Hungarian paprika. I looked around, thinking about my grandmother and wondering, *are these my people?* The thought didn't last long. I already knew that when it came to "people" the only one who mattered was standing beside me on the journey.

The trips in May 2015 re-energized me, and I returned to the office with a fresh outlook. The summer started off uneventfully, but it wasn't long before the general contractor reverted to their old trouble-causing ways. When they cut costs at the start of the project, some services had to go. I made sure everyone understood exactly what that meant and clearly documented it in the contract.

The impact of those cuts was hitting the construction team, and politely reminding them of the clause did not go over well. Their strategy of ignoring the contract and bullying me quickly reminded me why my "long weekends" were so important. By the end of the summer, their badgering and complaining to my management grew so loud that I finally relented and flew a low-cost designer in from Poland to silence them. As for the result of having to deal with their bullying, I took a deep breath and began planning my next series of trips.

September brought a brief week-long home leave to Oregon. While I took the brunt of the general contractor's bad behavior, Adrian excelled in the background. He had earned a chance at greater authority, and I began focusing my efforts on mentoring him. For my own sanity, I considered the new arrangement a necessary optimization. Given my executive authority as the company's top manager on the project, I unilaterally implemented the new structure. The home office didn't need to know.

Prague wasn't on my radar, but people at work couldn't stop talking about it. The city sounded exotic, like something out of an old spy novel. I couldn't resist.

Once October arrived, I notified Adrian about my next "long weekend." When it came to vacations, he remained suspicious about the length. We joked about what the term really meant, and to keep him off guard, I decided to limit the time away from work to only two days.

Our hotel sat along the Vltava River and was perfectly situated within walking distance of all the main sites. First up was a trip into the New Town. Karen and I had never given much thought to the Christmas song about good King Wenceslas, but a statue of him mounted on a horse stood in front of a large government building.

Below sat a bench with a saying that caught our attention: Truth and Love Must Prevail Over Lies and Hatred. It was a tribute to the Czech Republic's 1989 revolution, but it spoke of a universal hope. Based on my job, I needed hope.

We then made our way to Old Town Square and looked up at the medieval Astronomical Clock with its intricate wood carvings. On the way back to the hotel, we passed by a synagogue that was supposed to be the site of the first golem, a creature from Jewish folklore said to be formed from clay or mud.

On the second day we crossed the Charles Bridge and found our way to the Lennon Wall. This colorful, graffiti-covered tribute to peace seemed out of place within the narrow streets and old buildings, but it fit with the city's tributes to love and peace.

Our journey continued with a stroll up the steep narrow roads of Castle Hill where churches and replicas of medieval shops awaited. Upon finding a toy museum, we couldn't help but laugh at a display with President George W. Bush placed among The Three Stooges. At the souvenir shop on the way out, we added to our Christmas ornament collection by purchasing an oversized Santa Claus carrying packed suitcases with the word Praha on them.

That night, we walked back to Old Town Square to sample some food. My favorite was the potato chips on a stick, while Karen liked the Trdelnik, a cinnamon-and-sugar-coated pastry rolled on a tube and cooked over an open fire.

Our time in Prague may have been short, but after returning to work, I could feel how much the travel helped center me. While enjoying dinner one evening, Karen casually mentioned there were direct flights to Italy, and if I knew anything about Florence. My ears perked up. The last time I'd been in Florence was on a high school trip. Sharing the city with my wife brought a new sense of excitement.

The next day at work I noticed how much Adrian enjoyed his greater levels of responsibility. By this time, he had become used to my long weekends and didn't question them anymore. The site felt calm enough, so after a few weeks passed, I notified him of my next "long weekend."

The trip started with a visit to the museum housing Michelangelo's David. It wasn't just the beauty of his sculpture that caught our eye. The museum was filled with rooms of other lesser known works, from a period when art flourished in the city. Shelf after shelf of well-chiseled stone heads stared back at us, waiting for someone to reunite them with their torsos.

Afterward, we made our way over to a small restaurant beside Florence's Duomo. Not far from view, guides waved their paddles high in the air to capture the attention of their wayward flock. Watching the ballet of tourist groups move past the basilica's multicolored marble walls and red-tiled roofs felt like something out of a dream. As we sat under our table umbrella, rain and a ridiculously overpriced breakfast didn't matter. We had front row seats.

Fortified from our morning meal and more importantly, her cup of coffee, Karen agreed to climb to the top of the Duomo. We ascended uneven stone stairs to our first plateau and circled the base of the dome. There was barely time to catch our breath and look down at the tiny people below, before the guide encouraged us toward the next nearly vertical passage. Once at the top, we could see the entire city and surrounding hills spread out before us. I looked across the way at a large tower whose bells began to chime and gently suggested we go there next. Karen's mouth didn't utter a word. It didn't have to. Her eyes clearly said no.

The second day didn't slow down. We hopped a bus and headed to the Tuscan countryside. Our tour started with a farmhouse lunch and fine wine. A visit to San Gimignano gave us the chance to see olives being harvested. Karen's legs were too tired from the day before, so I scaled the steep stairs and took a video so she wouldn't miss anything.

By the time our bus made it to Pisa, Karen caught her second wind. We circled up the ramps until arriving for a view at the top. My interest leaned toward the structural integrity of the building and the marvel of how modern engineers had stabilized the structure. Before leaving, we took the photo every visitor takes. We each posed as if we were holding up the tower with our hands.

One more day remained, and we chose to use it to take the high-speed train to Venice. Once there, the Vaporetto shuttled us to Saint Mark's Square. We toured the church and stopped at the Hard Rock Café, but those felt like the obligatory things to do.

At lunch, we sat at an outdoor table among flocks of pigeons in the square, and listened to a band playing "Moonlight Serenade" in the distance. The melody of the saxophone froze me to my chair as I looked around and wished the moment would never end.

Our long weekends were doing exactly what I'd hoped for. Work didn't seem so bad anymore. The focus of my life changed from the struggles of work to the joy of travel.

Longer Weekends

While balancing a stressful project with seeing the world, I lost sight of an important responsibility. Getting back to Pittsburgh to see my parents drifted from every year to every other year. There were emails and weekly phone calls, but something wasn't right with my mother. Over the months, the phone calls became more and more repetitive. She spoke of concern about my brother John finding a job and wanted to know if I'd found a church in Israel.

Frustration often clouded those drifting conversations until Karen helped me see what I hadn't been willing to admit. Time had caught up with my mother. She had recently celebrated her eighty-fifth birthday, and her sharpness had faded. Once I accepted the change, the frustration vanished. Patience and understanding took its place. Phone calls were no longer enough. A visit was necessary.

In December 2015, Karen and I planned a nine-day trip divided between time in Pennsylvania with family, and Christmas cheer in New York City. Our journey didn't go as expected.

In Pittsburgh, I developed the worst headache in my life, and asked Karen to drive me to a hospital. After ten years together, she never saw me knocked down so completely, and hurried us to the car. An MRI showed nothing wrong, so the doctor prescribed a painkiller. It wasn't effective. The side trip cost me a day with my mother. I spent the rest of the afternoon sleeping in the room. That evening, even though my head still pounded and standing caused dizziness, we attended dinner at a nearby restaurant with my father. While battling through the pain, I observed noticeable changes since we last saw each other. He walked with a cane, had a hearing aid, and spoke with a lisp due to some poor-fitting dental work. Except when openly flirting with the waitress, he'd lost his spark.

Although my mother welcomed us the next day, I felt tired. My brother John stopped by the house, but couldn't stop speaking angrily about his wife, who sat beside him. Karen and I couldn't imagine sniping at each other like that, and it was painful to watch. When we left the house, the visit had unsettled me.

I can't say what caused my terrible headache, but the pain cleared by the time we boarded the plane for New York. Deep down, I hoped the family drama hadn't triggered the symptoms. What I knew for certain was that the Big Apple awaited, and the city was decked out in its Christmas glory.

In Israel, the city of Ashkelon didn't celebrate Christmas. Karen and I used to look for what we called hidden Christmas. To us, red and white striped curbs didn't mean "No Parking," they meant "Happy Holidays." Russian stores sold chocolate Santas and small Christmas trees, but those items remained tucked away in remote corners of the city.

New York offered us everything Israel didn't provide, and we anticipated our trip like two kids waiting to open their presents on Christmas morning. We started with a Circle Line tour of the city, walked under the Brooklyn Bridge, and stared up at the flashing neon signs of Times Square.

The windows at Macy's displayed scenes from *A Charlie Brown Christmas*, and the large tree in Rockefeller Plaza was something we had only seen on TV. To make the week feel even more special, Karen pre-purchased Skip-the-Line passes for the Empire State Building. It didn't matter that a line didn't exist. We were VIPs.

On another day, we rode the subway to Coney Island to experience a Nathan's Famous hot dog. Although I made the mistake of ordering oysters that smelled like low tide, the red ketchup and green relish kept our Christmas theme alive. We filled every spare minute. After checking out from the hotel, a visit to Radio City Music Hall to watch the Rockettes perform their traditional holiday show ended the adventure.

When we returned to Israel, travel dominated my thoughts. In college, I missed earning a minor in classic cultures by just three credits. A trip to Athens provided the opportunity to rediscover my passion. Since Greek Orthodox Christmas extended into January, and I had visions of seeing fireworks over the Parthenon on New Year's Day, the trip would allow us to keep our holiday momentum moving forward.

We started by walking through the Temple of Zeus and then made our way to tour the Parthenon. As we ascended the hillside, I started realizing that many of Europe's most amazing sites required arduous uphill climbs. At the top, construction scaffolding surrounded the ruins, and an icy breeze took away from my romantic visions.

On the way back from the tour we stopped at a "Greek yogurt" shop and laughed. It felt like seeing a sign for "French croissants" in Paris. We knew better than to say anything.

Athens offered us other fun with food. At a restaurant in Syntagma Square, we sat down to breakfast. After looking at the menu, we placed our order. The waiter stared at us in disbelief and loudly said just one word, "Breakfast!" We tried telling him how we wanted our eggs, and again he repeated the word. After about the third try, we realized there were no choices, just a set breakfast. Substitutions or additions weren't an option. We laughed at ourselves and were reminded how much we loved the world of international travel.

On New Year's Eve, from the comfort of our hotel room, fireworks lit up the sky over the Parthenon. A pair of binoculars helped make it all look bigger than life.

We spent our final day traveling to the Temple of Poseidon at Cape Sounion. On the way the tour bus operator didn't have much to say, so she droned on about obscure laundry shops and long-forgotten movie stars who had stayed in someone's uncle's, brother's, friend's, nephew's cottage. Snow fell around us as we stood shivering among the ruins and staring out to sea.

The next day pulled us back into reality as it was time to catch a plane. Taking so many trips pushed my luck, but the worst anyone could do was send me home, and that didn't seem like a bad consequence. Two months passed without going anywhere. That was enough.

To pass the long lonely days in Israel, Karen spent much of her time reading. She loved the stories about Catherine of Aragon and her visits to the palace of Alhambra in Granada, Spain. My limited knowledge of the country came from reading *Don Quixote.* That didn't count.

In March 2016, we launched into the world once again. Our trip began in Madrid with a tour of the Royal Palace. We had seen royal residences before with their canopied beds, tapestry-covered walls, and gold-plated dining sets. This one didn't stand out.

The following morning marked the beginning of a four-day bus tour south into Andalusia. At a stop for gas, I took photos with Don Quixote statues and metal cutouts. In the distance, windmill vanes spun and I could almost see the brave knight charging toward them.

Córdoba was our first stop where we toured the Mezquita-Catedral. Christian and Muslim architecture blended together. Endless red and white striped arches stood beneath ceilings filled with Christian imagery. It was an odd mix, yet the idea of two religions sharing one roof somehow worked.

We spent the first night in Seville. As we stepped off the bus, I noticed a barber shop next door. I knew *The Barber of Seville* was a famous opera, but could only picture the version with Bugs Bunny and Elmer Fudd.

Our stop included all of the requisite tourist activities such as taking a brief boat cruise on the river and visiting Columbus's tomb. In the evening, we were shuffled to a flamenco show. The performers looked like a group of angry people stomping their feet, and we realized it just wasn't our style.

Granada sat a short drive south, and once there we took a guided tour inside the grounds of Alhambra. Nothing about the palace or the surrounding gardens spoke to me of the peaceful refuge it was supposed to be. All I saw were crowds of tourists and ornately decorated walls. Karen had a different view. She loved seeing the intricate geometric tilework inside the palace and could picture stories coming to life.

That evening, we strolled through a neighborhood overlooking the Alhambra. As the sun set, the distant mountains faded into shadows while the white walls of the palace glowed on the hill above. Had I lived in the era of royalty, the view from that neighborhood would have satisfied me more than the palace itself.

Later that night, we gave Flamenco another try, which turned out to be our one mistake. The performance took place in a small cave crammed with too many tourists. Karen felt claustrophobic, the band blocked the only exit, and the furious stomping of the dancers made it worse. By the end of the show, she was sweating and desperate to leave. When five other caves emptied at the same time, the crush of people became unbearable. I grabbed her hand and led her outside where she could finally breathe. We made a few notes to ourselves. No more caves and no more Flamenco.

After the bus returned to Madrid, two days in Spain remained. We spent one taking a fast train to Barcelona. Most of our trips were carefully planned, but this one wasn't. We hopped on a Red Bus Tour and after about thirty minutes realized it was nothing more than a glorified city transit. When we could no longer keep our eyes open through the dull stop announcements, we hopped off to explore on our own. In front of us stood a building with an unusual looking façade designed by the famous architect, Gaudi. Inside, oddly shaped rooms and low curved ceilings forced us to duck. On the roof, chimney stacks looked like strange sentinels guarding the housetops. It wasn't somewhere we'd want to live, but the home was weird enough to remember.

Later, on a subway ride to the Sagrada Familia, we experienced a surprise. While on the packed train car, I kept my wallet deep inside a jacket pocket while Karen tightly gripped her purse's zipper. We knew about petty theft and wanted to be extra careful. That didn't stop a young pickpocket from targeting us. A man nearby pointed to a young girl and said something that made Karen look down. Despite gripping the purse tightly, the zipper had been pulled back a few inches and her wallet sat on the floor. As she looked up, the child and the man vanished into the crowd.

We had mixed feelings. The little thief showed the worst of the city, yet the man who helped Karen showed the best. The experience left us uneasy about Barcelona, and we were anxious to return to Madrid.

Because the tour company had made a few small mistakes on the Andalusia journey, they volunteered a self-guided food tour as compensation. We still had a free day left in Madrid, and snacking our way through the city sounded like a great adventure.

Each stop offered something new. One had Spanish hot chocolate and churros, several served unique tapas with a glass of wine. At one bar, we posed beside a pig's leg while a server cut thin slices of Serrano ham for tasting. The tour ended with olive oil and crusty bread at a small shop. The flavors lingered long after we finished. Our trip wasn't perfect, but we never tired of the joy found in travel.

Even Longer Weekends

At work, no one seemed to notice my many trips. I wasn't sure whether that was good or bad, but being around less seemed to earn more respect. The daily lack of organization wore on me. I began taking half days off on Thursday, using the excuse that it gave the team time to work without my interference. When the general contractor heard my logic, they nodded as if I were some wise old sage. Adrian did the same. My absence meant I trusted him, and he liked that. Karen liked it more.

A month after our trip to Spain, we ventured out again. Karen found a tour in Cappadocia, Turkey, that looked unlike anything we had done. The trip centered on an early morning balloon ride over cave-filled hills and valleys. The basket held eight people. As we floated above a landscape that looked inhabited by trolls and hobbits, dozens of balloons drifted quietly along. Upon touching down, a champagne toast celebrated the successful flight.

That afternoon, we visited an underground city with sprawling tunnels and rooms stretching in every direction. It reminded us of what it must feel like to live inside an anthill.

On the way back to our hotel, the bus stopped at a pottery shop. We had been on plenty of tours where guides funneled visitors into stores like this. There was a tea shop in Taiwan, a perfumery in Egypt, and an olive wood store in Israel. When Karen spotted a large hand-painted vase known as a ginger jar that made her smile, I told her to go for it. The shop owner's eyes lit up as we signed the papers for payment and shipping. Once the ink dried, his pleasant demeanor vanished and he disappeared into the back. The shift didn't bother us. We expected it.

As the minibus pulled away from the shop, I glanced to my right. Sitting proudly on the side of the road sat a thirty-foot statue of a pigeon. I continued staring when suddenly, the symbolism struck me. I didn't have the heart to tell Karen.

Nobody truly needs a large decorative ginger jar and we knew it. The purchase had only to do with making Karen smile. The "folly" adorns our dining room to this day with the same results.

Back in Israel, challenges persisted. A business manager from Oregon arrived unannounced. He had no history of working in Israel. The general contractor disliked one of my proposals and pushed to cut costs on work that was already stretched too thin.

I wasn't sure how the business manager obtained the authority, but without any discussion he reduced my budget by half. I wasn't happy. The proposal was based on years of experience and my detailed staff plans. Every hour and every expense could be clearly justified. Ignoring my advice ensured the project would lose money. He told me not to worry about it.

Not worry about it?

That was not how it worked. When he left, I would still own the project's financial performance. Pushing further felt pointless. Leadership had brushed aside my expertise, and if they didn't care about the cost, why should I?

That evening, I gave more thought to why cutting the budget bothered me so much. During his visit, this same manager had bragged about saving the client relationship on my prior project in Oregon, as if he forgot who he was talking to. It reminded me how just under two years ago, the company had broken a sacred trust. They were breaking it again.

The business manager left after only two days and the work returned to normal. I still listened to songs in the car about going home, yet as long as travel remained an option, work felt manageable.

In May 2016, I told Adrian about my plans for a long weekend. He knew those words well and immediately questioned what the phrase "long weekend" actually meant. Cornered, I changed course. "The trip shouldn't be considered a long weekend," I said. "A better description would be calling it a strong one." He smiled and playfully insisted I confess to the length. It was an eleven-day trip across Italy from Rome to Milan. Upon hearing my plans, he became excited. His wife was Italian, and he had visited the country many times. My decreased presence onsite was starting to look like a viable long-term strategy.

Karen and I had been to Rome before, though only for a quick overview. This time, we planned to take it slowly. We began at the Vatican, walking through vaulted passages where every inch of the ceilings and walls was covered with framed portraits, landscapes, and biblical scenes. Inside the Sistine Chapel, we stared upward, never feeling there was enough time to take it all in. In Saint Peter's Basilica, we saw Michelangelo's statue of Mary holding Jesus. The marble folds looked so much like cloth that it was hard to believe they were stone.

At the Colosseum, our tour went to both the top and bottom. The structural engineer in me was still alive, and I caught myself studying the arches and wondering how they stood. My pace quickened as the group moved beneath them.

A day trip south of Rome led us to Mount Vesuvius. When Karen came within a few hundred yards of the top, she stopped to rest on a bench beside a small souvenir stand. I desperately wanted to finish the journey, but that meant quickening my pace, and I wasn't willing to complete the ascent alone. I sat down on the bench with her and took in our surroundings. The extra steps wouldn't have revealed anything new. We were close enough to the top that claiming she conquered the volcano fully counted.

In the valley below, we ate Margherita pizza before touring Pompeii. I had visited there in high school. Our trips were updating my past to include her in it.

Next came a short flight to Milan. Seeing *The Last Supper* lost some of its luster once we learned how much had been damaged by weather and war. What remained was a heavily restored version of Da Vinci's original, more suggestion than certainty.

From Milan we took three day trips. The first was to the colorful seaside towns of Cinque Terre. As the guide warned everyone about pickpockets, Karen and I remembered Barcelona and exchanged a wary look.

At Lake Maggiore, a torrential downpour tried dampening our spirits. Generous quantities of the region's sparkling wine refused to let that happen and nearly made me miss the ride back across the lake. When we boarded the boat, several travelers gave us a disapproving glare. I checked my watch. We were one minute early. They might not have appreciated our timing, but I had enjoyed the wine.

Our final excursion was the Bernina Express train ride to Switzerland. Karen loved how the train wound through mountain passes and climbed into the clouds. At the Saint Moritz station, the tour guide abandoned us before we disembarked from the train. It was summer in Saint Moritz. With the town mostly empty, we just followed the signs and searched for people who could tell us when to meet back at the train. None of the aimless wandering stopped us from buying plenty of Swiss chocolate for the trip back.

Once back in Israel, five months remained in my assignment. The project could no longer support two project managers, so Adrian returned to Ireland. He had done a fantastic job throughout the project. I knew he had earned the opportunity to run his own job one day.

The next several months moved quietly along. Karen and I didn't like traveling in the summer months because we preferred avoiding the worst of the crowds. When September finally rolled around, we knew our time in Israel was coming to an end. We had taken so many trips over the past year that we were running out of ideas. Seeing more churches and museums no longer excited us. Our thoughts drifted to places like Madagascar, South Africa, or the Seychelles, but flights to those destinations were painfully long. Taking a train under the English Channel sounded fun. There were things in London and across England we hadn't done yet, and Amsterdam waited on the other side. In September 2016, arrangements were made for our final trip.

London began with a tour of Buckingham Palace and a spot of tea. Karen loved watching the changing of the guard, then seeing the tower of small finger sandwiches placed before her in the tea house. It had been a long time since we had visited London, and no trip there would be complete without a play in the West End. We watched *The Lion King* and enjoyed how the performers brought the animals to life. From the London Eye, we saw the city from high above and grinned at the thought of riding in an egg-shaped car on a giant Ferris wheel.

Branching out, we visited Bath and saw the colonnaded Roman pools. Bathers would feel as comfortable there now as they had hundreds of years ago. At Stonehenge, we walked the massive circle of monoliths. We'd seen smaller versions in Donegal, Ireland, but they didn't compare to the scale.

The train under the English Channel was more about the concept of what we were doing. It might have been more fun with windows to see the sea life zipping by, though I knew how unrealistic that would be.

In Amsterdam, we walked through the Red Light District during the day, then made our way to Anne Frank's house. We almost didn't go because World War Two history was everywhere in Israel. After visiting Yad Vashem, we weren't eager to see more. Anne Frank's house told the story without the same harshness, and we didn't regret the visit.

Towards the end of our stay, a tour took us through small towns where we watched wooden shoes being made and climbed through a working windmill. Sampling Edam cheese and stroopwafels topped off the day. By the time our trip to England and Amsterdam finished, we felt as if we'd seen enough. That was a first.

When the suitcases were unpacked in Ashkelon, mysterious visitors made their presence known in our apartment. Every morning, Karen noticed several new red marks on her skin that itched like crazy. Whatever attacked her left me alone. We finally decided it had to be bedbugs.

Karen washed every sheet and piece of clothing in hot water while I sealed off the bedroom doors. Once everything was cleaned, we moved into the second bedroom, and the bites started to fade. This was not the deciding factor for our departure, but it was an unwelcome reminder that we needed to leave.

The final month in Israel ended the way the project began. I was the only one left from my company. The other staff had gone home, and the local consultants were finishing their remaining responsibilities. When the general contractor asked me to transfer the contracts to them, I didn't object. The project was winding down, and my job here was essentially complete.

Without any fanfare, just before Thanksgiving 2016 Karen and I flew home.

CHAPTER 19

THE BEGINNING OF THE ENDINGS

There comes a time when a person realizes their career has plateaued. A choice needs to be made. Leave for a new company to keep climbing, or accept where you are and live with it.

The past three years may have been personally enriching, but professionally miserable. There was every reason to leave. The projects were high stress. They offered no new skills. The company provided no recognition. Performance reviews were fine, but watching others around me being promoted made it clear the company had no intention of giving me more responsibility. I should have left.

I was tired.

Karen was happy to be home.

I stayed.

Trusting My Instincts

Within weeks a new opportunity appeared. The company needed a project manager with international experience for a three-month study. I would split my time between Oregon and Italy. Karen knew the early phase was always the busiest and decided to stay home. In early December 2016, I boarded a plane.

Before arriving in Milan, there was one small detour I had to make back in Israel. The general contractor I'd previously transferred my contracts to needed help. They were shocked when consultant invoices blew through their budgets. Even though I'd left the project and no longer had any responsibility, I still felt ownership of the local engineers.

After meeting with all parties, the problem became clear. The general contractor didn't follow my advice on how to look after the contracts. My instructions weren't complicated and could have been handled by an intern. That didn't mean they were unimportant.

When my consultants realized the general contractor wasn't tracking their progress, they acted like sharks that smelled blood in the water. I hadn't expected my old consultants to behave so poorly, and firmly let them know. Out of respect for our past work together, they agreed to reduce their invoices.

I reported the results of the visit to my company. The negotiations had been successful. They were either too busy with other problems, didn't believe my report, or didn't care. I wasn't surprised.

Before leaving, I sat down with the general contractor and explained what had been negotiated. After all this time, they still hadn't learned how to apply basic management principles. It was just a continuation of the problems I had solved for them before.

With the Israel detour complete, I headed to Milan. Taking care of small details in advance had served me well in the past, and I approached the project in Italy with the same care. Before the plane landed, I had already asked the client their advice on the nearest hotels, the best restaurants, and where to park at their facility. The questions all seemed normal to me. Not everyone thought the same. The team's Oregon-based business manager, Craig, believed the parking question was strange and made a point of letting the entire team know.

Upon our arrival at the site, cars filled every parking space. We stopped by the front office, obtained visitor passes, and waited for the security guard to find a way to squeeze us in. One of the engineers patted me on the back, thanking me for asking silly questions. I didn't respond.

During the initial presentation, I mentioned that on a prior project in France, the engineers' lack of lunch options acted as a distraction. They grumbled about eating vending machine junk food, which in France should have been a crime. Attending to the team's basic needs was critical to keeping them focused. Craig looked at me in horror. After the presentation, he scolded me for embarrassing the client's visiting French project manager, who had been listening attentively.

That afternoon, my Italian counterpart gave everyone free access to the site's cafeteria and coffee machines. The French project manager thanked me for being direct.

At breakfast the next morning, Craig mocked me in front of the junior staff for trimming the fat from my bacon. I did not understand what he had against me. After everyone left, I told him not to behave that way in front of the team again, and that he owed me an apology. He stared, changed the subject, and walked away.

His unprofessional behavior confirmed what I already suspected. He felt politically untouchable. I didn't know how to manage a person like him, but I now knew exactly what I was dealing with.

When the initial four-week trip ended, I returned to Oregon for a month and ran meetings remotely. Dropped video feeds, late arrivals, and people talking over each other drove inefficiency. My prior projects had succeeded because when physically present, I could read body language, and address team needs quickly. None of that could be done through a computer.

Clients located nine time zones away liked remote work even less than I did. They wanted to see engineers in action and have their questions answered immediately. A meeting occurring at the end of the day in Milan took place during Oregon's early morning. Without seeing my team, the client imagined engineers constantly drinking coffee and eating donuts.

As frustration grew, I proposed a solution. A few of my supporting team members were located in Glasgow. Inviting the client to join everyone in Scotland for a progress review caught the client's interest. Many hadn't been to the U.K. before, and the project gave them the excuse they needed.

It worked for me too. When Karen and I lived in Glasgow years earlier, we hadn't toured the highlands. She was excited to return with me, even if just for a few days.

The client meetings went well, as did touring the highlands. The project was moving in the right direction. I returned to Portland to wrap up the remaining pieces, then traveled to Milan in early April 2017 for the final presentation.

One item I managed carefully was the estimate. To keep overall project costs reasonable, our proposal had only allowed for an unconventional method, but I understood the logic. During the discussion, the client couldn't follow the numbers.

Craig sat across the table and said he thought it was garbage. As a business manager, he had a tendency to agree with anything the client said. I couldn't believe it. My own team member was actively undermining the project. Unfounded client concerns sprang to life. I felt like a firefighter with a squirt gun. By the end of my discussion, the client had calmed down. Their senior management thanked me, then said they needed to slash the estimate by a third.

My eyes grew wide. The numbers wouldn't support their strategy. I voiced my concern as respectfully as I could, but it fell on deaf ears. There was nothing more to be done.

Normally, I would have followed up with my client counterpart to confirm her satisfaction with the presentation. Before I could do that, the phone buzzed. My brother Rick had bad news. My eighty-five-year-old father had fallen and was in the hospital. I needed to get home.

The Blur Part I – My Father

Rick said there was nothing I could do. My father told him he felt dizzy and just wanted a quick checkup. He didn't like doctors. Years earlier, one of his friends had gone to the hospital in good health and never came out. My father didn't want the same fate.

My brother John visited him in the hospital in Pittsburgh. We heard it hadn't gone well. John always resented how my father walked out on our family. I don't know what was said, only that there was yelling.

Over the next few days, we received news of problems unrelated to the fall. Surgery was needed. The first attempt didn't go well. One led to another. We were told his condition wasn't serious enough for us to fly across the country.

In Portland, Karen and I waited. There hadn't been time to speak with my father before he went unconscious. Outside on the rail of our balcony deck, two turkey vultures perched. We had never seen them there before. I knew what they symbolized, even if I didn't want to believe it. Two days later, my father was gone.

***

I didn't know why, but I was devastated. It wasn't as if anything was left unsaid. The last time we were together, the words just uncomfortably ran out. He wasn't part of my everyday life. He rarely reached out, but somewhere in my mind, he was always there.

My feelings were mixed. He abandoned his family and left lasting scars. He manipulated me to get my mother to sign mortgage papers. He turned his back on me in college when I bought a motorcycle. There were plenty of reasons to be upset, yet he was still my father. Warm memories lived within me that couldn't be forgotten. Even when I remembered the bad, the good always pushed its way in.

I loved working at the animal hospital with him and wanted to embrace his charismatic manner. He taught me it was alright to enjoy a little indulgence every now and then, even if it was as simple as Rocky Road cookies and chocolate milk. When I showed up at his country club to play golf in a tee shirt and shorts, he didn't blink an eye when upgrading my outfit in the pro shop. He made me feel like I belonged. When I was learning about discipline, he showed me a spontaneous side by taking a whirlwind vacation to the Caribbean. My other siblings didn't share these experiences. They belonged to just my father and me.

My project in Italy had finished, so I told the office I'd be out for the next month. It was nice of my father to pass away when work was light, though I doubted he considered that. The thought made me smile. Humor often shielded my grief.

Karen and I had a decision to make. After arriving home from Italy, we had bought tickets to Pittsburgh. The funeral was going to be held only a few weeks before our scheduled trip. Rescheduling the flight would have served only two purposes: to be around people who showed no interest in my life, or to find my own personal closure.

My mother always said we must respect our father, and I always had. I decided that grieving would be on my terms, no one else's. His choices with me in life made last-minute airfare changes seem distasteful.

I wondered what others might say about a son who skipped his father's funeral, but I could live with any fallout from my decision. When the time came, we didn't go to Pittsburgh. Karen and I spent the day on our balcony, talking through memories and privately honoring his life.

In the days to come, my brother John's wife called to tell us about the funeral. She said my other siblings made fun of Rick because he broke down over the coffin. She also said my brother Mike and younger sister Kathy huddled in the back, whispering like they were telling each other inside jokes.

Some of the people who had worked with my father stood up and said he always spoke of the pride he had in his children. This struck me as strange. He didn't like taking phone calls, rarely wrote, and never asked about my work. While driving home at the end of the service, she said Mike teased my mother about her poor memory.

When the conversation with John's wife started to feel like she was judging my family, I politely ended the call. Her words only reaffirmed the sanity of my decision to stay home. It also made me feel sorry for my mother. I hoped my father's death would bring her closure, but I doubt it ever did.

A few weeks after the funeral, Karen and I met my father's widow and her daughter for lunch in Pittsburgh. She was still bothered by how upset John had been at the hospital. I explained that my family's relationship with him was complex, and that John never forgave my father for walking out on four children and a pregnant wife. She stared at me across the table.

Her reaction stirred something that had been bothering me. Kathy told me the funeral only covered my father's life after he met his fifth wife. At the service, she said my siblings felt like an afterthought. When I received the obituary, it read the same way. What remained elusive was whether she chose to stay in the dark or if he kept her there.

Time passed uneventfully until a box arrived. Karen had reached out to my father's widow and asked if there were any mementos I could have. Most of his belongings had already been donated to charity, but she packed up a few remaining items and put them in the mail.

Donating his belongings without any consideration for his children rubbed me the wrong way. Especially since a few months earlier, he had written about being halfway complete with a memoir. Inside the box were letters, small keepsakes, and a few of the canes he used in his final years, but no memoir. I sorted the items and shipped what he had kept of each child to my siblings.

The wallet-sized portrait of him in the army that he had asked for when I started working at the animal hospital wasn't there. He had promised I could have it when he died. Instead, the box contained a page-sized portrait of the same picture. I didn't understand why he wanted my wallet-sized photo when a larger version existed. It was a question that would never be answered.

In fact, he hadn't left me anything. The man who owned airplanes, joined country clubs, and took cruise vacations left only memories. Years earlier, he told me of a plan to spend every penny and leave his family nothing. I laughed. I didn't need anything.

His will included detailed instructions for his own funeral, but nothing for his children. It closed the book on his story. It summed up his life perfectly for me.

The Blur Part II – My Mother

The trip to Pittsburgh wasn't only about my father. We hadn't visited my mother in two years and wanted to celebrate Mother's Day with her. She loved cherry tomatoes, so as a surprise, I planted some in her backyard garden. We brought her empty flower beds to life with a variety of flowers from a nearby garden center. It was the type of simple, practical thing my mother always appreciated.

I liked getting back to Pittsburgh, but never felt I did it enough. There was always one more crisis at work or another trip overseas. On this visit, my mother seemed more frail. Her shoulders were hunched, and her clothes showed their wear. There were still moments of playful teasing, but they faded quickly. She sounded tired and constantly looked worried.

Seeing her like this made me sad, but her stubbornness and pride prevented anyone from helping. While giving a faint smile, she said she was happy. That's usually how the conversations ended.

My sister Kathy was there for Mother's Day, too. We all went to church together, which was probably the best Mother's Day gift we could have given her. Afterward, we went to a restaurant and had fun taking photos at the table. That was the first sign that something was seriously wrong. My mother didn't like to eat out, and she never wanted anyone taking her picture.

The next day, while standing in the kitchen, she suddenly looked at me and said she didn't understand why my father had left her. We hadn't been talking about that. With an underlying sadness and her head bent down, my mother asked what she had done wrong. She believed only a terrible person could have made my father leave the way he did.

Hearing her blame herself for his abandonment broke my heart. I wasn't sure she knew who she was talking to. I told her what a wonderful mother she had been and still was. It didn't seem to help relieve the pain I could see in her eyes. After a brief pause, she went back about her business.

In the afternoon, my brother Rick stopped by. He told us he had called a social worker.

He called a what? Why?

He thought John had taken a loan against the house and burdened our mother with the payments. The social worker was going to come to confirm she wasn't a victim of elder abuse. I couldn't believe it. I knew John had lost his job at the bar and wasn't working. He could be grumpy, but he wasn't dishonest.

I thought about when Rick had called the police on John for drinking and driving, and wondered if this could be related. It seemed like more than concern for our mother's welfare. If there actually was a problem with the mortgage, Mike or I could make things right. Rick could have made his concern known before calling in outside help. Now, it was too late for that.

Things grew worse later that day when my mother and Karen were in the basement doing laundry. My mother hurried up the stairs insisting my brother Mike was out front and she didn't want him to leave. When Karen told her he wasn't there, my mother became uncharacteristically angry. Karen was shocked.

When I caught up with my mother, she looked confused. We walked to the door and she slowly realized her memory was playing tricks. She began to calm down and returned to her errands. The emotional swing and confusion went far beyond anything I'd seen with her. That evening, my niece shared her own stories about my mother's mood swings.

The social worker arrived the next day. I explained to my mother who she was and why she was there. During the conversation, my mother acknowledged the loan to John and said she wasn't happy he hadn't paid her back. She answered every question without confusion. I assured the social worker that if my mother had financial issues, the family could handle it. When the interview ended and the social worker left, a sense of relief surged through me.

John didn't know about the visit, and I wasn't about to tell him. He stopped by later that day looking like a shadow of the brother I once knew. His hair was uncombed and his clothes hung on him like a scarecrow. The smell of cigarettes and alcohol followed his every step. When I asked about the loan, he said he used the money to help his daughter through college. That was good enough for me.

Over the next twenty-four hours, another issue arose. The senior care home where my mother volunteered for over twenty years called and asked if we could tell my mother she could no longer volunteer there. They didn't want to watch over an old person who wasn't a resident, and were embarrassed to tell her directly.

During our visit, enough issues had arisen that something had to be done to help my mother. After Karen and I returned to Oregon, Kathy stayed in Pittsburgh for an extended time. What she saw made us more concerned. She asked our mother to visit her in Colorado, hoping she might agree to permanently move out west. After a month, Kathy convinced her to make the trip. She put the dog in her car along with as many things that would make her comfortable, and began the long drive.

When Karen and I flew to Kathy's home for a brief visit in July 2017, I noticed how confused my mother was. She spoke of flying to Colorado and how the dog behaved on the plane. It wasn't true. She had driven with Kathy. At times, she thought she was at a summer camp. Another time, she said my sister's husband was a girl because of his long hair. That one made me laugh, but underneath I knew my mother was deteriorating.

As we prepared to leave, I could see my mother wanting to come with us. She was confused and thought we were all going for a ride in the car. I explained we needed to return to Oregon, and let her know how much I loved her. Those were the last words I spoke to my mother.

A short time later, I received a call. My mother had fallen down the stairs during the night. She couldn't speak but was conscious. An ambulance was called. She didn't survive the trip to the hospital.

***

My mother's passing hit me much harder than my father's. It had only been three months, and there were no mixed feelings with her, only overwhelming grief. She had been a steady presence in my life, never turning her back on me and never doing anything other than showing love and support.

Growing up and throughout my adult life, it always felt as if an aura of sadness hung about her. I could see it in the worried expression constantly etched into her features. Despite that, she always said she was happy, and only wanted the same for her children.

My mother had taught me about love and forgiveness. Her values would live within me, but there would be no more comically sung versions of Happy Birthday. No more chocolate-covered Oreos mailed at Christmas, and no more routine weekly phone calls. A hole opened up deep within me, one that could never be filled. One that I would have to learn to live with.

My mother never let us see her cry. She must have passed that trait along to my sister. During the phone call from Kathy, I didn't need to see. I could hear her tears through the phone, and it told me everything I needed to know. Karen and I flew back to Colorado. We knew my mother's death would affect Kathy deeply, especially since the fall had happened under her roof.

Karen and I didn't want our trip to be surrounded by sadness. We needed to step away from grief, even if just for a few days. Seeing the strange and beautiful corners of Colorado felt like catching our breath between waves. We used the opportunity to visit the ghosts at The

Stanley Hotel in Estes Park, the monumental rock formations in the Garden of the Gods, and have honey-drizzled sopapillas at the irreverent *South Park* restaurant called Casa Bonita.

When the funeral occurred in late August, it felt more like a family reunion than a service. Before it began, we took family photos. For one of the pictures, my brother Rick came up beside me and placed an arm around my shoulders. His hair was long. Just like when we were younger, I wanted to tell the hippie to get a haircut, but it didn't feel like the right time. His arm was more comforting than words could express.

I don't remember much about what was said at the service except at one point the minister called her Sister Agnes. That wasn't a term I ever heard used in our church, and it felt like he was talking about someone else.

Looking around the sanctuary caused an uneasy feeling. This was the church I grew up in, and it had once felt like a second home. Now it just felt like a big empty space. A picture of my mother I hadn't seen before sat on a small table near the pulpit. The family decided her ashes should be spread on the church grounds near a small plaque listing her name. She would have approved of the simplicity.

Afterward, one of the older ladies approached me and asked if I had found a church yet. She must have been channeling the spirit of my mother. It was something she asked me on almost every weekly phone call. Just like during the conversations with my mother, I politely dodged the question.

Back at the house, the family gathered to go through my mother's things. Looking around, the rooms all seemed smaller and less alive. Curtains were torn, and the furniture showed signs of having survived four rambunctious boys and one little girl. Holiday dishes that had once sat proudly on the formal dining room table were faded and chipped.

Standing by her bed on the well-worn carpet I had once played on, the conversation turned to the clothes she wore and the Danish silver tucked away in her closet. Mike's wife pawed through my mother's jewelry, turning her nose up at the humble possessions. Mike stared at me from across the room with no emotion as he claimed my grandfather's watch for himself. It was too much. Cold transactions didn't belong here. I wanted to say something, but didn't trust what would come out. Tears started to flow. I needed to leave the room.

There were some things no one else wanted that we gathered to remember her by. Karen said she would like to take the holiday candles that had once decorated my childhood home. I saw some jewelry that had been given to my mother by one of her aunts. I also took a few rose-decorated salt shakers that always accompanied every formal holiday meal.

Before leaving, I saw my brother John outside. He still looked gaunt and walked with a cane. As the eldest, it should have been his responsibility to administer the estate, but his descent into alcoholism had stripped that right from him. He used to say he returned to Pittsburgh to look after our mother. Now, his demons made it so he could barely care for himself. It looked as if he felt the burden of failure.

I walked over to him, and as we slowly made our way along the front of the house, I let him know I remembered the kind things he had done long ago, like how he took over the mortgage payments when I was in high school to keep us in our home. He nodded and grumbled, but seemed appreciative of the memory. We stood there a moment longer, sharing a private, final exchange of respect, and then we were gone.

***

The duty of executor fell on Mike. He handled the estate with precision. I knew it was what was needed, but every letter he sent was cold and transactional. They felt more like something from my legal department at work than from someone who had just lost their mother. I wasn't surprised. It was exactly who he was.

Back in Oregon, I was responsible for distributing the Danish silver. I considered it an honor. Every piece was researched, photographed, and logged. I created a flash drive for each family member with the information to ensure the history would be preserved. Some bore the initials of the great-aunts my mother was named after, while others were so worn that their stories would forever be lost to time.

It felt sad mailing the silver out, almost like splitting apart a family that had sat silently in my childhood home for decades. Everyone received pieces I felt were special, along with a note detailing what I knew about the history.

A few pieces remained with me. My mother had always protected the silver and kept it in her care. Now I would do the same. Some were proudly displayed in my home. Others were wrapped and placed back to sleep in a closet.

The Treadmill

My mother's passing hadn't occurred in the middle of a project. The office was slow. I needed something to focus on and push forward. An unexpected test and a new project answered the call.

The engineers held professional licenses. My company wanted project managers to carry credentials, too. In October 2017, after attending six weeks of classes and studying manuals, I took the Project Management Institute's exam. The instructor said getting anything higher than a passing grade of seventy percent meant we had studied too much. Just phoning it in wasn't acceptable to me. When the scores came back, mine was in the upper nineties. No one in my company who took the exam scored higher.

As December rolled around, I could feel unease spreading at work. The president of our division announced the company had been bought out. This news didn't help. Even the most senior project managers weren't told. It felt like another break in trust. I found out with everyone else.

The new company claimed to share our values. They were bigger, slicker, and far less personal. I had been embedded with them over two decades ago in Ireland. They reminded me more of a good-old-boy network than the closer, more personal nature of my firm. Adrian had worked for them also, and used to tell me stories about their culture that confirmed my experience. Over the years, their company hadn't changed, only scaled up.

I don't remember much about early 2018, only the confusion about what the buyout meant. After twenty-seven years, I felt myself detaching from the company. Something was needed to get my head back in the game. In March, a new project in New York appeared on the horizon. It was a chance to regain focus.

The Pittsburgh office wrote the proposal and won the job, so most of the team came from there. It would be supplemented by 3-D modeling in Portland, a New York civil engineering consultant, and engineers from one of our biggest competitors. I had no idea how managing this mixed crew would work, but it wasn't the first time a job required bringing a diverse group together.

Meetings in New York came together surprisingly well. The local civil engineering company let us use their office as a home base and were gracious hosts. They were respectful and diligent. Compared to what I had experienced with Craig in Italy, it was a pleasant reminder of how welcoming the engineering community could be.

Toward the end of the project, the client manager said our designs would be carried through the halls of the state capital. They wanted to portray importance by being big and impressive, and requested the entire project be placed into binders. The format was unusual, but if that's what the client needed to be successful, they could rely on me.

Once back in Portland, I had copies printed. They were hauled around the office for a week as I shuttled down hallways and between floors. The books were dropped on tables, paged through, and tested every way I could think of. When one binding failed, a sturdier one took its place. I laughed at myself, thankful for a way to release some energy. It might have been silly, but it felt like I had my mojo back.

With the New York project well under control, my mind moved to another vacation. In May 2018, Karen and I took a trip to Banff, Canada. When I suggested Banff, I made sure to over-pronounce the final letter, turning it into a two-syllable word. I called it Banf-f, which made Karen laugh every time.

The hotel turned out to be more like a large bed and breakfast. We passed through a busy kitchen into a warmly decorated dining room, with shelves of books and board games covering one wall. The dark hardwood floor creaked with each step. Our room was downstairs. When we pulled back the curtains, a firepit surrounded by chairs filled the window, which was at ground level. The brochure said it was a view room. It forgot to mention we were the view. Karen and I smiled and kept the curtains closed. It wasn't going to ruin our trip.

The next day, we took a cable car to the top of Mount Sulphur and enjoyed the most tender bison steak we had ever tasted. The panoramic view of the surrounding snow-covered mountains added to the atmosphere. We hiked along roaring streams of clear blue glacier water, circled a lake where chunks of ice clinked against one another, and ate lunch at the Fairmont Hotel on Lake Louise. Banf-f was beautiful.

When I returned to the office, the client called to say the project in New York would not be going forward. I wasn't sad. It was going to be a difficult job to complete. Not finishing meant I could once again claim that my project was a brilliant success. There were no contractor questions or lawsuits. Only profit.

Something else happened during my shuttling back and forth to New York. Rick started reaching out. After my mother's passing, he wanted to reconnect. He had remarried, gone back to school for a counseling degree, and moved to North Carolina. When I texted him to say I was traveling the country, his replies appeared within minutes. They always arrived with a small dose of his humor. I'd missed him over the years, and it was nice to have him back.

In the coming months, the texts didn't stop. I traveled to Wisconsin for a project that seemed sketchy. Nothing came of it because it was. The company sent me to Texas to take part in a proposal interview where they wanted me to act like someone I wasn't. The only good that came out of that was the barbecue. One assignment required me to spend a few weeks in Arizona, followed by a flight to Israel for a final presentation.

At the end of a successful week, the client's team invited everyone for a celebratory meal at a nearby restaurant. My counterpart and I wrapped up final details and left forty-five minutes after the rest of the group.

When we arrived, his team had ordered a meal for him. As he began eating, my team stood up to leave for the airport. Our flights left at the same time. People in the Phoenix office could be cliquish, but this even surprised me. Seeing what was happening, the client insisted I share in his food. I ended up eating quickly and heading for the airport. The people I worked with might not have been reliable, but Rick's texts always were.

The Blur Part III – Rick

By October of 2018, rumors of a major project swirled in Portland. It was for the same client who wanted me removed from a job in 2013. I was hesitant to accept the new assignment and let management know why. They looked at me with puzzled expressions. The client was specifically asking for me. Assurances were made that what had happened before had nothing to do with me. I reluctantly accepted.

A few weeks before the official start, the company decided to shuffle people's desks around the office. It wasn't unusual. Project teams were constantly being organized into their own spaces, and the company didn't ever want an employee getting too comfortable in one spot. With me, getting comfortable in one spot had never been an issue.

When the work started, the company didn't have a desk for me. That was unusual. I was one of their most experienced project managers, preparing for one of their biggest jobs. It grated on me that among the seven floors the company occupied, they couldn't find a single place for me to sit. After three weeks, I commandeered a conference room.

By this time of my career, projects felt completely predictable. They all followed the same basic script. As part of the process, I documented anything that could possibly go wrong, and came up with ways to avoid them. An extensive list stared back at me. Managing this client's insecurities and my own team's was going to be a challenge. It shouldn't have felt unusual, but my history with the Portland office told me nothing was ever as simple as it seemed.

Days stretched past eight o'clock during the initial planning sessions. Workload in the overall office was reaching a breaking point. When I told the division president we did not have enough staff to execute the work, he brushed me off.

By October 31st, most of the planning was complete. I told my colleagues to leave early, hoping they could be home before trick-or-treaters filled the streets.

At five o'clock, I knew Karen would be arriving any minute to hurry me home. The office had already emptied out. The buzzing phone in my pocket meant she was parked by the front door. My coat was already on and both feet were headed toward the stairwell. I didn't answer.

Upon reaching the car, Karen was in tears. She told me Rick had suddenly passed away. Doubts ran through my mind about the reality of what she had just said. I went numb.

***

The manager in me took over. My brain shifted to logistics, because my heart couldn't manage the truth. I thought about returning to the office to notify them I'd be gone, calling my brother's wife back, and contacting family. Returning so late in the day after most everyone had left seemed ridiculous, so I focused on calling my brother's wife.

She was distraught and wanted family phone numbers. I asked what happened. Rick had been gardening in their backyard. She had spoken with him only fifteen minutes earlier. When she went out to look for him, he had collapsed on the ground, already gone.

When I offered to help call family, she sounded relieved. The first person on the list was my oldest brother, John. Strangely, he simply responded that Rick was five years younger.

We discussed who would contact whom. Although John wasn't the most eloquent communicator, he wanted to share the responsibility. As the oldest brother, he needed to actively help. We made a plan to split the calls.

As darkness fell over Portland, trick-or-treaters began showing up at our door. The neighborhood children shouldn't lose their fun because of my pain. Candy was handed out with smiles, but a deep sadness weighed on my heart.

That night, I sat in bed distraught. Karen comforted me as best she could. Rick had been the brother closest to me. We laughed while playing ball games in the backyard, won a Little League trophy, tossed pizza dough together, and sat quietly at a bar on the eve of his first marriage. We had only just reconnected after years of his struggling. At fifty-four, he was too young to die. I felt broken. The family I had once known could never be again.

Karen and I arrived in North Carolina a day early for the funeral. We wanted to spend some time with his wife, and she seemed very appreciative.

The service didn't feel like the reunion that had accompanied my mother's passing. John didn't bother showing up. His relationship with

Rick had always been turbulent, so it wasn't surprising. I respected his choice to grieve in his own way.

Before everyone took their seats, there was a viewing. My brother Mike approached Karen. Instead of offering condolences, he made a cutting remark about me. She didn't find it funny or appropriate. When she told me much later, neither did I.

As the room settled, Kathy and Mike didn't join Rick's wife, Karen, and me in the family section. They sat in the back of the room, maintaining their distance. John's wife mentioned this behavior at my father's funeral. I watched them huddling together, but no longer sought to understand the logic behind their separate alliance. The distance spoke for itself.

There was a meal after, lots of hugs, and a brief stop back at Rick's house. His mother-in-law looked over and said I looked just like him. I knew it wasn't true. Rick had my father's charisma. He could always flash a smile and the girls would swoon. With me, they ran. I smiled politely at her compliment.

We were shown a small room Rick had claimed for his own. It held a board game from Ireland we had sent him years ago. I couldn't believe he'd kept it.

As the evening wound down, I knew we needed to leave but I didn't want to. Some part of me still expected Rick to come out and say it was all a joke. It wouldn't have been beyond him, though I knew that wasn't going to happen. That night, I sent one final text to Rick, letting my brother know I missed him. For the first time, there was no reply. It was time to go.

CHAPTER 20

THE ENDING OF THE ENDINGS

Over the course of eighteen months, I had lost both parents and my closest brother. We don't always get to know how a person's story ends. I knew theirs. Each one closed with sadness.

By mid-November 2018, I wasn't sure if what I had gone through were endings, beginnings, or something in between. A sadness had settled in. My family felt shattered. The only steady part of life I could hold onto was my wife. When I needed her, Karen was there.

Stepping Back In

The week after returning from North Carolina, Karen and I attended a performance of Walt Disney songs by the Oregon Symphony. Though small, the concert was a perfect reminder of innocence. I needed that.

Work wasn't so sweet. On average, I received around sixty emails per hour. Every one of them needed to be either filed, ignored, delegated, or answered. Missing a day meant over four hundred messages piling up, all screaming for immediate attention. I'd managed the pressure before, but this felt different. I knew I had to press forward so there wasn't time to figure out what was different.

As I guided the engineering team through their initial two-month study, a proposal had to be submitted for the next phase of work. There was another major job in the office competing for resources. A decision was made to use staff in India and Pittsburgh, two offices that had never supported this demanding client before.

A few months earlier, the president of my division brushed aside my staffing concerns. Shortly after, he gave a speech to the project managers promising never to do a project without proper staffing.

On past jobs, I was often an integral part of the negotiating team and could help a client understand the constraints. This time, he was negotiating the contract, not me. Before the proposal was submitted, I told him there weren't enough people to execute my plan. Once again, he brushed me aside. My stress levels rose.

In Israel, when those above me didn't listen, I disengaged from the project and traveled through Europe. In December 2018, the company issued an unexpected bonus. Karen gently encouraged me to treat myself. I agreed. I wanted to see a play on Broadway, so on Christmas Day, we boarded a plane for one week in New York City.

We had been to New York before, but there was much more to see and do. I scheduled a Broadway play every other day. Karen knew I liked being close enough to see the actors' expressions, and she was able to secure tickets in the front sections for *My Fair Lady, Anastasia, and Wicked.* She liked that I had chosen plays centered on strong female characters with familiar stories and toe-tapping music.

Between performances, we strolled through Central Park and wandered the galleries of the Met. A framed poster of one painting hung in our home office, and hunting for the original became a game.

We also took a skip-the-line tour that included climbing to the top of the Statue of Liberty and having lunch in the Ellis Island food hall. One evening, under the Brooklyn Bridge at dusk, we looked out toward Lady Liberty as the sky behind her turned fluorescent orange.

On December 30, the day before our departure, we walked through Times Square to see the preparations for New Year's Eve. We called it New Year's Eve Eve. We had all the fun, with none of the crowds, and no stress. It counted. The entire trip was a huge success.

During the first three months of 2019, I could see challenges growing. My management was holding meetings with the client about how to make the project run more smoothly, but they weren't including me. I had seen this before in Israel in 2007, upper management meeting behind closed doors, disconnected from the work being done in the trenches. My presentations and input didn't seem to matter.

I was later asked to attend a senior client meeting that mattered even less. The other major project in the office was struggling, and their client was throwing fits each week, complaining about imaginary problems. Our senior managers were desperately trying to calm them down.

My project was on the agenda, but the topic always centered on the lack of staffing. Talking about how not having enough people affected the schedule wasn't acceptable. Since no one wanted to hear reality, there was no reason for me to be there. To make things worse, my client counterpart wasn't in those meetings either. He attended a weekly report-out session with the rest of my team three floors above where I sat. They reviewed the real problems and then identified possible solutions. That's where I should have been.

Not all meetings caused stress. There was one I actually enjoyed. The client came to the office each week to review the design. I knew the power of free food and provided lunch for everyone. Sometimes we had ribs, sometimes deli sandwiches. I chose the menu.

As March rolled around, I decided to liven things up. The client constantly emphasized the importance of staying on budget. To reinforce the idea, I decided that week's lunch would be Happy Meals from McDonald's. It seemed like a playful way to make a point.

My team loved it. Happy Meal toys littered the engineers' desks, and the designers could be heard laughing within their cubicle walls.

The client had a different reaction. My counterpart appreciated the humor, but his team viewed the lunch as an intentional slight, distracting them from the actual discussion.

Providing lunch wasn't required. They could have eaten at the food carts across the street or one of the restaurants nearby. My attempt at lighthearted budget reinforcement had misfired by inadvertently suggesting a lack of professional respect. I quickly ordered two dozen pizzas to shift the focus back to the design review. They might not have enjoyed the Happy Meals, but thinking about that lunch still makes me smile.

While McDonald's provided amusement, one meeting didn't. When most of the design was complete, the client invited the engineers to an appreciation dinner. It sounded like a generous offer. I remembered the times awards had been presented to me and hoped my team could now experience what I once had. They worked hard to deliver the design faster than anyone thought possible, and I strongly encouraged them to attend.

The event was held at a popular restaurant in one of their presentation rooms. Plate after plate of appetizers arrived and several speakers offered high praise. As the evening progressed, I noticed something odd. The client was only congratulating themselves. They gave each other awards and pats on the back, but acted as if the design team didn't exist.

As they took credit for the engineers' hard work, it hit me. My group hadn't been invited to receive appreciation. They were invited to give it. I politely finished the evening, applauding in the right places and smiling at their jokes, but it felt like my team was being used to satisfy the client's ego. Nothing could be said, but it showed me how much the client's values differed from mine.

There was another disturbing thing I saw in the client's organization. Years earlier, I worked with a bright young woman who had just started. Her open and honest approach resonated with the engineers. When I saw her on my new project, her personality had changed. She was aggressive and no longer cared to collaborate.

Watching this once reserved individual high-fiving her colleagues made me wonder about myself. I had worked in and around this client for years. My company's culture was closely aligned with the client's. How had it changed my behavior? I hoped it hadn't, though I knew that was wishful thinking.

***

Karen knew the minefield I sometimes walked at work and understood I needed an outlet. In April, she found the perfect event. We would go tiptoe through the tulips at the Wooden Shoe Tulip Festival, just a short drive from home.

We had never been there before and couldn't believe the color. Field after field and row after row of colorful tulips spread out as far as the eye could see. We set up the tripod and nestled together among the flowers. It might not have been Amsterdam, but it was the next best thing.

More travel was in store. In early June, we flew to Nevada. Carson City served as our base, and we drove to Lake Tahoe from there. I had never been on a California wine tasting tour before, and Karen thought it would be fun for me. The bus took us to five different wineries in the Sierra Nevada mountains. At one stop, I could actually taste the subtle notes being described. That was a first. Some of the presentations were a bit cheesy, with one host treating her wine like it had a sassy personality. I loved it, but Karen didn't appreciate me fraternizing with another woman, especially if she happened to be a wine.

One day, we visited a silver mining town and explored a historic schoolhouse. That evening, at an isolated spot on Lake Tahoe, our private guide set up a telescope and told us stories about the stars. Her tales were accompanied by hot chocolate and marshmallows.

By July 2019, work wasn't getting any easier. Schedule pressures were mounting. It was a small miracle the team had accomplished as much as it had in such a short time, but I knew we couldn't meet every deadline.

I prioritized the team on delivering the most critical designs a few days early since those would best support the construction group. It didn't matter. When the less important designs were issued a week late, the client started sending legal notices. They were technically correct, but it was the worst thing they could have done. Instead of focusing on getting the job done, efforts had to be diverted to the notices.

No matter how chaotic things became at work, nothing was going to stop me from celebrating Karen's birthday with her. She had often talked about visiting Victoria, Canada when she was younger and how she wanted to make a new memory there with me. I was more than happy to oblige.

The best part of the trip was high tea at Butchart Gardens. We entered a building surrounded by an expansive rose garden and settled at our table, which looked toward a large picture window overlooking the grounds. After ordering tea, a multi-tiered tower of sweet and savory bites arrived, each level more inviting than the last. When we finished, we strolled through the endless gardens and paused on the lawn to listen to musicians preparing for a concert. The weather cooperated, music filled the air, and we found happiness among the flowers once again.

The Breaking Point

Over the past twelve years, every major success came with a senior manager working behind the scenes who smooth-talked the client and advocated for the project. They always closely coordinated all communication with me, and acted as a kind of pressure relief valve for those times when a client just needed to vent. Sometimes the role was filled by business development, sometimes it was an operations manager. Several months into the project, the person fulfilling that role was reassigned. My objections fell on deaf ears. I knew that decision wouldn't end well for me.

By August 2019, months of staffing shortages were taking their toll. Senior management acted surprised, although they had been informed. Charts and graphs were projected onto large conference room screens as they tried to explain to the client why progress had slowed. It was painful to watch.

Construction had started. The general contractor began surprising me by announcing problems for the first time during client meetings. Senior management told me I couldn't fight back. They wanted the client to believe the engineer and construction teams were one big happy family. I hadn't been forced into silence like this on a project before, and didn't like it. They couldn't see the politics being played, or the pressure the client placed on me because of it.

It wasn't the only way I was being silenced. After asking for more engineers, I was given additional project managers instead. The problem wasn't oversight. They addressed a chronic shortage of production staff by increasing administrative overhead. Since pushing back wasn't an option, I joked with others about how I'd asked for engineers and got *manage-eers* instead.

The new managers didn't report to me. They reported to the division president. I asked why I'd been assigned to the project if they weren't going to let me run it. There was no reply.

To relieve the stress, I spent lunch walking the remote stairwell in the nine-story office. The exercise tired me out physically, but it didn't help mentally. The meddling in my project was undermining every attempt to bring it back under control.

In early October 2019, I received an unexpected phone call. My brother John's wife had passed away. She used to call complaining that John's smoking, drinking, and diet were going to kill him. No one thought he would outlive her.

I'd had enough death over the past two years. John constantly fought with her, and she retaliated by posting embarrassing pictures of him online. It was a strange relationship I wanted no part of. Her death didn't affect me directly, but it did make me concerned for my brother. She might have been toxic, but she looked after him.

By November, John stopped responding to my texts and calls. I heard he was struggling financially, and became concerned about his housing situation. Reaching out to his daughter let me understand that she was checking in occasionally to make sure he was alright. Her visits included doing his laundry and cleaning the apartment. She made no mention of needing any assistance.

Having her shoulder the burden of caring for my brother alone didn't seem fair, so I wrote to Mike and Kathy and shared my concerns. I thought the three of us working together could provide financial assistance to at least ease that burden. They had different ideas.

Kathy wanted to contact church groups and ask them to pray. That didn't sound effective, but I didn't discourage her. Mike shared that he had traveled to Pittsburgh, and described the filthy apartment conditions. Predictably, Mike also mocked my suggestion of any support. He didn't think help should be given unless asked for. I knew how proud John was. No matter how bad his situation became, he wouldn't reach out. From over three thousand miles away, there was nothing more I could do.

November did hold a small ray of happiness. Rick's daughter got married. Her wedding was one year to the day after her father's funeral service. She wanted to turn a sad remembrance into a joyous one. She succeeded. My closest brother would have been proud.

Before the ceremony, when Mike entered the church I greeted him politely. Despite his unkindness toward me, he was still an older brother who deserved respect, even though he hadn't earned it. Karen and I sat up front in the family section with Rick's first wife. Mike and Kathy huddled in the back of the sanctuary, whispering secrets. I'd heard about this behavior at my father's funeral, seen it at Rick's funeral, and here it was again. Saying something didn't feel productive.

In mid-November, I was invited to an unexpected client meeting. One of their senior managers was making unreasonable demands. The meeting was called by a business development manager who was meddling in the project. The division president had recently elevated him above my level, and he felt no need to coordinate his actions with me.

Before it started, everyone sat cordially around the table. I knew the client manager from Israel. He had once brought me the most delicious box of locally made baklava I had ever tasted. Once the meeting began, he was like a race car driver stomping on the gas. His voice rose, and as his excitement grew, he started talking about problems that only existed in his mind.

I was familiar with the Israeli way of conducting meetings, but the business development manager directed me not to push back. The shouting that followed was relentless. Without having anyone to return his energy, the client grew more aggressive. There were real problems to handle, and it bothered me having to be passively sitting in a room taking this abuse.

In my college days, there were times when I could feel a strong urge to run away. After a few deep breaths, the anxiety always subsided and I managed to regain focus. It hadn't reappeared for a long time, until recently. During the past few months, that old "run away" feeling had been creeping back into my life. It showed up again in the meeting, but this time there was no opportunity to take a deep breath.

I broke.

Knowing I was about to say something inappropriate, I stood up, excused myself, and walked out. As the other managers from my company looked my way, the yelling followed me out the door. Never before had I walked out of a meeting. For a moment, I stood outside, trying to understand what had just happened.

I approached one of the senior managers and explained where my head was at. Leaving the meeting was serious to me. The feeling of anxiety hadn't fully left and I knew something was wrong. The senior manager hadn't been in the meeting and didn't seem to care. When I returned to my desk, I no longer wanted to engage in the project.

Over the next month, contact with others in the office was limited to a bare minimum. I spent most days working alone in private conference rooms and walking through the nearby park blocks. At times, I would sit on one of the benches and watch students walking by. They still had hundreds of promising choices lying before them. I didn't feel like I had so many. As a light rain fell around me, my mind drifted with the falling leaves.

Why was I still working? These jobs were killing me. Was it the money?

I ran the numbers a dozen times. My boyhood dream of being a millionaire was never about a number or a label, it was about security. Karen had always helped to keep me centered. She never cared about being wealthy. She just wanted us to have enough, which meant not having to worry about food, housing, or health. For both of us, it was about having a safety net.

My own definition of "enough" had been complicated by my parents. I didn't need my father's Country Club memberships. I no longer carried my mother's worry about paying bills on time. The truth was simple. I didn't need to work anymore. I already had "enough."

Sitting on the bench or walking the park blocks didn't end until my mind stopped wandering, or until I started getting too cold and wet. Back in the office, the project kept moving forward. I was still there, but at the same time I wasn't. My mind had disengaged. I was running on autopilot.

Yearly reviews began in December. They were usually written by people who only knew my work by reputation. A manager who had been promoted ahead of me sat across the conference room table and showed me what he wrote. Most of it was complimentary, but one line stood out. The company's senior management found me defensive.

When I asked for clarification, he justified the comment by reminding me of a conversation we'd had months earlier.

The structural engineers struggled with calculations that in my younger days gave me no problems. I still maintained my engineering license, and when he told me how insurmountable their challenges were I pushed back by explaining my experience with the issue. The engineers were using their struggle to hide a different problem. The manager was not a structural engineer and wasn't sure who to believe. He chose the engineers' excuses over my first-hand knowledge. My words were dismissed, and he said that at the time, my tone sounded disrespectful.

Disrespectful?

Shock set in. When we had the original conversation, I had done nothing more than objectively state facts. My response was rooted in technical expertise and personal experience, but he had taken it as attitude. Now, it was showing up in a performance review.

By the end of our meeting, he acknowledged the misunderstanding and offered to rewrite the review. His second version was more accurate. I appreciated the effort, but the damage was done. The initial conversation revealed what senior management truly thought of me, breaking whatever little trust remained. My emotional detachment deepened.

At the company Christmas party, I sat at my desk. A colleague came by and suggested I join everyone in the lobby. Beer and wine flowed, a photo booth had been set up, and hundreds of people mingled. I couldn't bring myself to join in the holiday cheer. After pausing at the glass enclosure overlooking the festivities two floors below, I packed my bag and left. Karen was waiting for me in the car outside.

The Off Ramp

Work may have cast a dark cloud, but it didn't stop Karen and me from planning a small vacation over the Christmas holiday. We had enjoyed our holiday visit to New York City the year before so much that taking another trip while families gathered in their own homes just felt right. We had visited the capitals of seven countries, but never our own.

Strange reports about a virus spreading in Asia were beginning to surface, so we quickly made a plan and packed our bags for Washington, DC.

On Christmas Day we started at the Jefferson Memorial. From there, we followed the path along the edge of the Tidal Basin and uncovered a surprise. The Roosevelt Memorial was larger and more relevant than we expected. The most vulnerable citizens were under attack by the current administration. One quote carved into the wall spoke to us:

> *"The test of our progress is not whether we add more to the abundance of those who have much; it is whether we provide enough for those who have too little."*

Further along, another quote by FDR's wife, Eleanor, caught our eye.

> *"The structure of world peace cannot be the work of one man, or one party, or one nation... It must be a peace which rests on the cooperative effort of the whole world."*

I smiled at Karen and thought, never underestimate the wife.

At the Lincoln Memorial, we climbed the steps and stared up at the statue we had only seen in movies. From the hall, the full length of the National Mall stretched out before us. Along the way down the left side, we stumbled upon another memorial. The Korean War Memorial was as striking as any of the more well-known monuments. Figures of soldiers draped in sculpted rain gear patrolled through low bushes, frozen in time.

At Martin Luther King's Memorial, we found more inspiring words:

> *"I believe that unarmed truth and unconditional love will have the final word in reality."*

> *"The ultimate measure of a man is not where he stands in moments of comfort and convenience, but where he stands at times of challenge and controversy."*

It was Christmas Day. Without the crowds, there was time to reflect. These weren't monuments to people. They were monuments to ideals. Each one reminded me there was a bigger picture than my own struggles at work.

We had five more days to explore the capital and its surroundings. One day, we drove to Mount Vernon to walk the halls where our first president once lived. I had just finished reading a book about Thomas Jefferson, and on another day, we visited Monticello. Seeing the house and grounds brought his story to life.

We even found time to visit the Manassas Battlefield, a place where almost thirty years earlier, on my first business trip, I had charged across the field attacking imaginary enemies. Now I walked it at a more leisurely pace, hand in hand with my wife, appreciating the sacrifices that had been made.

Tours of the Capitol Building, the Supreme Court, and the Library of Congress immersed us in history. On our last evening, tired and content, we sat on the cold ground, staring up at the Capitol Building's yellow glow as the sun slowly set.

The trip was wonderful, but everything hadn't exactly gone to plan. Important items were left on the plane, and we had to return to the terminal to retrieve them. Our first rental car had to be returned because the gears made a funny sound. Finally, in the airport departure lounge, Karen received a notification about fraudulent hotel charges hitting the credit card. All was resolved, but I was starting to feel less invincible than in years past.

In January 2020, I returned to work and started to transfer my responsibilities to younger managers. One of my goals had been to mentor them and work myself out of a job. If I could leave, it meant my efforts were a success. By the end of the month, they were ready.

I still walked the office halls with trepidation. No one treated me differently, but being back didn't feel comfortable. A new project in Israel was being talked about. Senior management asked me to help with the proposal. They wanted to understand everything about my past assignments, and how I structured the project management teams.

I sketched extensive diagrams on a white board and explained in detail why I did what I did. Understanding the organizational structure of my management team wasn't as important as understanding what drove the strategy. They only wanted the chart.

I was questioned about how I calculated Israeli taxes and negotiated contracts. They tried to extract everything they could, but I was more than just words on a page. Their attempts to drain my knowledge felt both intrusive and offensive. The information, without the why, was useless. My values, experience, professional judgment, and context behind the decisions couldn't be captured in a document.

When senior management assigned me to handle computer infrastructure, it was clear they weren't serious about having me lead the new effort. Preparing computers was only a small part of what I had done for projects in 2009 and 2014. The division president and his business development counterpart were acting as if they were going to run the project themselves.

In early February, I was told to get on a plane for Israel. Enough rockets had been fired at me to last a lifetime. If I were going, I wanted to know why. When no explanation came, I declined the trip. It was starting to feel like they didn't want me for anything beyond my reputation.

Like years earlier, words from Johnny Mathis' song *Coming Home* ran through my mind. I felt like the company had taken everything I had to offer until there was nothing left. I wasn't going to be anyone's puppet, or try to please people who didn't care about me. All that remained was leaving the company and going home.

By late February 2020, I stopped going into the office. The pandemic was picking up speed, and I could see where it was headed. I removed all my belongings from my desk. No one noticed.

In March, the entire company transitioned to remote work. They mostly forgot about me. I called into meetings, listened to corporate directives, and enjoyed long walks through the neighborhood with my wife.

By April, management finally noticed my absence. They needed something for me to do, and assigned a menial task working under a senior engineer. I spent the next day staring at my computer.

***

I woke up thinking of nothing other than starting another day. When I looked in the mirror, I saw the dark circles under my eyes. They had been there for years. I knew what the stress of these projects did to me. At just 55, I looked older than I felt. My brothers, at this same age, still had darker hair. The person staring back at me had hair that was snow white. If I wanted to live a long and healthy life, this couldn't continue.

By noon, I walked into our home office where Karen was working on her computer and showed her an email I had written. It was a resignation letter. My message was brief and professional. I had seen people leave before and knew that once a message was sent, there was no turning back. Karen looked up, smiled, and slowly nodded. She saw I was serious, and told me she would support whatever decision I made.

I always told her I would know when it was time to go. I didn't believe I could give my best anymore. It wasn't fair to the company or to me. It was time to end thirty years with one company that had spanned careers in structural engineering, construction management, and project management.

After taking a deep breath, I pressed send.

The Aftermath

The company was surprised. During a video conference, I overheard engineers in the background saying they thought I would be the one to turn the lights out. Management treated my decades of service as an inconvenience to be processed. It gave me the impression they were saying, "Don't let the door hit you on the way out."

There were final phone calls and emails. Promises were made about keeping in touch, though everyone knew it wouldn't happen. People were told I was retiring. I wasn't fully convinced of that myself. What I remember most from that time is an overwhelming sense of relief.

As my final day passed, there weren't any colleagues patting me on the back, or speeches about past glory. That's how the company treated my friend Lee when he retired. The company hosted two celebrations for him. One at a restaurant overlooking Portland's city lights, and another in a downtown bar with a screen showing photos from his career.

For me, the company acted as if I didn't exist anymore. In the end, it was just Karen and me. It always had been. I wouldn't have had it any other way. We pulled out a small bottle of champagne and some party hats. Frank Sinatra's song *My Way* played in the background. The pandemic was in full swing and we were on our own. That wasn't much different from how it felt when she first joined me in Ireland.

We pulled each other close, grateful for what had been. After a lifetime of work, I was finally free.

POSTSCRIPT

Karen said I spent my first year recovering by napping the days away on the couch. Between naps, we spent weekends at the Oregon Coast, watching the waves crash and just being together.

By mid-2022, the pandemic was winding down, and people emerged from their bubbles, but that wasn't what I remember most about that year. In 2022, I lost both of my older brothers.

John came first in July. He was found in his apartment after a wellness check. His health had been ravaged by years of drinking, smoking, and surviving on a diet of Boost, a nutritional drink meant to supplement meals.

His life felt like a tragedy. A brother who carried the burden of being the eldest. Some of it was placed on him, some he placed on himself. Over time, it broke him.

I didn't want to remember what he had become. I wanted to remember who he was. John was the one who hid in his room and, to the delight of his younger siblings, pretended to be a talking tree. He was the brother who shared superhero comic books and handed out Christmas gifts that had been purchased from a gas station and were wrapped in a paper bag. John sat beside me at endless Pittsburgh Pirate and Penguin games, cracking peanuts and drinking beer. He taught me how to drive a stick shift and took over the mortgage payments to keep me in a stable home through high school. Whether it was playing one-on-one basketball together or turning his head and delivering a grumpy, "Bah," he was my next closest sibling after Rick.

His daughter organized the funeral. It didn't feel like a sad occasion, the way the other family funerals had. It felt like it was something everyone had expected and it had finally happened.

At the lunch afterward, the family gathered in the back room of a small bar. Kathy sat emotionlessly beside me without saying a word. She was glued to her phone, playing Pokémon with Mike, who sat across the table. I knew everyone grieved differently, but I shook my head in disbelief.

Mike passed in November. He was found in a stairwell at work. At John's funeral, we noticed that Mike carried far more weight than could be considered healthy. Whiskey sipping, cigar smoking, and lack of exercise hadn't helped. A volatile personality also likely played a role.

His was a life of academic excellence. He earned a doctorate from an Ivy League school and advised the upper echelon of foreign governments. He thought he was better than everyone else and wasn't afraid to let anyone know it.

Going to his funeral was a difficult decision. Over the years, Mike had lost my respect. Kathy had a unique bond with my older brother. I knew she would be hurting, so I also went out of respect for her. Through all of the funerals, Karen and I had reconnected with one of my cousins. I wanted to see her. The one person I didn't go for was Mike.

At his funeral, I listened as people spoke of a wise man who knew something about everything, and helped little old ladies shovel snow. It wasn't my version. I remembered a brother, who when we were growing up, violently pummeled me with his fists. As a young engineer, I remembered the rented workspace in Massachusetts, and the way he shouted at me as if I were an enemy instead of his brother. I remembered the edge in his voice when he spoke to his wife, or anyone who didn't agree with him. His teasing was often at my expense, and he didn't seem capable of writing or saying anything kind or supportive.

I felt no sadness at his death. It was more like relief. Or joy? That couldn't be though. I brushed the thought aside. When I told my cousin how I felt, she couldn't believe brothers could feel that way. She said it would change in time. Years have passed. It hasn't changed.

At the dinner after the service, Kathy sat beside me at the table. Her experience with my brother was different than mine. She worshipped him. I couldn't relate.

In the weeks following, Kathy started reaching out more, an attempt to reconnect now that her closest ally was gone. My writing her back was done with a genuine hope for the future. I had always maintained a deep desire for connection, and the simple fact that she is family was enough to compel me to try. Kathy is my sister, her story with me is still being written.

Shortly after we arrived home, Karen came down with COVID. I followed a week later. We felt it was Mike's last gift to us. It felt consistent with who he was.

After recovering, it hit me that over the last five years, five of my family members were gone. All three older brothers passed before their sixty-fourth birthday.

***

John drank heavily and chain-smoked as his health deteriorated. Mike puffed on cigars, sipped whiskey, had a volatile temper, and was overweight. Rick fought through past addictions to oxycodone and alcohol, but never stopped smoking. My brothers were all undone by their vices. I'm thankful that they taught me what not to do. I didn't share their vices, but it still feels like death is watching. My vice was a career that was slowly killing me. I like to think I got away.

The anxious feeling of wanting to run away stopped appearing the day I decided to leave work. It hasn't returned. These days, I find happiness in simpler things, like just being with Karen. It doesn't mean I've given up on bigger adventures, like someday exploring Machu Picchu.

Every morning walk we take, every meal shared at home, and every classic TV show we laugh at together reminds me of the joy I've had and still have in my life. I'm not sure where my story will end, but for now, I'm just glad it's still going.

www.ingramcontent.com/pod-product-compliance
Lightning Source LLC
LaVergne TN
LVHW100509110826
845146LV00002B/567

* 9 7 9 8 9 9 6 1 3 6 3 0 8 *